TITANIC LIFE

MIKE HARRIS

Mike Harris

Titanic Expedition Leader

1980, 1981 & 1983

ISBN:1461150159
ISBN-13:9781461150152

This book is dedicated to my wife Evelyn who stuck by me
through the good times and the bad.

MIKE HARRIS

CONTENTS

FORWARD

We are pioneers of the deep, becoming older as deep ocean technology is developing before our eyes in the direction of computerizing of the methods of research, implementation of robotic technique: remotely operated, autonomous vehicles, etc. Young generations are coming into the field of ocean exploration. But they have different way of thinking.

Some of them don't accept real diving of people underwater. They think unmanned systems are much easier and more reliable than manned vehicles.

They also believe this type of unmanned technique reduces the risk for human life practically to zero.

But they are mistaken.

These new scientists have never felt what it's really like to dive, feeling the viewports of the submersible. Seeing life through the viewports is different than seeing it on the TV screen.

In every discovery the spirit and presence of the human brain and human eye must exist. Also the presence of man in the process of the research or observation

Dr. Anatoly Sagalevich

gives an ability to obtain the most trustworthy information of the highest quality.

This aspect of the book TITANIC LIFE by Mike Harris is very vital, because all expeditions and observations are based on real-life experiences.

The author devoted his life to exploration: diving on wrecks at Bikini Lagoon, climbing on Mt. Ararat looking for Noah's Ark, and most importantly, searching for and helping to discover the wreck of the RMS Titanic. Mike was the first to organize the salvage of Titanic artifacts and was instrumental in forming the company, RMS Titanic, Inc., that exhibits artifacts today.

I had the pleasure to work with Mike's son, G. Michael Harris, in 2000, when we made several dives together in the Mir-1 and Mir-2 submersibles. During the dives we recovered a number of Titanic artifacts for museum expositions. I remember every time we found something interesting, Mike's son would be very happy, smiling and even laughing like a kid. Obviously, enjoying the thrill of life and exploration, taught to him by his dad.

On the basis of our dives together, Mike's son organized a very nice museum in Orlando, which is one of the best Titanic museums in the world!

I like the fact that Mike Harris considers not only the present, but also the future. He wants to transfer his life experiences and love of exploration, not only to his son, but to new generations of the Harris family as well.

I had the pleasure to dive in Mir-1 with Mike's 14-years old grandson, Sebastian. It was a marvelous dive for the young boy. He was the youngest person in the world to ever dive to Titanic at 12,850 feet depth. His name is now in the Guinness Book of Records, which makes his father and grandfather very happy.

Mike Harris now plans to dive in the near future to the Titanic with his son and grandson. Mike knows the experience of diving and exploring should not be allowed to disappear, it must be kept alive in younger generations!

TITANIC LIFE is very interesting and useful for a wide circle of readers, but not only for the deep ocean professional people. It's a real story about the investigations of the Titanic. TITANIC LIFE also allows the reader to understand that the organizing of deep ocean exploration is not an easy job, but in the end the person who is doing these operations has a great prize: real dive on great depth, which is incomparable with anything else.

An additional prize awaits after the deep dive: the opening of the hatch and view to blue skies. Life is started again!

Thanks Mike for a great story!

Professor Anatoly Sagalevich
Head of Deep Manned Submersibles Laboratory
of P.P. Shirshov Institute of Oceanology of
Russian Academy of Sciences

Mir 1 and Mir 2 Submersibles

PREFACE

Titanic Life. It's no secret that a good part of my life has been associated with looking for the Titanic, or recovering artifacts from the Titanic, one of the most famous shipwrecks of all time. But what causes one person to grow up wanting to lead a group of people off on some unknown adventure, not knowing if it's going to lead to success or failure, while other people (most other people) could care less about taking such a chance?

Ever since I was a little kid growing up in Tampa on the West Coast of central Florida, I've always been curious. I can't remember a time when I didn't want to see what was around the next corner. I couldn't wait to become old enough to join the Cub Scouts and then the Boy Scouts.

Camping outside with my friends, tramping around palmetto scrubs and swamps looking for snakes to catch, staring up at a sky full of stars at night was just something I loved to do from as far back as I can remember.

I know that sounds crazy to a lot of people (and I guess it is), but maybe you can begin to understand why someone like me would one day want to grow up begin leading people on adventure expeditions around the world.

One of the first expeditions I ever led was to Bikini Atoll way out in the Marshall Islands. You've got to fly forever across the Pacific Ocean just to get there. I chose Bikini as my first expedition because that's where the U.S. tested their atomic bombs after World War II. When I had done a little research and found that the Bikini people could no longer live on their Atoll because of lingering radiation and sharks out in the lagoon had mutated into fierce monsters, I was hooked! Leading a team of divers and filmmakers to such an infamous destination had the ring of a most wonderful and exciting adventure!

I learned about my second expedition almost by accident. One day I was reading in the *Christian Science Monitor* about people wanting to climb Mt. Ararat in Turkey to see if they could find Noah's Ark. I thought that sounded like a good idea. So before too long I put together a different film team (this time with mountain climbers) and was headed off for what turned out to be another very interesting and promising adventure.

After several expeditions to Turkey searching for the religious treasure, someone told me about a different type of treasure that was sitting not too far away in Mexico. Well, Mexico is a lot closer to Florida than Turkey, so I put together another team of filmmakers (this time with a group of die-hard treasure hunters) and led them on an exciting adventure through the mountains of old Mexico in search of Pancho Villa's treasure.

Ever since I led my first expedition back in 1971, I had heard stories about people planning to locate and raise the famous RMS Titanic in the North Atlantic. When I started doing research on where the Titanic might be located, I found out that she sunk in water that was more than 12,000 feet deep.

I had experience taking divers into Bikini Lagoon, but the ships we dove on at Bikini were sitting in water that was no more than 250 feet deep. At 12,000 feet, there's no light whatsoever, the water is freezing cold and the pressure is about 6,000 pounds per square inch. In the early 1970s technology didn't exist that could find something 12,000 feet under the sea -- even something as large as the Titanic. Consequently, I busied myself looking for objects that were indeed famous -- like Noah's Ark and Pancho Villa's treasure -- but maybe a little easier and not quite so dangerous to find.

Near the end of the 1970s, technology was changing and the possibility of locating the Titanic became a real possibility. *Deadly Fathoms*, my film from the Bikini expedition, had won a Silver Medal at the Atlanta International Film Festival. I had also made films of our Expedition to Ararat and my Search for Pancho Villa's Treasure. Consequently, with three expeditions completed and three documentary feature films produced, I finally had enough experience to pull together my biggest expedition yet: locate and film the unsinkable Titanic on the bottom of the North Atlantic.

Leading the first expedition to search for the famous ocean liner in 1980 was truly a wonderful experience and unforgettable thrill. I was able to pull together another very professional film team, as well as oceanographers from Scripps Institute of Oceanography in California and Lamont Doherty Geological Observatory. Since that first Titanic expedition was so historic, I was able to get writer and actor Orson Welles to be my on-camera host and narrator for my film *Search for the Titanic*.

On my second Titanic expedition, which we conducted in 1981, James Drury of TV's The Virginian joined us on the voyage, as did my financial benefactor, Texas oil-man, Jack Grimm.

Along the way I found time to lead two additional expeditions: one to explore the mystery of what happened to aviator Amelia Earhart, and another religious expedition, this time trying to find the location of the Ark of the Covenant in Jordan and more Dead Sea Scrolls in Israel.

All of these stories are told in the pages you now hold. But where should I start? You probably won't believe this, but I got started leading expeditions around the world and producing films of my expeditions because of legendary Hollywood movie star Mickey Rooney.

How I went from being a stargazing kid in Tampa to leading expeditions around the world is what *Titanic Life* is all about.

1 EARLY YEARS

I grew up in Tampa, Florida, before air-conditioning, before television and before Tampa had professional football, baseball and hockey teams. Who would have thought that a small city on the West Coast of Florida would have made such impressive strides in just fifty years?

I was born in1936. When I was 18 months old, my father was struck by lightning and killed while playing golf in Temple Terrace, a small community on the east side of Tampa. Three weeks later my brother, Dudley, was born. I've always thought of what a traumatic event that must have been for my mother to have her husband die at twenty-nine and having to raise two young boys.

When my mother and father graduated from the University of Iowa in 1934, my mother got a job working for a regional theatrical company out of Des Moines. Her job was to go around Iowa to the various towns, talk the local people into putting on a play which she would produce and direct, then collecting the money, half of which would go back into the community and the remaining half to her theatrical company.

Dudley, Mother and Michael

I don't really know how she pulled off such an entrepreneurial stunt. But I can imagine it took guts for a woman to go out onto the road all alone in the early 1930s and take on the challenge of organizing people she didn't know into putting on a play that other people would pay good money to see.

When my parents came to Florida, my mother decided that she wanted to learn to fly a plane. So, she went out to the Davis Island airport near downtown Tampa and took flying lessons in a Piper Cub. But when her Cub ground-looped while landing one day, she decided that maybe learning to fly wasn't really what she wanted to do!

Maybe loving adventure is in the genes. I became an Eagle Scout at 13, and received my private pilot's license by the time I was 16.

While a member of Troop 22 in Tampa, my first really exciting adventure was traveling on a train with eight other scouts to the Boy Scout World Jamboree in Valley Forge, Pennsylvania. What a thrill it was for me to meet other scouts from around the world, each of us trading something from our state or country with

Mike Harris (far left) with Tampa Scouts

another scout from another state or country. I can't remember exactly what I brought from Florida to trade (probably a coconut, small turtle or toy alligator), but I do remember making my trade with a scout from New Mexico who gave me the neatest looking horned toad I ever saw!

One memory from that trip that remains the most vivid is seeing President Harry Truman addressing boy scouts from all over the world during opening ceremonies. We were all sitting on a large grassy hillside looking at a stage that had been set up way down below. I can't remember what his speech was about, but I do remember that when the commander-in-chief started speaking, five thousand scouts pointed their new Kodak box cameras at him and started taking his picture. This caused almost five thousand flash bulbs to start popping in Truman's face, all at once!

Everyone says the president was a salty character and I can certainly attest to that, because when all those popping flashbulbs startled him, he barked an order into the microphone to all the scoutmasters present: "Tell those damn scouts to stop taking pictures!" Every scoutmaster jumped to his feet to make certain their "damn" scouts put away their cameras.

Not only did we get to see the president and meet interesting scouts from around the world, we got to see live television for the very first time. Coming from Tampa, nobody had television. I'd heard of it, but certainly neither my family, nor any of my friends had ever seen anything like live television. At the Jamboree, there was a large tent that had two black and white TV sets—one at each end—set up for viewing. I remember looking up at that TV picture and wondering what it would be like if I could have one of those things in my home someday.

I graduated from H.B. Plant High School in Tampa in 1953. I wasn't a very good student, but was a pretty good swimmer. I set a few high school records and even was elected captain of our swim team.

Plant High Swim Team (Mike upper right)

Upon graduation I attended the University of Florida and worked my way through school by being a lifeguard at the University pool. It was a real tough job, but somebody had to do it!

When I graduated from the University of Florida in 1957, with a Bachelor of Science Degree in Advertising and Radio-Television Production, I married my college sweetheart, Barbara Burton, and headed off to spend three years in the Marine Corps as a newly commissioned Second Lieutenant.

While going through flight training in Pensacola, our first child, Lisa Gail, was born. Later, when stationed at Quantico, Virginia Barbara and I were blessed with a second child, John Michael, who I named after my grandfather (John Alfred).

Mike Receiving an Award as "Student of the Week"

Being an officer in the Marine Corps was a great honor and a terrific experience but making a career in the military seemed a little too structured for what I was beginning to think I wanted to do with my life. Consequently, when I received my Honorable Discharge from the Marine Corps, Barbara and I and our two kids returned to Tampa where I got a job with the Henry Quednau Advertising Agency writing and producing radio and television commercials. In the early 1960s, Henry Quednau was the largest AAAA advertising agency in the city.

It was an interesting job and I was able to create a few memorable ad campaigns, but after several years, I began getting a little antsy and looked around for something that, hopefully, would afford me a little more opportunity and responsibility.

I was offered a position as Assistant Advertising Director with Mary Carter Paint

Company. In the late 1960s the Tampa company was famous throughout the United States for its popular "Buy One Get One Free!"marketing slogan. For the first time, I felt like I was really beginning to get someplace.

During my first year at Mary Carter, the company bought a chain of Biff-Burger Drive-In fast-food restaurants, and I was named Advertising Manager for the new division. In the 1960s, however, the fast-food industry was still relatively new. Consequently, we were always coming up with different promotions to increase customers. To draw kids and young families into our fledgling Biff-Burger restaurants, I dreamed up a character called Biffy-the-Clown and started featuring him in all of our radio, television and newspaper advertisements.

Since I was the Advertising Manager for Biff-Burger, I named myself to play the part of Biffy. Plus, whenever we opened a new restaurant in Florida, Georgia, Tennessee or Kentucky, I'd show up wearing my Biffy costume, while giving away buttons, balloons and my Biffy picture for the kids.

How I came up with my Biffy-The-Clown costume and makeup is a story in itself. Since I didn't know anything about being a clown I figured I'd better get some advice from a professional.

Consequently, I drove 45 miles south of Tampa to Sarasota to meet with one of the top clowns in the Ringling Brothers, Barnum & Bailey Circus. He taught me how to apply my clown makeup and also helped me come up with a costume and identity for Biffy-the-Clown.

Mike as Biffie-the-Clown

Biffy became a big hit. Biff-Burger customers increased like crazy throughout the south, partly because of their unique broiled burger—but also, I'm sure, because of the celebrity status that Biffy-the-Clown quickly attained. Biffy became so popular with young kids and their families that Biff-Burger was adding a new store in a different town throughout the South every week.

This was in the days before Ronald McDonald. So, jokingly, I like to tell folks that before Ronald McDonald, there was Biffy-the-Clown!

Eventually (like my previous endeavors) I grew tired of being Biffy-the-Clown, and also having to wear a coat and tie as Assistant Advertising Director of Mary Carter Paint Company. I never liked wearing a coat and tie, not even when a military uniform with a tie and "piss-cutter" cap were standard uniform apparel for an officer in the Marine Corps.

I knew I wanted to start doing something different, but at the time, I really wasn't sure of just what. I had been out of the Marine Corps for several years, trying to do something positive with my life, but not everything was coming up roses. Sadly, my marriage to Barbara collapsed, but I did end up with my two kids, Lisa and Michael.

I began searching for something that would take advantage of my advertising degree and my work experience with Mary Carter Paint Company. It didn't take me long to land a job with the Jim Walter Corporation. Jim Walter, also located in Tampa, was the largest builder of shell homes in the world. I was named one of their Regional Advertising Managers, responsible for all Jim Walter advertising in Florida.

Now a single dad with a new job, I began looking around for a wife for me and also a mother to the two little kids I had at home. It wasn't long before I became acquainted with Renee Roderer, a girl from Wiesbaden, Germany. Renee had recently come to America hoping to marry a U.S. soldier who had been stationed in Germany. She seemed to be just the girl I was looking for, so we married and within three years had two kids, Gerald Michael and Stephen Herschel.

Here I was, still a young man in my early thirties and already I had four kids. But having to raise four young kids at home began taking a toll on Renee. When Jim Walter sent me to Atlanta, most of the burden of raising four kids fell to Renee. Jim Walter put me in charge of all the company radio, television and newspaper advertising, not only in the State of Florida, but Georgia, Tennessee and Kentucky as well.

I liked working for the Jim Walter Corporation, as it gave me the responsibility I enjoyed, but whatever good it did for my career, did absolutely nothing to help my marriage. In all the turmoil, I left Jim Walter and came back to Tampa hoping to keep things together with Renee. But nothing worked. Renee and I divorced, Jerry and Stephen went to live with their mother, and my two older kids, Lisa and Michael, left to go live with their mother, Barbara.

My life was in the toilet. Two failed marriages. Four young kids. Whatever I was doing, it obviously wasn't working.

Then I heard about a movie producer named Ron Gorton who lived in Clearwater, twenty-five miles from Tampa. Never lacking in confidence, I marched right over to meet this Hollywood mogul and talk myself into a job! And it worked. I did talk myself into a job and ended up being Ron's right-hand man.

In 1964, Ron produced Panic Button with Jayne Mansfield and Maurice Chevalier. When Mr. Chevalier came to Tampa in the early 1970s on a worldwide tour, Ron and I picked up the famous actor at the Tampa airport and drove him over to St. Petersburg where he was scheduled to hold a concert. Spending the day with such a distinguished celebrity was a very nice perk that I've never forgotten.

Maurice Chevalier

While working for Ron, Tampa attorney Vince Thornton came to Clearwater and pitched Ron on helping to bring an all-star football game to Tampa. Back then, there were no professional sport played in Tampa, but the movers and shakers of the community longed for the day that such a dream might become a reality. One way to build toward that dream was to get the Hollywood producer living in Clearwater to help them produce the football event they envisioned.

Ron and I quickly brainstormed and came up with the idea that we should call the all-star game the American Bowl. "Let's make it a red, white and blue affair," I added, with Miss America present and All-American football players from the northern colleges battling All-American football players from the southern colleges.

For the first American Bowl, Ron Gorton and Vince Thornton were the Executive Directors, and I was its Director of Advertising and Promotions. The game was an artistic success, but not a financial one. Consequently, Ron and Vince dropped out. But I believed the American Bowl represented a great opportunity for Tampa, so I wanted to do whatever I could to keep it operating.

Consequently, I approached the Lions Club of Florida and sold them on the idea of becoming sponsor of our patriotic game. Because of my efforts, the Lions named me as the game's Executive Director.

One of the first things I did was persuade a friend of mine, Bob Dudley, president of the Meeker Television Network in New York City, to broadcast our game on national television each year. This enabled Tampa to receive national recognition and local Lions Clubs all across Florida to make money for their charitable activities. The American Bowl was the forerunner of what is now the popular Outback Bowl, which features top teams from the SEC and Big 10 on New Year's Day. But back in the 1970s, the NCAA wouldn't allow us to put on a bowl game that matched two teams. We were only allowed to feature senior All-American football players from the north and south.

Consequently, in order to boost ticket sales throughout the West Coast of Florida—and also to put on a decent game and halftime show for Bob Dudley's national television audience—I made it a point to hire, not only top college coaches, but movie and television celebrities as well. In keeping with the patriotic theme, I arranged for an "American of the Year" to be showcased each year and presented with a huge trophy by a famous celebrity during halftime ceremonies.

One year I arranged for the Lions Clubs to invite Ray Croc, Chairman of McDonald's, to be our "American of the Year". When I met with several of the fast-food giant's top advertising executives at their headquarters in Oak Park, Illinois, I asked them if Ronald McDonald was copied after Biffy-the-Clown. They told me a lot of people over the years

Ray Croc

had claimed that Ronald McDonald was copied after them, but admitted, that I was probably the only one who got it right! They confided to me that Biffy-the-Clown was killing them in the south, so they had to invent Ronald McDonald to counter the competition.

On the athletic side of the production, I was smart enough to name another good friend of mine, Marcelino .Chelo. Huerta, as my Director of Coaches and Player Procurement. Chelo was a member of the College Football Hall of Fame, so he had a personal rapport with most of the college football coaches in the country.

Every year Chelo was able to bring in celebrity coaches like Paul "Bear" Bryant from Alabama, Darrell Royal from Texas and Charlie McClendon from LSU to coach the senior All-Americans from the south, and Duffy Doherty from Michigan State, Bo Schembeckler from Michigan and Woody Hayes from Ohio State to coach the All-Americans from the north.

Chelo, Joe Almand, Mike Harris (back row)

With a name like American Bowl, I made sure there was plenty of red, white and blue everywhere. Each year I had talent like soul singer Lou Rawls, Margaret Whiting (singer of "My Foolish Heart" among other hits) or Crooner Jerry Vale to sing the "National Anthem". Composer Paul Lavalle came in for several of our games and led a large ensemble of local high school bands that covered the field in a huge formation in the shape of the U.S.A.

Don DeFore with Bowl Game Director Mike Harris

Movie star Burt Reynolds, TV personality Don DeFore famous for several TV hit series Hazel and The Adventures of Ozzie and Harriet and Twilight Zone's Rod Serling were just a few of the Hollywood celebrities I invited to participate in

22

halftime festivities. Lions Club members did their best to sell tickets, but no matter how much patriotism and show biz I threw into every game, I still could not get a lot of people into Tampa Stadium. Football fans wanted to see two successful football teams playing each other, not two teams made up of a collection of senior college All-Americans even if some of them were the very best football players in college on that particular year.

After about six years of directing the American Bowl, I started looking around for a different type of challenge. I had always been interested in show business ever since my mother put my younger brother, Dudley, and I in stage plays at the Tampa Little Theater.

With the American Bowl becoming increasingly harder to keep afloat, my desire to accomplish something in show business began to grow. Out of the blue one day, I decided that what I really wanted to do was produce movies in Florida. I'd never produced a real feature film before, but I'd certainly produced and directed a lot of commercials over the years (and even acted in a few) so it really wasn't too big a stretch for me to believe that I could produce a "real" movie for distribution in theatres.

This is where the Hollywood movie actor Mickey Rooney comes into the picture. I'd heard that Mickey had recently moved to Ft. Lauderdale with wife number six (or seven), and was looking for movie projects. Since I've never been shy about calling anyone on the phone, somehow I was able to find Mickey's phone number and set up a meeting with him at his home in Ft. Lauderdale.

Over several months of conversations, I convinced Mickey that I could raise the money we needed to produce a feature film together. What a thrill it was for me, a local kid from Tampa, getting to meet Mickey Rooney and actually become friends with a famous Hollywood star.

Mickey Rooney

During my first visit to his home, I was immediately struck by the fact that Mickey Rooney was always "on stage". He was always pitching movie ideas, acting out parts, telling me how he was going to promote our film, making up lines for the film, reciting them, singing, dancing, whatever. He was always bubbling over with such incredible energy that it actually made me tired just being around him.

Mickey had a screenplay about a man who was a compulsive gambler. Mickey, of course, would play the lead. I thought it was a good idea and knew that I could shoot the whole film economically in and around Tampa. I got in touch again with my friend, Bob Dudley, the New York television executive who provided broadcast coverage for the American Bowl and told him that I wanted to produce a movie with Mickey Rooney. After I explained to him what it would be about, Bob said he liked the idea and agreed to back me financially.

When I received Bob's check, I immediately flew back to Tampa and couldn't wait to call Mickey in Ft. Lauderdale and let him know I had the money we needed for our movie. When I called, there was a slight pause on the other end of the line— unlike any of the other phone calls I'd made to my usually boisterous Hollywood friend.

"Uhhh, Uncle Mike," he stammered. I don't know why he called me Uncle Mike, but he always did. "Uncle Mike, I just sold that screenplay to someone else. But don't worry," he gushed confidently, "we can produce a western together! I've got a western I've been thinking about that will feature me with three of my sons! I'm telling you," he continued excitedly, quickly getting up to speed, "it will be a great film, Uncle Mike, just great!"

I was flabbergasted! I wanted to produce the contemporary gambling film that Mickey and I had talked about, not a western with his sons that I didn't know anything about. How could I shoot a western in Florida? And most important, I had sold my TV friend, Bob Dudley, on backing me on a gambling film with Mickey Rooney in Tampa. Now I couldn't do it! With my mind reeling, I was the one stammering on the phone. "Ahhh, Mickey", I mumbled, "let me get back to you about that." I then hung up on my Hollywood friend, terribly disappointed.

It was a long flight from Tampa back to New York City. Here I had received a check from Bob Dudley to produce a film with Mickey Rooney and now I had to give it back. All my dreams of being a full-fledged movie producer were going up in smoke.

When I got to Bob's office in downtown New York, I explained to him what happened and handed him back his check. But surprisingly, he didn't take it. Instead, he asked me one question: "What other film would you like to produce?" I was flabbergasted, again!

Thinking quickly, I told him about this documentary film I had in mind, where I'd lead an expedition to Bikini Atoll, out in the Central Pacific. I told him about atom bomb testing the U.S. had done there after World War II. Gaining confidence, I started regaling my friend with stories I'd heard about all the famous ships that were sunk by atom bombs and now lying in relatively shallow water, just waiting to be filmed. I also told him I'd heard stories about huge mutant sharks that were rumored to be swimming the waters at Bikini.

Without hesitation, Bob said it sounded like a good idea to him and he was sure he could sell a good documentary on TV. Keep the money," he replied firmly, "and produce the documentary. He then added, You've got to remember, Mike, when I gave you that check, I wasn't backing Mickey Rooney. I was backing you!

2 DEADLY FATHOMS

With my confidence and enthusiasm restored, I flew back to Tampa and immediately started rounding up the best divers and underwater cinematographers, I could find. Within a few months, I scheduled a seat on Air Mike (Air Micronesia) and flew out to Majuro, the capital of the Marshall Islands. Once there, I rented a Grumman Widgeon seaplane and flew around to several atolls to see what interesting World War II relics might look good in our film.

The first location I checked out was Maloelap Atoll. When my pilot set the twin-engine Grumman down in the lagoon and slowly taxied up to the beach, I felt as if we had, somehow, flown back in time. There, spread out before me, were dozens of Japanese fighter planes and bombers, each obviously damaged none able to fly. It was as if World War II had ended yesterday! When I opened the door and stepped out, it was eerily quiet.

I walked up to two Japanese Zero fighters that were sitting on the nearby bombed-out coral runway. Both aircraft had rusted landing gear with flat tires. One fighter was missing its wing; the other, its tail. A short distance away a Japanese G4M "Betty" bomber sat silently in the tropical heat with one engine, one wing and its tail missing.

Not far away were two more Japanese bombers, both sitting nose down on rusted gear and rotted tires. Each had wings and looked like they could fly, but neither had a tail. Except for the rusted condition of these aircraft, it was difficult to believe that World War II had ended just 26 years earlier. I don't know if we were the first people to set foot on Maloelap Atoll since the war, but it looked like nothing had changed. Bomb craters were still in the runway. Damaged aircraft still sat everywhere waiting to be discovered.

I took several rolls of pictures with my 35-mm camera, climbed back into the Widgeon and asked my pilot to take me to Wotje Atoll. I knew I didn't want to fly all the way out to Bikini Atoll, where the atom bomb testing took place, because I already knew for sure that I wanted to film the sunken warships and supposed mutant sharks there. But I did want to check out Wotje and Kwajalein Atolls to see what each had to offer.

When we flew over Wotje lagoon, I noticed there was a large, four-engine aircraft sunk in relatively shallow water not far from the beach. This time when we landed, there were a few Marshallese families waiting for us on the beach. When I asked them about the large aircraft in the lagoon, they said it was a Kawanishi flying boat.

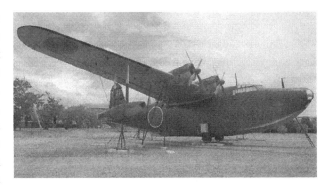

Kawanishi Flying Boat

I could hardly believe it. The Japanese Kawanishi flying boat was the largest four-engine flying boat in the world. I couldn't wait to dive down and film her.

The Marshallese also told me about a Japanese freighter that was sunk at Wotje by U.S. troops when she tried to leave, prior to the atoll being attacked by U.S. Marines. They said she was sitting in about one hundred and eighty feet of water. They also said no one had ever dived on her before, which was very good news to me!

Flying over Kwajalein, I was surprised to see what looked like a very large ship in the lagoon, with her stern section sticking out of the water. After landing, I learned she was the German heavy cruiser, Prinz Eugen, which also happened to

German Heavy Cruiser Prinz Eugen

be the sister ship of the famous German battleship Bismarck.

The Prinz Eugen was captured after the war and taken to Bikini Atoll to participate in atom bomb testing. She was damaged by the testing, but not sunk and was being towed back to the United States when a typhoon unexpectedly struck and sunk her in the lagoon.

Having decided that both Wotje and Kwajalein Atolls would be good locations to film, we flew back to Majuro where I made arrangements to lease a 100-foot island freighter called The Mieco Queen. The Mieco Queen didn't look like much, but I was assured she was a seaworthy vessel with a good Marshallese crew.

While scouting locations in the Marshall Islands, I was told I needed special permission to go to Bikini. So when I flew back to the States I immediately got back in touch with Bob Dudley in New York and let him know what I had found out about needing some kind of special permission to go to Bikini. He said he didn't believe that would be too big a problem and to just keep him advised as to my progress.

I did find out on my trip that the U.S. government was a little skittish about letting anyone go to the infamous Bikini Atoll. In 1971 the Marshall Islands was classified as a U.S. Trust Territory. I had also heard that Bikini Atoll was located in a restricted area and that visitors were strictly forbidden.

That sounded a little ominous, but being a dyed-in-the-wool optimist, I also thought I was smart enough to figure out how to get whatever permission I needed. All I wanted to do was make a simple documentary film in the middle of the Pacific Ocean. How difficult could that be?

After a few phone calls, I flew off to Washington, D.C., and made an appointment with a Navy admiral at the Pentagon, confident he would give me the permission I was seeking.

When I arrived outside the admiral's office, I took a deep breath, stuck out my chest as I was taught as a Marine officer, and boldly walked in for my meeting. Needless to say, the admiral wasn't happy to see a fledgling filmmaker arrive in his Pentagon office—especially a fledgling filmmaker who wanted to film at Bikini Atoll. He told me sternly that it was too dangerous to dive on sunken ships in an atoll that had been subjected to intense atomic radiation. In general, he did all he could to discourage me from going. When I didn't back off and continued to ask for permission to film at Bikini, he switched tactics and said that such permission wasn't up to the Navy. It would have to be given by the Department of the Interior. Then he edged me out the door.

Baker Atom Bomb Test at Bikini Atoll

Well, the admiral had not actually said, "No". So, retaining my confidence, I headed for the Department of the Interior. But officials there gave me basically the same story as the admiral at the Pentagon. They also said it wasn't a safe place to dive and reminded me that Bikini Atoll was located in a restricted area. When I asked the Interior Department for permission to film, they too said they didn't have the proper authority and suggested that if I really wanted to go to Bikini Atoll, I should get my permission from the folks at the Atomic Energy Commission.

My meeting with officials at the Atomic Energy Commission was no more productive than my meeting with officials at the Department of the Interior. They did tell me, though (with a completely straight face), that if I wanted to film at Bikini Atoll, I would have to get permission from the…United States Navy! Needless to say, the admiral at the Pentagon was not pleased to see my face when I showed up at his office for a second meeting.

I ended up riding on this government merry-go-round twice—not counting a meeting I had with a Mr. Johnston, the High Commissioner of the Trust Territories, in Honolulu. Mr. Johnston met with me after flying to Honolulu from his headquarters in Saipan. Just like the admiral at the Pentagon and the other government officials I met at the Department of the Interior and at the Atomic Energy Commission, Mr. Johnston advised me strongly about going to Bikini Atoll—but didn't actually say that I couldn't go.

I was confident that I had done my due diligence, and quickly reasoned that although no one in the government had given me permission to film at Bikini Atoll, no one had directly told me that I couldn't. So, I contacted Bob Dudley again to let him know no one had said we couldn't go, and immediately began making final plans to get my newly assembled film and dive teams to Majuro in the Marshall Islands.

I rented a DC-8 four-engine prop cargo plane that I found in Miami. We painted "Bikini Gal" on her nose, loaded two submersible mini-submarines inside, along with two dozen professional divers and filmmakers, all their equipment and supplies and two decompression chambers. I made sure we took along enough provisions to enable us to dive and film in the Marshall Islands for at least 30 days. When everyone got on board in Tampa, we took off for the Marshall Islands—with stops along the way to refuel or clear customs in Los Angeles, Oakland and Honolulu.

When we arrived in Honolulu, government officials asked to see my permission papers. I told them who I had met with over the last few months, including the Trust Territories High Commissioner, Mr. Johnston. I emphasized strongly that no one had ever said we couldn't go. The officials fussed and fumed and didn't seem at all happy that we had flown all the way from Tampa to Honolulu without official permission to go on to Bikini, but weren't particularly sure of just what they should (or could) do about it. They especially weren't happy to learn that I intended to take my expedition team on to Majuro Atoll in the Marshall Islands.

In 1971, Majuro was pretty close to the end of the line as far as communications were concerned. When we arrived, two young government representatives quickly met us at the plane and wanted to know who we were and what were we planning to do. When I showed them all the equipment we had on board and told them about making a documentary film at Bikini, they immediately asked me to show them the document that gave me permission to dive and film at Bikini Atoll.

Unloading Bikini Gal at Majuro Atoll

I thought to myself, these people never give up. When I told them how I had tried to get permission from everyone I could think of in Washington, including the

High Commissioner Johnston in Honolulu, and that none of them had ever said "no", they also weren't sure what they should do next.

To get through to the outside world from Majuro, it was necessary to go to the only radio shack on the atoll, try to dial up Guam via short wave radio, then, if the atmosphere was just right, get connected to a phone line on Guam that could be patched in to Honolulu. It was not every day that government folks on Majuro could successfully get patched in to Honolulu so they could reach their superiors in Washington. Consequently, when we kept unloading our DC-8 and loading everything onto our island freighter, Mieco Queen, there wasn't too much the young government lackeys figured they could do.

Before heading out onto the high seas, they hurriedly typed up a few papers for me to sign that stated, "if anyone gets hurt or killed while diving in the Marshall Islands, it's our fault and not the fault of the U.S. government or Trust Territories." We were, as they stated succinctly, "on our own!"

That was fine with me, but I didn't breathe a full sigh of relief until the last line was thrown from the Mieco Queen and we were heading towards the vast open waters of the Central Pacific.

Mieco Queen at Sea

Our first stop was Wotje Atoll, where the Japanese had built a seaplane base during World War II. The few Marshallese villagers still living on Wotje told us the U.S. Marines never attacked there, but they did bomb them repeatedly and wouldn't let any Japanese supply vessels in or out. Consequently, most of the soldiers on Wotje starved to death, except for a few who boarded a Japanese freighter named the Fujian Maru, which was sunk by Marine fighter planes when it tried to leave.

Just as the Marshallese islanders had told me on my first visit, no one had ever dived before on the Japanese freighter. Few government people (and certainly no tourists) had ever been to Wotje Atoll since World War II. Consequently, we were the first to dive in the crystal clear waters of the lagoon and experience what turned out to be a spectacular highlight of the trip.

Calvin Hiashakawa

The Fujian Maru was resting upside down on the bottom in about 180 feet of water. We recovered dozens of sake cups and saucers and untold numbers of green bottles that hung eerily from the floor of the vessel. There were also large, hand-painted plates of different shapes and sizes, which I personally brought on board the Mieco Queen and kept in my small cabin for safe-keeping. But our most unusual encounter involved the discovery of a human skull. We filmed the grisly reminder of the Fujian's last voyage, but were careful not to touch it or remove it from its watery grave.

When I dove on the four-engine Kawanishi Flying Boat, I settled myself in the cockpit of the huge plane, grabbed the controls, and tried to imagine what it must have been like to fly her during World War II. I also wondered what caused her crash. Was she taking off?

Was she trying to get back to her base before the Marines attacked? I would never know, but I've never forgotten what it was like to sit at those controls, underwater, and pretend I was flying a giant Japanese Kawanishi.

The next stop on our great adventure was Kwajalein Atoll. This was the final resting place of the German heavy cruiser, Prinz Eugen, On any of our dives, it was necessary to organize exactly what each diver and filmmaker planned to accomplish before ever getting in the water.

My two main diver/filmmakers were five-time U.S. national skin-diving champion, Bruce Mounier, and Rick Frehsee, expert diver-writer for major underwater magazines. Assisting them were professional utility divers, Van Smith, Robert Schaefer and Skip Norwood.

Bruce Mounier Diving on Flying Boat

Calvin Hiashakawa, a third diver I picked up in Honolulu, was a Japanese diver I would need at Bikini when we dove on the Japanese battleship Nagato. The flagship of Yamamoto's fleet, Nagato was sunk by atom bomb testing in 1946.

I also brought along Dr. Norman Ahl, a Navy officer who was on leave from the submarine base at Pearl Harbor. Dr. Ahl was a specialist in decompression sickness. I hoped, of course, his specialty wouldn't be needed.

When diving below 100 feet, there's a considerable amount of coordination that goes into making the dive successful. At 180 feet, the depth of most atolls, there's very little light. Diving at that depth requires underwater lights and hundreds of feet of electrical cords. Our two utility divers had to maneuver the heavy electrical cords and lights, while the other two divers remained on alert with loaded bang-sticks, ready to protect the other four divers in the water against shark attacks.

Prinz Eugen Torpedo Room

Sometimes I was in the water with the divers, but I remained on board the Mieco Queen most of the time helping direct topside filming. Norm Virag, a professional documentary filmmaker from Michigan, was on the team to handle the majority of the creative work out of the water.

At times it was necessary to film divers entering or exiting the water from one of the Zodiac inflatable boats we kept at hand, but mostly Norm filmed their diving activities from the deck of the island freighter.

The filming we did at Wotje inside the Fujian Maru and at Kwajalein on the Prinz Eugen

was excellent practice for what we knew would be much harder and more technical dives needed to film the multiple warships and planes resting on the bottom in Bikini Lagoon.

When we finally arrived at Bikini Atoll, site of the 1946 Operation Crossroads "Able" and "Baker" atom bomb tests, everyone pressed against the Mieco Queen's rail trying to be the first to get a glimpse of the infamous location. The weather was perfect for the occasion: rainy, cloudy and gloomy. I'm sure that each of us began to worry, just a little, that maybe being the first to dive into Bikini's graveyard of ships, which were doused with ample doses of radiation during the Operation Crossroads, wasn't necessarily the smartest thing to do. But we had come a very long way for the historic opportunity and I wasn't about to let anything stop us. We weren't afraid of radiation! We weren't afraid of mutant sharks! We weren't afraid of anything! (Well, maybe mutant sharks!)

Mieco Queen at Sea

Eventually the weather cleared and we were able to begin planning our dives. The first thing we had to do was locate the ships that were sunk in the lagoon. We knew generally where the tests took place, but had no idea where the large ships we wanted to dive on were located. With no sonar equipment, all we could do was drag our ships anchor, back and forth in the search area and hoped we snagged onto something important.

The first ship we snagged that we wanted to dive on was the U.S. battleship Arkansas. She was considered an old ship when World War II started. So when the war ended, the Arkansas was towed to Bikini and placed within the target area.

The "Able" atomic bomb test involved a B-29 flying over Bikini Lagoon and dropping a four-ton bomb on ships that were anchored close to each other in the target area. There were large ships and small ships, facing different directions. There were a few submarines and a few merchant ships.

Several of the large ships were war prizes—like the Prinz Eugen and the Nagato. Even the U.S. aircraft carrier Saratoga was sacrificed for the sake of the experiment. She was towed into the target area with Hell fighter aircraft tied down on her flight deck outside and Avenger dive-bombers tied down in her hanger deck below. All ships and planes were fully fueled and loaded with live ammunition, just as they would be in a real wartime scenario.

Plane on Hanger Deck of Saratoga

The U.S. government chose to have such a large and diverse group of ships, each battle ready, in order to determine what might actually happen to war ships arrayed on the sea and under the ocean when attacked with an atomic weapon.

When the "Able" test was conducted, surprisingly, only a few war ships sank. Others were only slightly damaged. Consequently, the U.S. conducted a second test called, naturally, "Baker." During the "Baker" test, they took the same ships, those still afloat in the target area and detonated an atomic blast underwater. The huge explosion lifted the Arkansas straight out of the water, before crashing her down to the bottom in a furious rain of explosive might and radiation.

The mighty aircraft carrier Saratoga didn't sink right away, but within hours, slipped beneath the waves and came to rest on the bottom, sitting upright with her communication mast above the conning tower resting just ten feet from the surface.

The hellcats and Torpedo dive-bombers on her flight deck were knocked off by the terrific underwater blast, but those tied down in the hanger deck below remained curiously in place.

The first ship we dove on was the Arkansas. Filming the huge ship on the bottom, lying on her side, partially upside-down, reminded our divers of what a magnificent ship

Bruce Mounier in Plane Cockpit on Saratoga Hanger Deck

the Arkansas must have been in her glory days. The barrels of mighty twelve-inch guns remain on alert, still pointing skyward, reminding each of us of her ominous display of Navy might.

Our Japanese diver, Calvin Hiashakawa, was given his chance to star in our movie when he was featured during a long, deep dive on the Nagato. Prior to his dive—which was longer and deeper than Calvin had ever attempted before—Dr. Ahl went over all the decompression rules he should be aware of when diving to such depths. Calvin must have learned his lesson well because during his time hanging on the decompressing line at thirty feet, no problems were encountered.

However, the divers did run into one problem late one afternoon while hanging on the decompressing line waiting for nitrogen to escape from their bloodstream. Topside on the Mieco Queen, a Marshallese sailor was banging a hammer on the deck, trying to straighten out a metal fastener. The divers waiting underwater could hear the banging as the sound loudly reverberated from the metal hull through the water.

Unfortunately, a 12-foot tiger shark also heard the banging and came to investigate. The men below were sitting ducks. They couldn't surface without taking a genuine risk of developing the bends. Luckily, one of the men topside saw the deadly creature approach, grabbed two loaded bang sticks and dropped them to the defenseless men 30 feet below. Thankfully, the tiger shark wasn't interested in such an easy meal, and slowly meandered off into the depths below.

The highlight of our dive at Bikini was getting to go inside the hanger deck of the Saratoga, finding the Avenger dive-bombers and sitting inside several of the aircraft as they remained tied down in the hanger deck approximately one hundred feet below the surface.

When I left on my expedition to Bikini, my third wife, Evelyn, was eight months pregnant with our first child. I knew it was going to be close to get back to Tampa in time for her delivery. I had planned to be gone for 30 days, but ended up returning three weeks late. Somehow, through a lot of prayer and perseverance, Evelyn managed to wait until I returned from my first big adventure. Just one day after I returned, our baby girl, Madalene Elizabeth arrived!

Rod Serling

During the next six months, I stayed busy editing and compiling Deadly Fathoms, the 90-minute documentary film of our adventure, which featured famed television personality Rod Serling as host and narrator. I entered Deadly Fathoms in the 1973 Atlanta International Film Festival—and was stunned to win the festival's Silver Medal!

Evelyn at the Atlanta International Film Festival

It was tremendously gratifying for my first documentary film to win an award. My producer Bob Dudley was also happy because it enabled him to distribute the film on television and recoup his investment. Because my first expedition and *Deadly Fathoms* turned out to be successful, I explored my options for another expedition I could lead—and another documentary film I could direct and produce. I was no longer thinking about trying to make a film with Mickey Rooney. Leading expeditions was too much fun!

That's when I came up with the idea searching for the Titanic. The only thing I could think of that would be better than diving in Bikini Lagoon would be to find the famous ocean liner Titanic in the Atlantic and try to recover her artifacts.

I knew that trying to find the Titanic at the bottom of the Atlantic Ocean would be a much bigger deal than locating and diving on ships in Bikini Lagoon. But I was young. I had good health and I genuinely believed there wasn't anything I couldn't do! I also had a loving wife who was crazy enough to let me chase my dreams. With an over-abundance of optimism sitting squarely on both shoulders, I started looking into how I was going to find the Titanic in the North Atlantic—a challenge which turned out to be much harder than I ever could have imagined.

Deadly Fathoms Promo Sheet

3   TITANIC RESEARCH

In the early 1970s, when it came to finding something underwater—even if that something was as big as the Titanic—technology wasn't what it is today. I had just led an underwater expedition to Bikini Lagoon. But Bikini Lagoon had a maximum underwater depth of between 180 and 200 feet. The water where the Titanic went down—400-miles off Cape Race, Newfoundland—was 12,000 feet deep or deeper. There was no way a diver could strap tanks on his back and dive to a depth even close to that. Besides, the 6,000 pounds of pressure per square inch would crush the life out of anyone who tried. Even if I could talk someone into backing me on the expedition, actually finding the historic ship on the bottom was going to be a very difficult proposition.

I started by calling my high school buddy Dick Greenwald. Dick and I were on the Plant High School swim team together in Tampa in the early 1950s. He graduated in 1951 and went off to The Citadel in Charleston, South Carolina, for his undergraduate studies.

Dick Greenwald

Dick's father was an early pioneer in Navy aviation, having flown experimental flights in small biplanes that were designed to hook onto large dirigibles while in flight. He had high hopes that his son would have a successful career in the military like he did. But poor eyesight kept Dick from receiving a commission upon graduation. He did obtain a degree in accounting, but I'm certain that not being able to get into the military was a very big disappointment—not only to Dick, but to the Greenwald family as well.

I remember going to New York City one summer and staying in Dick's basement apartment in Greenwich Village. A big water main or sewer pipe ran right through his small one bedroom efficiency, which you always had to duck under or you'd bang your head. Back then, with all the hippies and beatniks running around the Village spouting poetry, New York seemed like a really neat place to live.

Dick wasn't working in accounting at the time. He had taken a job as a stage hand on one of the off-Broadway (or maybe I should say, "way-off-Broadway") theatre productions.

After doing his New York thing for a few years, Dick returned to Tampa and got a real job as an accountant. When he tired of accounting, he entered law school at the University of Miami in Florida and graduated with a degree in Admiralty Law. That's when his career really took off.

Dick eventually became Secretary and General Counsel for Deepsea Ventures and Ocean Mining Associates in Gloucester Point, Virginia, a company in the forefront of searching for and mining manganese nodules on the deep ocean floor. (Having developed a reputation as the leading authority on international mining rights, in 1985 Dick was asked to speak before the Subcommittee on Oceanography of the Committee on Merchant Marine and Fisheries in the U.S. House of Representatives.)

In the 1970s, Dick and Deepsea Ventures were very much on the cutting edge of searching for manganese nodules and developing ways to mine them in 20,000 feet of water. So when I started thinking about how I was going to find the Titanic in 12,000 feet of water, I naturally thought of my old high school buddy.

When I contacted him, he thought I was a little nuts for wanting to find the Titanic. People had talked about wanting to find the famous ship for years, especially a man in England named Douglas J. Faulkner-Woolley. It seemed that on every anniversary of the Titanic's sinking (April 14, 1912), Woolley would get his name in newspapers and magazines around the world by announcing how he was going to lead an expedition to find and salvage the famous ocean liner.

One year Woolley said he was going to find the Titanic and raise her off the bottom by filling her hull with ping-pong balls. Another year his plan included building large ocean barges, equipping them with very strong cables and hauling the sunken ship back to the surface. Each year the intrepid Englishman had a different scheme to find and salvage the Titanic. But while Woolley and others were talking about finding the Titanic and getting publicity, none had ever followed through and actually conducted an expedition at sea to locate and salvage her.

So in 1974, when I visited Dick Greenwald in Virginia and told him about our successful expedition to Bikini Atoll and *Deadly Fathoms*, my friend was duly impressed. He was further impressed that I had actually met and worked with the famous television host Rod Serling.

Deep Diving Submersible Aluminaut during Sea Trials

But when I started telling him of my plans to search for the Titanic in the North Atlantic, his enthusiasm, understandably, became tempered. Dick knew full well that diving on ships in 200 feet of water was a whole lot different than trying to find a ship in the middle of the North Atlantic at 12,000.

But Dick also knew me well enough to know that when I wanted to do something, I wasn't someone who was easily discouraged. He suggested I try to get an appointment with Art Markel, skipper of a deep-diving submersible called Aluminaut that was owned by Reynolds Aluminum in Richmond, Virginia. He said the Aluminaut had been designed to dive to 15,000 feet, could cruise on the bottom at three knots and—at 51 feet in length—was large enough to carry a crew of six.

I immediately became interested in what Dick had suggested and quickly asked him how he knew so much about the Aluminaut. Putting on his best business face, Richard told me that it was his business to know what capability all the submersibles in the world had. He then said that the Reynolds Aluminum deep-diving submersible might "possibly be" what I needed to dive on the Titanic.

I didn't like the sound of that! "What do you mean it could 'possibly be' what I need?" I quickly asked. Dick then told me that even though the Aluminaut was designed for 15,000 feet, she had never been deeper than 7,000 feet.

Seeing that I was becoming a little less enthusiastic about taking him up on his suggestion, Dick decided that giving me a little of Aluminaut's history might be in order. He asked if I remembered the publicity about the U.S. bomber that accidentally dropped a hydrogen bomb in 3,000 feet of water off the coast of Spain in the early 1960's? I told him that I vaguely remembered the incident. Dick revealed that it was Reynolds' Aluminuat, along with a Woods Hole submersible called Alvin, that made the difficult recovery.

I asked Dick if the Aluminaut was the only submersible that could dive to 15,000 feet. He said there were actually two others that could go much deeper—all the way down to the bottom of the deepest part of the ocean. In the Pacific Ocean, the Mariana Trench drops to an astounding depth of 35,000 feet. Two submersibles— one owned by the U.S. Navy and the other by the French—have gone down to the very bottom of the Trench. But Dick quickly added, "I don't think you'll find that either of them will be available".

Dick knew so much about working in the deep ocean, and I knew so little. It was clear that I had a lot to learn if I was ever going to lead a search for the Titanic. I was experienced enough to know at this point in my life there's never a shortcut to success. If I was ever going to fulfill my dream, I'd better start educating myself right away.

Imposing on my friendship with Dick a little more, I cautiously pressed him for more information. Rolling his eyes playfully, Dick took a deep breath and suggested that we get some lunch. "If I'm going to start teaching you about working in the deep ocean," he said, "let's at least have a little lunch together!"

Over a hamburger, fries and a coke at the local McDonald's, Richard explained to me that a Belgian scientist named August Piccard invented what he called a bathyscaph. The bathyscaph would enable Piccard to drop down into deep depths of the ocean, deeper than man had ever been able to go before. He was able to do this by filling a lightweight material with liquid petroleum, which was lighter than water. This petroleum liquid enabled Piccard's device to have lift.

Bathyscape Trieste

To get the devices to go down, the Belgian scientists hung heavy metal ballasts on them, attached by electromagnets.

Whenever Piccard wanted to rise back to the surface, all he had to do was release the metal ballast and the lightweight material holding the petroleum lifted him safely back to the surface.

Anyone who knows me knows that I always carry a yellow note pad with me wherever I go. I use it to take notes, keep track of appointments, telephone numbers, brainstorm ideas… anything. With Dick Greenwald teaching me about deep-diving submersibles, you can imagine, I was writing in my yellow pad like crazy.

In 1953, August Piccard joined forces with his son, Jacques, and the two of them built a new bathyscaph that they called Trieste. In 1958, the two Piccards sold Trieste to the U.S. Navy. U.S. Navy lieutenant Don Walsh, along with Jacques Piccard, set a world diving record when they took Trieste down to 35,800 feet. The very bottom of the Mariana Trench.

Don Walsh and August Piccard

Dick also told me about the French submersible Archemide. It was similar to Trieste, but neither, he added quickly, would be safe to dive on the Titanic.

He explained that if the soft cover surrounding the envelope of gasoline that provided the submersibles their lift ever became punctured from a jagged piece of wreckage, there would be absolutely no way the vessel could get back to the surface. On a shipwreck like the Titanic, there were almost certainly broken masts or ruptured steel plates with jagged edges. If just one of them accidentally punched a hole in the soft envelope and released the gasoline, Dick said there was only one thing a person could possibly do "Just bend over and kiss your ass goodbye!"

I asked Dick if the Trieste had ever been used to find anything like a sunken ship in the deep ocean. He said that in 1963, the American submarine Thresher sank off the coast of New England and all hands were lost. The Trieste located the Thresher, took a large number of pictures and recovered a few small pieces of the sub for identification purposes, but made sure she stayed well away from any large portions of the wreck.

He then told me again about the American B-52 bomber that was carrying a hydrogen bomb off the coast of Spain in 1966, when it collided with a refueling tanker and accidentally dropped the potentially lethal weapon into 3,000 feet of water.

The Aluminaut and the Alvin were instrumental in finding and recovering the devastating device, much to the great relief of the U.S. Navy—not to mention folks living on the coast of Spain.

Deep Diving Submersible Aluminaut

I then asked Dick about the possibility of using the Alvin. He said I should probably stick with the Aluminaut. The Alvin was owned by Woods Hole, one of the most prestigious oceanographic schools in the country. Getting to use her to find the Titanic would be like trying to talk the U.S. Navy into renting out the Trieste. "Both", Dick said, "would think you were a crackpot and wouldn't want to waste their time!"

He encouraged me to visit Art Markel at Reynolds Aluminum in Richmond. "They might be able to get some publicity out of searching for the Titanic," he said.

Well, I followed Dick's advice. I knocked on the door of Reynolds Aluminum and asked for Art Markel. Art turned out to be a big guy, with a big heart and lots of enthusiasm for his baby, the Aluminaut.

When I told him I wanted to dive on the Titanic, Art was immediately interested and saw it as a ticket for him to get his submersible dive program up and running. It turned out that the Aluminaut's hydrogen bomb recovery mission back in the 1960s was the high-water mark of Reynolds' deep submersible program. The Aluminaut was now sitting, unused, in a storage facility at Green Cove Springs, Florida, just outside of Jacksonville, much to the dismay of Art Markell and his small team of deep submersible believers.

Thankfully, Art was a personal friend of Louis Reynolds and David P. Reynolds, the two top executives at Reynolds Aluminum. When Art introduced me to the two brothers, I told them how I thought Reynolds Aluminum could get a lot of favorable publicity if their deep submersible was used to find the Titanic. They both asked a lot of good questions, which I could only dance around with my very limited knowledge of working in the deep ocean. Actually, I had no knowledge of working in the deep ocean, but I was smart enough to tell them them that I'd get back to them with answers to their specific questions.

Mike and Art Markell at Green Cove Springs

Art was only too happy to take me to Green Cove Springs to get inside the Aluminaut and see for myself how big it was to accommodate equipment and personnel. When I asked him if the Aluminaut could dive down to the depth of the Titanic at 12,000 feet, Art was the one who started dancing with his answer.

"Well," he countered cautiously, "the Aluminaut was designed to dive successfully to 15,000 feet, but she has been sitting out of the water now for several years." I was afraid to hear what was coming next. "Consequently, to bring it back up to proper specifications, it would need considerable modifications." I asked him how much he thought the considerable modifications would cost. Again, he started dancing, but eventually came up with a figure of about one million dollars.

When I asked him why he thought it would cost so much, Art began regaling me with his knowledge of the Aluminaut. Both the forward and aft hemispheres would need inspecting, preserving and reinstalling. Plus, the main ballast tanks, both port and starboard, also needed work. Then there was the vertical motor and compensating assembly that needed overhauling. In addition, the stern plane motor, rudder motor and manipulators needed to be gone over thoroughly— especially if the Aluninaut was going to be certified to dive safely to 12,000 feet.

Art Markell Sitting at the Aluminaut Control Panel

Facetiously, I asked if that would just about do it. Unfortunately, Art must have thought that he was talking to a financial angel, because—now very enthused—he started rattling off more work that needed to be done!

"We need to redesign and install a 38-inch Acrylic hemispherical main view port at the Aluninaut's bow", he said, "so we can see and film the Titanic better!" He also said it would be a good idea to add jet bow thrusters for sediment control, double the power with a new fuel cell, and boost the current penetrator capacity up to 60 kilowatts. When he took a rare pause to catch his breath, I stopped him.

It was already clear that making all those modifications to the Aluminaut was going to be rather expensive, not to mention that Art's growing list was starting to make the entire undertaking a little "iffy". But I didn't tell Art that. I just shook his hand enthusiastically, thanked him for the informative tour and let him know—just like I told the Reynolds brothers—that I would be back in touch with specific information just as quickly as I could.

Gee! This was not going to be as easy as I thought. There was so much I didn't know about working in the deep ocean and there was so much more that I needed to know! Leading an expedition to Bikini Atoll and diving on ships in 200 feet of water wasn't quite the same thing as trying to find the Titanic in water that was

12,000 feet deep. I thought I was smart enough to figure out what needed to be done, but was somewhat surprised to learn that the technology for finding the Titanic wasn't as developed as I thought it would be.

When I began my research into how to actually look for the Titanic, everyone I talked to said that the only way to search a large area of the ocean bottom was with side-scan sonar. Using a submersible, they said, would be much too expensive, and you could only light a ten-foot area in front of the sub at any one time.

I discovered there were several different models of side-scan sonar devices. The most reliable was said to be the Klein side scan sonar device, which Klein called Hydroscan. It could be used for both shallow and deep water and was popular for providing relatively high resolution of various underwater targets.

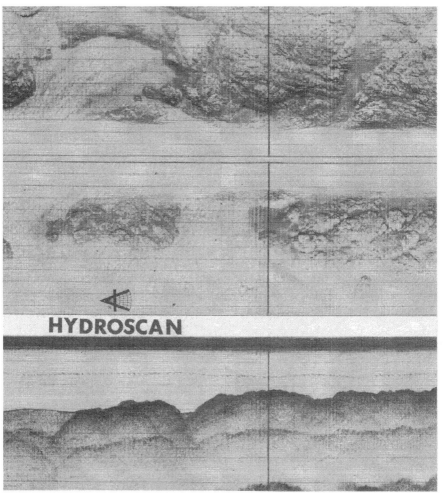

Klein Side-Scan Sonar Images

In those days, most sonar devices could cover a high-resolution search swath of about a half-mile. It would take a long time to search for something on the bottom of the ocean if you could only search a half-mile swath at a time. A half-mile is certainly better than looking at just ten feet of lighted area out of a submersible's port hole, or through the lens of a camera, but trying to cover a search area thirty miles by thirty miles in size, would still be a very expensive and time-consuming endeavor.

It had cost my investors about $250,000 to dive on sunken ships at Bikini Atoll, and that included the production of Deadly Fathoms. Having a ship like the Mieco Queen worked out just fine in the Marshall Islands, but I knew it wouldn't work at all as an oceanographic vessel in the North Atlantic.

I was quickly learning that renting a research vessel with the right equipment was not going to be cheap. At a minimum, I would need to hire a fairly large crew of oceanographers, which meant the ship had to be at least 180 to 200-feet in length. Plus, the ship would need to be equipped with sophisticated navigation and deep ocean search equipment.

I also found out that to tow a camera sled or side-scan sonar unit in 12,000 feet of water would require leasing a drum that was large enough to hold at least 20,000 feet of wire. It didn't take me long to figure out that navigation equipment, specialized deep ocean search equipment, plus oceanographers and a sophisticated research vessel was going to easily cost over a million dollars, not to mention what a feature documentary would cost to publicize such an historic expedition. On top of all this, I wasn't entirely convinced that early-1970s technology that could make searching for the Titanic an acceptable risk actually existed.

Consequently, I felt I had no choice but to put my plans to find the Titanic on hold and begin scouting for another expedition I could lead and film. Hopefully, scaling down my expectations would be a little more in keeping with my level of experience and capabilities.

4 NOAH'S ARK

When I was a year-and-a-half old my father, Dudley Harris, was struck by lightning and killed while playing golf at the Temple Terrace Golf Club on the outskirts of Tampa. Eventually my mother got married again, to a man named Don Shreve. Don legally adopted me and my younger brother, Dudley. Consequently, growing up in Tampa, going to Gorrie Elementary School, Woodrow Wilson Junior High School and Plant High School, I went by the name Mike Shreve.

During that time my mother and stepfather attended St. Andrews Episcopal Church in downtown Tampa. In my early years I sang in the church choir, eventually becoming an altar boy during Sunday services. But I was never particularly interested in Sunday school, or even going to church. I had always believed in God, but just never wore my religion on my sleeve and wasn't too sure what organized religion I really believed in.

When I left home and was out on my own, I decided I would do two things. First, I would legally change my name back to Mike Harris; and I would quit going to church.

My wife Barbara, whom I met while attending the University of Florida, wasn't particularly religious either, so the two of us never developed the habit of going to church on Sunday. We never encouraged either of our two children, Lisa Gael and John Michael, to go to Sunday school as I had been as a boy.

Whenever anyone would ask me what religion I believed in, I always told them I believed in the Ten Commandants and the Boy Scout Creed. Being an Eagle Scout, I had long ago memorized the Boy Scout creed: "A Scout is trustworthy, loyal, helpful, friendly, courteous, kind, obedient, cheerful, thrifty, brave, clean and reverent." I have always believed that if people lived by the Ten Commandments and the Boy Scout Creed the world would be a much better place.

Like I said, my marriage to Barbara didn't work out and neither did my second marriage to Renee. I certainly wasn't proud that I had been married twice and fathered four children. In fact I was down-right ashamed of myself for the way my two marriages had turned out.

By the time I was in my early thirties, I was not particularly happy. I didn't drink, nor did I like to "run around," but I was definitely drifting without a rudder and didn't know what I really wanted to do with my life. Eventually I began to realize that I wanted to get back to the roots my mother had instilled in me when I was a boy growing up in Tampa. I slowly became aware that maybe what I was missing was going to church and having God play a more active and positive role in my life.

In my professional life, I was giving my time and attention to making the American Bowl football event a financial and professional success. I knew that if I was going to be able to do that, I would need to get Dick Pope associated with my college all-star game. At the time, Dick Pope was known as "Mr. Florida" and was a very big promoter of tourism throughout the state. I thought that if I could get him to help promote my American Bowl Game in Tampa, it would give me a big boost in both publicity and attendance.

The reason Dick Pope was so popular statewide was because he owned and operated Cypress Gardens, one of the major tourist attractions in all of Florida. Dick was a very charismatic character, who owned a collection of flashy sport jackets, all, of which, featured unusual flowery designs. Dick liked to wear one of these jackets whenever he went out to promote Florida in general, or Cypress Gardens in particular.

Cypress Gardens Water Skiers

I took a drive over to Cypress Gardens in Winter Haven, Florida, about thirty miles east of Tampa, to meet Dick Pope. When I arrived, the famous Cypress Gardens ski show was going full blast. Beautiful girls on water skis were zipping past the grandstand, all waving happily to the throngs of tourists who were enjoying their visit to the popular tourist attraction.

When I got to Dick Pope's office, the most beautiful girl of all wasn't in the ski show outside. She was sitting inside as Dick Pope's administrative assistant.

I introduced myself and told the assistant I was there for my appointment with Dick Pope. She said Mr. Pope was expecting me and would be free in a few minutes. I'm glad he was busy, because I wanted to get to know this very attractive young lady sitting at her desk just a few feet from me.

When I met with Dick Pope, he agreed to lend his name to the American Bowl and help me promote my all-star classic. But much more importantly, the beautiful young lady sitting in Dick Pope's office became my wife just three weeks later! Not only was she beautiful, she was religious and exhibited the wholesome family qualities that I had been looking for in a wife. Her name was Evelyn. Like me, she had been married before. She had three little kids, Carrie, Robin and Todd, to add to my four little kids, Lisa, Michael, Jerry and Stephen. We had what's been described as a real life, "yours, mine and ours" situation!

Especially when 14 months later "our" child, Madalene Elizabeth, was born. Wow! I now had eight kids. My first two kids, Lisa and Michael, lived with their mother, Barbara, in nearby Largo, Florida. My second two kids, Jerry and Stephen, lived with their mother, Renee, in Clearwater, also nearby.

On weekends, Evelyn and I would often have all eight kids under one roof—either camping out or sleeping over. To say it was interesting would be an understatement. But, somehow, as the years went by we all managed to survive, and the "yours, mine and ours" experiment surprisingly worked out just fine!

Evelyn, Carrie, Michael, Jerry, Elizabeth, Lisa, Robin, Stephen and Todd

Evelyn was a very staunch member of the Christian Scientist Church. When we first met, I asked, without thinking, if a Christian Scientist was one of those people who rang bells and collected money in pots during Christmas. "No," she said, only slightly miffed, "that's the Salvation Army". I quickly regretted opening my mouth without thinking.

Although I was not fond of organized religion, I wanted to please my new wife. So we made sure our kids went to Sunday school and received at least some basic religious training. I also started going to the Christian Science church in Tampa and eventually became a member myself.

It was not unusual, then, for me to read The Christian Science Monitor, the newspaper printed daily in Boston by the Christian Science Mother Church. Some may mistakenly believe it's a religious newspaper. There is one religious article in the paper each day, but the rest of the newspaper is devoted to national and international news. I loved reading the CSM because of its worldwide coverage and honest editorial style of reporting.

One day in early 1975 I saw an article about a man in Texas who planned to look for Noah's Ark on Mt. Ararat in Turkey. I immediately took notice. Looking for Noah's Ark sounded like a terrific project. In fact, it sounded like just the type of project I could easily be a part of: I loved adventure, I knew how to lead an expedition, and I knew how to produce a film. I didn't know the man in Texas, but I was convinced

Mt. Ararat in Eastern Turkey

he needed me to help him put together an expedition to find Noah's Ark.

Evelyn and I arranged for a babysitter to keep the kids for a few days and headed for a small town outside of Dallas, where we met with Tom Crotzer, the man I had read about in The Christian Science Monitor.

Tom, it turned out, was the head of a small clan of very religious people who lived together at what Tom called his Holy Ground Mission. It didn't take long for me to realize that finding Noah's Ark was a very holy mission for Tom and his clan. Tom had already made several trips to Turkey searching for the Ark. He showed me pictures that he and his followers had taken on Mt. Ararat that showed a large boat-like object sticking out of a glacier in the Ahora Gorge on Mt. Ararat. He was certain it was the long-lost vessel from the book of Genesis.

I was more than a little apprehensive of Tom's religious fervor, but my enthusiasm quickly gave way to common sense and I told him that I was sure that I could raise the money we would need to mount an expedition to Mt. Ararat. After Tom and I signed a short agreement to work together, Evelyn and I were invited to spend the night with Tom and his family and other members of his Holy Ground Mission. We hadn't expected to be invited to spend the night, but not wanting to appear rude, we cautiously accepted.

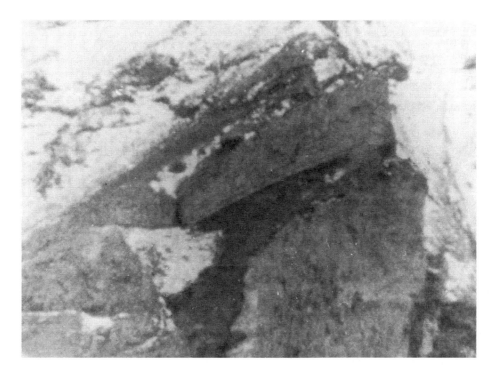

Tom Crotzer's Picture of Noah's Ark on Mt. Ararat Showing Wooden Planks

It didn't take long, however, to find out that the two-dozen or so husbands, wives and kids, living at the Holy Ground Mission were completely subservient to Tom Crotzer. Everyone got up at five o'clock in the morning and started reading the Bible for two hours. After a meager breakfast, the mission members who were old enough to work went into the community to perform menial tasks for money, which they brought back to the mission and promptly gave to Tom.

If a woman in the Holy Ground Mission needed bread, she was required to go to Tom and ask for a loaf of bread for her family. Everyone living at the mission seemed to be extremely religious, but Evelyn and I not only found this atmosphere unsettling, it didn't strike us as particularly Christian.

We hated to say anything, since we were their guests. But as soon as we left, we both confessed to each other that we were afraid we had stumbled into a strange, religious cult. Crotzer and his Holy Ground Mission seemed to be using their publicized search for Noah's Ark to further their unusual "Christian" beliefs.

I had an agreement with Tom Crotzer, and had given him my word that I would try to raise money for an expedition to find Noah's Ark. But getting involved with what appeared to be a bunch of religious goofballs had Evelyn and me doing a lot of praying and soul searching as we drove back home to Florida.

I did need a new project. And leading an expedition to Mt. Ararat to find Noah's Ark would certainly be a very interesting adventure. But I genuinely struggled with what to do. Maybe Tom Crotzer wasn't as goofy as he seemed, I reasoned. And maybe he was overly religious, but deep down he seemed to be an honest man.

I wanted to convince myself that working with Tom wouldn't be a problem, but just in case, I started trying to find someone who had worked with Tom Crotzer before. I started researching books and newspaper articles that described people or groups who had gone looking for Noah's Ark in the past.

I found quite a few stories about people who had searched for Noah's Ark. Some actually made claims that they had found Noah's Ark—or at least parts of it.

One notable book I found was *Noah's Ark: I Touched It*, by French industrialist Fernand Navarra. Mr. Navarra claimed to have found a plank of wood that had come from Noah's Ark sticking out of a glacier on Mt. Ararat. Later, when I was leading my own expedition, I met several people in Turkey who had been guides for

Navarra in the 1950s. Each one of them would laugh and tell me the Frenchman's audacious claim was definitely not true. They said Navarra had them carry several large wooden beams from a very old structure at the base of Mt. Ararat, up to the glacier in the Ahora Gorge. After the beams were tossed into a crevasse, Navarra took pictures that showed him "discovering" one of the old-looking beams as it was being dug out of the ice.

Eryl Cummings (l) and Fernand Navarra

Another interesting book I discovered was Noah's Ark: Fact or Fable? by Violet M. Cummings. Violet's book was about her research into the stories of Noah's Ark and about her husband Eryl's quest to find the ark for more than thirty years. Eryl was reported to have climbed Mt. Ararat more than any other explorer hoping to find the Holy relic. Because of his unflagging spirit, Eryl gained quite a reputation as the premier ark hunter—or "Arkologist" as he came to be known by Noah's Ark enthusiasts. Eryl was somebody I definitely wanted to meet.

Within a week of reading Noah's Ark: Fact or Fable?, I called Eryl and arranged to meet him in Farmington, New Mexico. I happily told him all about my interest in leading an expedition to Mt. Ararat and producing a film of the historic adventure. After Eryl said he would love to join me, I asked him if he knew Tom Crotzer?

Eryl smiled softly and told me that he did know Tom Crotzer and that Tom, for years, had wanted to be the man who discovered Noah's Ark. He then told me that he, too, hoped to be the first to discover Noah's Ark. But then added with a smile, "If it's God's will, it will happen. But not before!"

Eryl Cummings at Ahora Gorge on Mt. Ararat

I told Eryl about Evelyn and I spending the night at Tom's Holy Ground Mission. Again Eryl smiled (he smiled a lot) and suggested that their lifestyle was a little different than his, but didn't think there was anything wrong about being religious.

I told Eryl that Tom had said to me that he had permission to climb on Mt. Ararat. Eryl was immediately skeptical of his claim, but only shrugged and let me know he hoped that what Crotzer told me was true. Right about then, I started to worry. Why would Tom Crotzer tell me he had permission to climb Mt. Ararat, if he didn't?

Eryl told me that in those days it was very difficult for anyone to get permission to climb on Mt. Ararat to search for Noah's Ark. With Mt. Ararat sitting on the border of Turkey and Russian-controlled Armenia, the Russian government didn't like anyone climbing on the fabled mountain.

It was beginning to look like the first hurdle in this new adventure was going to be just gaining access to Mt. Ararat. Eryl, however, did not believe it would be impossible. Eryl said he was close friends with Dr. Zinnur Rollas, the personal physician of Turkish president Fahri Korutürk. "The president", Eryl said smiling, "has been known to give out permission. Dr. Rollas has also been known to help make it happen."

This was reassuring. If anything were to go wrong with Tom Crotzer's written permission, there may still be a chance we could get up on the mountain through Eryl's personal friendship with Dr. Rollas.

Within a couple of months I had raised the necessary money, hired about a dozen climbers and filmmakers and headed for the beautiful city of Geneve, Switzerland, near the Swiss Alps. I had traveled there many times before, often as a guest of Carlos Piaget, heir to the Piaget watch fortune.

Carlos lived in Michigan, but his family lived in Neuchâtel, northwest of Geneve. The Piaget family also owned several chalets in the Alps at Grimentz. Carlos and I had climbed in the Alps together many times. I knew I could find snow, ice and large

Mike at Piaget Chalet in Grimintz

glaciers in this region, which would be excellent training for my expedition team.

Training in Swiss Alps

After training and filming in Switzerland for two weeks, we took the fabled Orient Express for Istanbul and were finally off on our great "religious" adventure. After filming beautiful Istanbul sights like the Blue Mosque and Covered Bazaar, we hired two Turkish climbers as guides and headed for Ankara.

When time came for Tom Crotzer to show us his supposed permission document, not unsurprisingly, no document materialized. Again Eryl just smiled and suggested that maybe we should go have a little talk with his old friend, the president's physician.

Dr. Zinnur Rollas was a tall man with a friendly disposition, who seemed more than eager to help. He said he would do what he could to obtain a permission, but meanwhile, we should just be patient.

About that time, while we were waiting for Dr. Rollas to secure our permission, Tom Crotzer and his four-man team from the Holy Ground Mission just seemed to disappear. Eryl wondered if the round-trip flight to Turkey I had purchased for them might have been all they really wanted from me. He suspected they were probably hitchhiking their way out to Eastern Turkey to see if they could get up on the mountain "by the grace of God". Climbing on Mt. Ararat without proper permission, Eryl suggested, had never deterred them before.

After a day or two cooped up in our small Turkish hotel room waiting for our permission (and trying to be patient), I decided to venture out. Here I was in Turkey, the country that used to be called Asia Minor in the Bible, sitting around in a hotel room with a professional film team and just twiddling my thumbs. I decided that when permission did arrive to climb on Mt. Ararat, there would be plenty of time to get on with our primary expedition. In the meantime, I wanted to film some of the ancient Biblical and archaeological sights I knew were scattered around the far away country.

What a remarkable place Turkey turned out to be. We found two incredible, underground cities—one of which had never been filmed before. It still had huge round stones that rolled across doorways to seal entrances. The virgin underground city we filmed (which I guessed to be more than 2,000 years old) was dug downward into solid stone for more than nine stories. The city contained animal stalls, sleeping quarters, a large

Underground City at Derinkuyu

church and storage areas—all dug through more than 900 feet of solid limestone. We actually were able to film large earthen vats, still in their original place, which had been used to manufacture and store wine during the time of Jesus.

Another underground city we visited in a different part of Turkey didn't have any of the large round stones or original earthen vats. These had long ago been removed and placed in museums around the country.

Each week, Eryl and I continued to travel back to Ankara and check with Dr. Rollas to see if our permission to climb Mt. Ararat had arrived. But each week there would be one excuse or another, as to why we still weren't granted permission. So, never wanting to sit around and do nothing, I would immediately take off again with my film team and start roaming the country. We managed to capture on film an incredible variety of Biblical and archaeological sights from the Black Sea in the north to the Mediterranean in the South.

Amazingly, we were able to follow in the footsteps of the Apostle Paul and visit the first seven Christian churches he established 2,000 years previously in Asia Minor. I discovered there are so many ancient ruins throughout the country, many of them mentioned in the Bible, that to film them, I'm sorry to say, became almost ordinary and commonplace.

Once, when we approached an archaeological ruin said to be 6,000 years old, there was no one around but a farmer nearby plowing his field with a mule. A meager wire fence ran around the outside perimeter of the ancient ruin, but would not stop anyone from walking into the ancient site if they wanted to. When I asked the farmer if it was all right for us to take a few pictures, he said I would have to wait.

Off to one side of the two-strand wire enclosure sat a rundown-looking wooden shack no bigger than an average-sized outhouse. The farmer stepped inside then emerged a few minutes later wearing a uniform that consisted of an official-looking coat and rumpled cap. He smiled broadly, saluted smartly and announced in passable English, "I am now at your service".

Within minutes the meager fence gate swung back and we were allowed to film whatever and wherever we wanted. When we finished I gave the farmer a very nice tip and silently wished to myself that getting permission to climb on Mt. Ararat could be as easy!

Unfortunately, it wasn't. In fact, during the summer, we never did get permission to climb Mt. Ararat. I had to settle for returning home with plenty of good footage of ancient Turkish and biblical sights, but with no actual footage of our expedition team climbing Mr. Ararat in search of Noah's Ark.

Turkish Village Farm on way to Ahora Gorge on Mt. Ararat

As usual, Eryl was pragmatic about it. He said that he had come to Turkey many times hoping to look for the Ark, only to be denied for one reason or another. He said that I shouldn't give up and that maybe we should try again next summer.

Only during the summer months (mostly July and August)—when some of the snow had melted on the higher slopes of Ararat—was it possible to see the ark. And that wasn't every July and August. Actually, until you're able to get permission and make the arduous climb up to at least 12,000–14,000 feet, a climber isn't sure if conditions are right to see the ark, even if you know where to look.

 During other parts of the year, snow and ice on Mt. Ararat covers everything—especially above 10,000 feet. Only during certain years, after long spells of drought, does the snow melt enough that a successful search for the Ark can be accomplished.

When Eryl and I made our first trip to Ararat together in 1973, we never did obtain the hoped-for climbing permits from Dr. Rollas. Consequently, we never had a chance to find out if the climbing conditions were favorable that year for an ark sighting.

After that first trip, I never saw Tom Crotzer again. I have no idea what - if anything - he accomplished on Ararat, or even how he returned home. He and his mission members just disappeared, never to be heard from again.

After coming back to Tampa to prove to Evelyn that I didn't get killed trying to climb Mt. Ararat—and to get reintroduced to my kids—I flew out to Farmington, New Mexico and started going over all the film footage and photographs we had taken with Eryl Cummings in Switzerland and Turkey. I pulled out a copy of the photograph that Tom Crotzer had given me several months earlier that showed an ark-like wooden object sticking out of the ice in the Ahora Gorge on Mt. Ararat.

Eryl and I had looked at the photo together many times in the past. It did look authentic. It was possible to even see planks on the flat bow and part of one side of the object that wasn't completely hidden by the glacier. If that boat-like-looking object we were looking at in the photo was really the fabled Noah's Ark, then somehow we both needed to get back

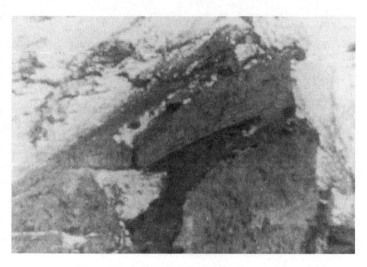

Tom Crotzer's Ark Object on Ararat

to Turkey, climb Mt. Ararat and find out. Wanting to find and film the ark wasn't a full-fledged obsession, but it certainly was something that I was now driven to do!

It wasn't necessarily a case of proving that the stories in the Bible are true. Just traveling around Turkey, following in the footsteps of Paul or Jesus' disciples was convincing enough of that. Many of the churches, tombs and places we filmed in Turkey can be found specifically mentioned in the Bible.

So why should I doubt the ancient story of Noah building an ark, riding out the great flood, and having it come to rest on Mt. Ararat?

There have been many stories over the years of people seeing the ark—and even some who have claimed they actually walked on the deck of the holy relic. I remember one story in particular about an Armenian boy named George Hagopian, who said that when he was young he used to ride on the shoulders of his uncle up the slopes of Mt. Ararat to the place where the ark was buried in the ice and snow.

George Hagopian with Ararat Painting

Once, he said, a small portion of the ark was sticking out of the ice, so his uncle helped push him up onto the deck. He said the wood was dark, almost black, and very weathered-looking. He said it must have been preserved for all those years, because of it being encased almost continually in ice.

I also unearthed more recent accounts of people claiming actually to have seen Noah's Ark. One story I learned about from Eryl Cummings was a sighting that happened in 1952, the same summer that Fernand Navarra climbed up on Ararat and made the claim of finding wooden timbers that came from Noah's Ark.

George Green, an American pipeline engineer hired by the Turkish government to look for oil, was flying a helicopter over the Ahora Gorge, when he saw a boat-like object sticking part way out of a glacier. The surprised engineer quickly swung the helicopter

George Green

around to take a closer look and also to take a few pictures. According to the story, when Green showed the pictures to several of his friends, none had any doubt they were looking at the same Noah's Ark mentioned in the Bible. But while on a mining job in Guyana several years later, George Green was mysteriously killed and all of his ark photos disappeared.

After Eryl and I returned from Turkey, we met David Duckworth, who said he had spent a summer working at the Smithsonian Institute in Washington, D.C. During that summer, he said, a shipment of wooden crates arrived on the loading dock. Word spread that the crates were from a joint expedition of the Smithsonian and the National Geographic Society.

The young man said he heard one of the supervisors announce excitedly, "Hey, they've got Noah's Ark out on the platform!"

Mike, David Duckworth & Eryl Cummings

Eryl and I filmed an interview with Duckworth during which he easily described what the wooden planks looked like— which were exactly as described by George Hagopian. "But after a couple of days," David said, "all the boxes were removed and word went out to everyone that if they wanted to keep their job, they better not mention anything about Noah's Ark to anyone again." David was only nineteen at the time and didn't want to lose his summer job, so never did mentioned it to anyone—until we filmed him

in the winter of 1975 in New Mexico.

Also that winter I interviewed Captain Clair Shaeffer , a Chaplain stationed at Tampa's MacDill Air Force Base. He stated that he was stationed in Samsun, Turkey from 1964 to 1965. He left to go on another assignment for a short period, but when he returned, his men told him that he had missed a very significant event. They said a National Geographic expedition came through the base on their way home from visiting Mt. Ararat in eastern Turkey. Clair said that when the men asked if they had found Noah's Ark, they replied, "We cannot answer that question now, but we can say that we've made the greatest discovery in the history of man!"

Chaplain Shaeffer went on to explain how he immediately took out an annual subscription to the National Geographic, fully expecting, one day soon, to see photos and extensive coverage of the discovery of Noah's Ark. But over the years, no such article appeared.

Facing a one-year delay in securing permission to climb Mt. Ararat—and with a wife and family to support—I needed to find another project. Our hope was that in a year Dr. Rollas would be able to get the permission we needed. Eryl remained optimistic that we would be on Mt. Ararat the following summer.

I hoped and wished that he was right. But I also knew that hoping and wishing wasn't going to feed my family for a year. I knew I had to find another expedition.

My treasure was in heaven. All I had to do was pray and wait for the answer. So I did, and before long my prayer was answered.

5 PANCHO VILLA

By the end of 1975 Eryl Cummings and I had become very good friends. Not only did he have a reputation as a leading "arkologist," he also liked to hunt for buried treasure (all kinds of treasure).

While I was working on editing my Noah's Ark footage in 1976, Eryl began sending me stories about The Lost Dutchman's Mine in New Mexico, Spanish Gold hidden in the Sierra Madre Mountains and even tales of treasure hidden in Mexico by the legendary bandito Pancho Villa.

When I read the stories Eryl sent me about Pancho Villa, I was immediately interested. Searching for Pancho Villa's treasure sounded like a great idea for an expedition and film. When Eryl and I met, he assured me the stories he had heard were true and that not only could we make a film, we would find the treasure and everyone on the expedition would become rich.

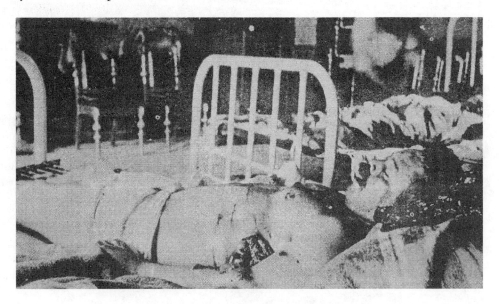

Pancho Villa on his Death Bed

Unlike needing clearance to climb Mt. Ararat, I didn't think I'd have to get any special permission from the Mexican government to search for treasure. I expected I might encounter local villagers in the area, but I didn't think they would be an insurmountable problem. So I set about researching everything I could get my hands on about Pancho Villa.

When I discovered Villa was killed in Parral, I immediately made plans to take a research trip to the small town south of Chihuahua.

Pancho Villa was the only person who ever attacked the United States. When General John Pershing was sent to New Mexico to run Villa back into Mexico, Pershing's chief aid at the time was a young lieutenant named George Patton—the same George Patton who later became a decorated World War II General.

When the brief border skirmish was over, both sides stopped long enough to have their pictures taken. I found an old photograph that had Pancho Villa looking into the camera, along with his notorious sidekick, General Zapata. Also smiling into the camera, on either side of Pancho Villa was General John Pershing and Lt. George Patton on one side and Zapata on the other side. It was strange to see these historic figures, each smiling happily for the camera, along with a dozen or so of Pancho Villa's Mexican bandito soldiers.

After visiting Chihuahua, I went to Mexico City and spoke with several potential investors about funding the expedition and film of the search.

Pancho Villa, General Pershing and Lt. George Patton

While there, I also talked with several notable Mexican filmmakers who I wanted to bring along on the expedition. One man in particular I hired was Juan Garcia, a cinematographer who had a terrific reputation for getting very good shots.

Finally, by the winter of 1977, I had my expedition team in place, which included a professional dowser named "Doc" Blanchard, and my good friend Eryl Cummings. Eryl was positive that Doc had the ability to successfully dowse for gold and silver. I didn't know anything about dowsing, so I just had to take Eryl's word for it.

I hired five additional local filmmakers to work with Juan to handle additional production duties—second camera, lighting, sound, etc. In addition, I brought with me two Australian roustabouts that I picked up in southern California. To round out our unlikely expedition team, I included two friends of mine, David Cory from New Jersey and Roberto Blanco from Tampa. We were a motley-looking crew indeed.

Mike (in hat) with Film Team in Mexico

Dave Cory was an independent businessman from New Jersey who had joined us on our expedition to Turkey. He had proven to be very resourceful in coming up with solutions to problems—especially when traveling through primitive areas.

There's no doubt we would be traveling through primitive areas in Mexico, so it was good to have Dave with us.

Bobby Blanco was a Cuban by birth, but moved to Florida when he was a young man. He and his mother lived together in a small house near the Tampa International Airport. Evelyn and I have always loved Cuban people, and we especially love Cuban food. Bobby was managing a restaurant in Tampa in the 1970s when we first met him, and the three of us immediately became friends.

Bobby was a great outdoorsman. He loved to boat and fish. Adventure was definitely in his blood. So he jumped at the chance to join our team—and reminded me that while we were traveling in Mexico, his Spanish would certainly come in handy.

My plan was to conduct the Pancho Villa expedition in the winter of 1977, then get back to Turkey in 1978 before the end of summer, when the snow on Mt. Ararat might have melted enough to afford us another go at finding Noah's Ark.

Excitement is always high at the beginning of an expedition. There's plenty of hope and anticipation, imagining all that might be accomplished during the great adventure. I'm always excited about leading an expedition, but I'm also excited about making another professional documentary film that will show our great adventure to the rest of the world.

Before leaving on our adventure to Mexico, I rented a twin-engine Piper Aztec plane (and pilot) in Texas, loaded it with tents, sleeping bags and other camping gear, then had the pilot fly all the gear down to Mexico City so it would be waiting for us when we arrived. The rest of us took a commercial flight into the Mexican capital and began pulling together all the additional equipment we would need.

For instance, I hired a Mexican helicopter pilot who owned a 4-place Bell helicopter. The chopper could not only get us into most inaccessible areas, it also had a special camera mount that would enable us to film out of the aircraft's side door. I knew we would be traveling through some very rugged mountainous country where Eryl had indicated several other treasures were located prior to heading into the area we thought Pancho Villa's treasure was located. I was confident the helicopter with the stabilizing camera mount would enable us to get some very spectacular aerial pictures.

The first treasure we looked for was a large amount of Spanish gold that Eryl said was hidden in a cave "where two canyon walls are so close together a large tree could cross!" Eryl figured that the easiest way for us to find the treasure was to fly in the Bell helicopter above the Aros River until we found the spot.

Mike with Helicopter Camera Mount

As our helicopter meandered through the northern portion of the Sierra Madre Mountains, we searched for two canyon walls that were so close that a large tree could cross over the divide. That certainly sounded easy enough, but after following the river down the canyon for nearly an hour, we found only one location that possibly could have fit Eryl's description. Unfortunately, the terrain was so rugged in that one particular spot there was no way we could even come close to landing the helicopter.

We had no choice but to fly ten miles upstream to our base camp. We planned to take the two inflatable rubber rafts we brought along (for just such an occasion) down the relatively calm river the next morning to that one special spot in the canyon where we anticipated the Spanish treasure would be.

Then it rained cats and dogs. For the next three days.

All we could do was sit in our tents and dream about finding all that gold that was waiting for us ten miles down the canyon. When it finally stopped raining, the little stream that three days earlier had meandered peacefully through the canyon was now a raging river crashing through the canyon in a furious torrent.

Some of team members were apprehensive about putting our rubber Zodiac boats into the boiling whitewater. But not me! Being an adventurous filmmaker, the thought of filming the surging floodwater was like manna from heaven. What an exciting film I could now make as we rode down the canyon in our two little boats, crashing along through roaring rapids.

The more I thought about it, the clearer my cinematic vision became. In that rushing water, it wouldn't take us long at all to travel ten miles downstream toward the waiting pot of gold.

After a little coaxing, I managed to get our two Australian roustabouts to push off from shore into the rapids to prove to the group that paddling in the whitewater wasn't too dangerous. Within 200 yards, the two men were thrust against a large bolder and nearly capsized. As quickly as they could, the Australians paddled for the opposite shore and exited their small craft as if their lives depended upon it.

After accusing my Australian teammates of being somewhat less than manly, I asked my Cuban-American friend Bobby Blanco to get into the front of the second Zodiac with a paddle. I told him I would sit in the middle with my trusty 16-mm Canon Scoopic camera to film what promised to be a great adventure.

I then asked my other friend Dave Cory to grab a second paddle and take a seat in the rear. Then, after waving gallantly to our anxious companions on shore, we pushed off into the charging maelstrom and headed for the gold downstream.

When we passed the large bolder our two Australian teammates had crashed into, I figured this wasn't going to be such a dangerous escapade after all. I began concentrating on trying to get some exciting film footage of our spectacular river adventure.

After about two miles, the river was still running hard and fast, but wasn't quite as full of frothy white rapids as it had been in the beginning. The three of us even started relaxing a bit and began joking about how easy it was going to be to find that Spanish gold. This part of the expedition was working out a lot better than even I had expected.

Bobby and Dave's expert paddling was keeping us right in the middle of the river as the high steep walls of the rocky canyon continued to sweep past. I stayed busy looking for spectacular shots to film and was delighted at all the adventure shots I was actually able to record. We all noticed that the river seemed to be picking up a little speed, but for me, that made the shots even more spectacular.

Then, while looking through the camera's viewfinder, I noticed that I couldn't see the river ahead and wasn't sure what I was seeing. When I looked up to get my bearings, I asked Bobby, "What happened to the river?"

He tried to stand up a little in the front of the unsteady Zodiac, so he could get a better look down stream. When he did, Bobby could hardly believe his eyes. We were being swept faster and faster because we were headed straight toward a twenty-foot waterfall. The river had disappeared because not more than fifty yards in front of us it was crashing straight down.

Bobby and Dave started paddling as fast as they could, desperately trying to reach the safety of a protruding bolder, but the water was now running way too strong and we were quickly swept past. All three of us started paddling for shore as hard as we could, Bobby and Dave with their paddles and me with one bare hand, since my other hand was still holding my Cannon Scoopic. But it was all to no avail. We were going to be swept over the waterfall and there wasn't a thing we could do about it.

Resigned to our fate, I did what any other documentary filmmaker would do. I immediately put my eye to the viewfinder and started filming. I figured that if we were going to die being swept over a waterfall, at least I would make sure I got some spectacular footage.

As we were swept over the precipice into the churning water and rocks below, I remember watching the horizon flip completely upside down through my viewfinder as our little Zodiac tumbled through the air.

When we crashed hard into the swirling water below, I felt a searing pain in my back. Instantly I started being tossed around in muddy river water. First I was pushed up, then immediately pulled back down. Over and over my body was flung every which way, with no possible notion of being able to help myself in the churning river—all the while holding onto my trusty Canon Scoopic camera.

I've always prided myself on being an expert swimmer. I was captain of my high school swim team, and put myself through the college at the University of Florida by working at the university pool as a lifeguard. But in that raging Mexican river, there was absolutely nothing I could do to save myself. I was completely at the mercy of the river.

Then, as if by magic, the angry waters pushed me to the surface, close to the Zodiac. Almost at the same time, Bobby and Dave popped to the surface close by. Instinctively, we all grabbed for the small rope that ran around the outside of the overturned raft and hung onto it with all the strength we had.

We were swept over rocks, down into whirlpools, then pushed back out, tossed over and around huge boulders that were hidden by massive volumes of cascading water. We were swept down the canyon with all the fury of a runaway locomotive. There was nothing we could do but try to keep our head above water and hang onto the bouncing Zodiac for dear life.

After about five minutes (which felt like an eternity) our raft crashed into a large protruding boulder about fifteen feet from shore. We did everything we could to hold our precarious position, because another fifty yards further downstream, the river made a sharp turn around a bend in the canyon and again disappeared.

My back was killing me. I could barely move. Bobby had a large gash on his forehead where he had obviously struck the rocks below the falls. And Dave's large knife had been pushed through its sheath into his leg when we went over the falls.

We weren't sure if we should let go of our tenuous resting place—allowing ourselves to be swept around the corner of the canyon into the unknown—or attempt to reach the rocky shore fifteen feet away. Maybe the river around the bend would calm down and we could reach the shore safely. Or maybe the ferocious churning went on for miles.

We had no idea what to do. I tried to pray, but prayer wasn't coming as fast as I wanted it to. And then inspiration that I can only call an "angel thought" came to me: we should try to reach the shore where we were. There was safety just fifteen feet away if we could somehow get to it.

Now all we had to do was figure out how to get to the rocky shore. With water rushing past us with such force, swimming would be impossible. I formulated a plan. Bobby seemed to be the least hurt, so I asked him to take the rope from off the Zodiac and tie it around his ankle. If he could climb up on the slippery boulder while Dave and I pushed the Zodiac toward shore, he might be able to jump onto the bottom of the overturned craft, take a quick step and leap for the shore. If he missed, Dave and I would try to pull him back to the boulder before he was swept away.

I knew it was tricky, and I knew I was asking a lot of Bobby, but with the water racing so fast between our boulder and the shore, there didn't appear to be any other way of escape. We had one shot. If Bobby missed the shore we could probably pull him back to the boulder, but the Zodiac would be irretrievably lost. I prayed a silent prayer.

Bobby steadied himself on the rock as Dave and I pushed the overturned Zodiac as hard as we could toward the shore and into the raging torrent. At just the right instant, Bobby jumped, made two quick steps on the raft bottom and leaped as hard as he could for the shore.

Somehow, barely, he grabbed a protruding rock and slowly scrambled to safety. After resting a few moments he untied the rope from his ankle and was able to pull Dave and me, one by one, across the raging stretch of water to the shoreline.

All three of us lay on the rocks, exhausted. My back and ribs were killing me, but I was still holding tightly to my waterlogged camera. Bobby's head was sliced open, as was Dave's leg. Both were bleeding badly but, miraculously, we were all alive. This looking for treasure was beginning to get a little too dangerous, even for me.

One by one we got to our feet and slowly climbed over the rocks to higher ground. Before heading back to camp I wanted to find a spot where I could look around the bend in the river and see if we'd made the right decision to get out of the raging flood waters where we did.

It wasn't easy, but when we were finally able to climb to higher ground and see around the bend, all three of us were shocked at what we saw. Downstream the rock walls of the gorge narrowed even closer, so that for almost a mile the water raged through the rocky gap with such force and fury it was plain that if we had gone that way we would all have been killed. There was absolutely no doubt about it.

I immediately gave thanks to God for giving me that little angel thought when I so desperately needed it. It ultimately saved our lives.

We eventually made our way back to base camp. There was no more talk about looking for treasure, at least not for that year. And there was also no more talk about going back to Mt. Ararat to look for Noah's Ark. We were all too beat up to go looking for anything.

I put the soaked 16-mm movie film into a bucket of water to keep it wet until I turned it over to a lab for processing. Surprisingly, the image on the film was still good. It was not great, a little scratchy in places, but it did show us surging down the river, going over the falls, then turning a complete flip in the air and falling upside down into the water. That's where the image dramatically stops.

I made a mental note to save the film for use in the documentary adventure I planned to complete when I returned to Mexico the following spring. Maybe by then my broken ribs would have healed and I'd be able to complete my search for Pancho Villa's treasure. I also planned to go back to Turkey so I could film the dramatic discovery of Noah's Ark. It's good to be a dreamer. There are always so many wonderful things to plan and dream about. But it does little good to dream if you're always afraid to act on them.

And I hadn't forgotten about my dream of finding the Titanic in the North Atlantic. It was still one of my major goals. But I knew finding it would cost over a million dollars. Leading an oceanographic expedition and raising the money for such an ambitious endeavor was not going to be easy—especially since I had led only one expedition and produced only one successful documentary film. Even though *Deadly Fathoms* was a pretty good beginning, I didn't think that one success gave me enough credibility to raise the money that would be needed to find and film the Titanic.

In the meantime, I'd let my body heal while I tried to figure out how I could raise enough money to get my two expedition teams back together. I was sure Pancho Villa's treasure was still out there somewhere in the mountains of old Mexico, just waiting for me to find it. And Noah's Ark was still sitting in a glacier on top of Mt. Ararat in eastern Turkey, waiting for someone to discover her as well. Being the consummate dreamer, I saw no reason why that someone couldn't be me.

6 STARTING AGAIN

In the spring of 1978 I got a little money together from several investors in Florida and New Mexico and set about putting our Pancho Villa expedition team back together. Once again, keys to any effort to find Villa's treasure were Eryl Cummings and Doc Blanchard. Eryl had memorized all the treasure stories by heart and had a pretty good idea where we should be looking. His faith remained strong that Doc, our professional dowser, could pinpoint Villa's treasure location once we got close enough up in the mountains for him to dowse for it.

I brought back Bobby Blanco and Dave Cory, my two compatriots who almost drowned with me the previous summer when we went over the falls. They, too, had healed and like everyone else remained infected with "treasure fever". The two Australian roustabouts were now nowhere to be found, so they were no longer a part of our reconstituted expedition team.

My local Mexican camera team also agreed to return. And, as before, I took along another 16mm Canon Scoopic movie camera. My first one was damaged so badly from our river adventure there was no way I could ever use it again.

I liked the size of the Scoopic. It was large enough to shoot 16mm film, but also not so large that I couldn't hold it in one hand and shoot the cutaway scenes I knew I would need when editing my documentary.

Missing from our 1977 expedition were the two aircraft and pilots. I had gotten plenty of beautiful aerial footage the year before, so figured I didn't need to hire the expensive Bell helicopter or twin-engine Aztec for this expedition.

We all assembled at Chihuahua, Mexico, about two hundred miles south of El Paso, Texas, and eagerly began final organization of that summer's expedition. I knew what I wanted to film first was right there in Chihuahua.

On my research trip more than a year previously, I learned there was a museum in Chihuahua that was run by one of Pancho Villa's wives who, surprisingly, was still living. It turned out that Pancho had several wives during his lifetime, but the lady in Chihuahua was reported to be his last. Since she spoke a little English I thought she would make a very nice interview for my proposed documentary.

When we got to the museum, I arranged to interview Mrs. Villa, who happily gave me a personal tour of her small, but very interesting museum. She pointed out a variety of old photographs, many of which featured her husband with a number of famous people he had been photographed with over the years. She also had on display several of her husband's uniforms, his personal pistols and even the bullet-riddled roadster he was riding in when he was ambushed and killed at Paral.

Pancho Villa's Roadster

I noticed two skulls sitting on a shelf, one obviously of adult size and the other a child. I asked Mrs. Villa, "Who did the two skulls belong to?" She smiled and said happily that the large skull was of her husband Pancho Villa. I was astonished. Mrs. Villa was keeping the skull of her late husband sitting on a shelf for all to see? Obviously shocked, I asked her, cautiously, "Who does the small skull belong to?" Without hesitation, she smiled again and told me proudly, "Oh that was when Pancho was a little boy!"

I had been had. Big time. And knew it. I couldn't wait to get my expedition team out of Chihuahua and head in the direction of the small Mexican town called

Cuauhtemoc, where Eryl said Villa's wagons passed on their way into the mountains. From there we took a dirt road that led us directly toward the mountains where I knew Villa's treasure was waiting to be discovered.

This time, instead of aircraft, I spent money on a large D8 bulldozer that I'd leased in Chihuahua and carried on the back of a flatbed truck. I figured we'd need the bulldozer because of a treasure story that Eryl and Doc related to me about Villa's Mexican hoard.

It seems that Pancho Villa amassed a fortune in

D8 Bulldozer

stolen objects made of gold, which he melted down into small gold bars. The bars were then placed into 20 wooden wagons and hauled to a cave in the mountains outside a small Mexican village called La Cacita. Doc said that peons were forced to carry the gold into the cave then a handpicked team of Villa's most trusted soldiers blew up the entrance to the cave, trapping the poor villagers inside.

Most intriguing of all was Doc's story that he had found the entrance to the cave by dowsing just two years earlier. But he was unable to get inside the cave because of all the rocks that had collapsed over the entrance when Villa's men blew it in. That's why I arranged to have the D8 bulldozer with us when we got to Doc's cave.

When we arrived in the dusty village of La Cacita we attracted quite a crowd of local men, women and children. They all came to the side of the road and watched as American and Mexican film team members, adventurers, treasure hunters and especially our huge bulldozer arrived. Old timers said they hadn't seen anything like our procession since Pancho Villa came through town with his group of bandito soldiers some fifty years earlier. They said that Villa and his men also had large wooden wagons with them—ten of them, each pulled by two mules. They all agreed that with all those soldiers around, the wagons must have been carrying something valuable.

I, of course, asked them if they thought Pancho Villa's wagons were full of gold. The old timers just shrugged and mumbled, "No se, no se". I asked Bobby what that meant. He wasn't sure if they were saying they didn't know what was in the wagons, or just didn't want to talk about it.

I asked Bobby to talk to the other villagers about the famous bandito and his gold. He asked around and discovered they didn't know any more than we did. They had heard stories growing up, but never had any idea if any of the stories were true. They also said that over the years, small groups of "gringos" would pass through La Cacita on their way into the mountains.

But so far, they told Bobby excitedly, none of the other gringos had a dozen people carrying supplies, equipment and a huge bulldozer. Our group of gringos, they agreed, was something special. I told Bobby that once we found the gold and made a movie about it, I didn't think the people of La Cacita would continue to have so many gringo visitors.

As we left the village, everyone eagerly anticipated the adventure that lay before us. The thrill of searching for the Pancho Villa's famous stash of gold was exciting for all of us. I could only imagine how exciting it would be to actually lead an expedition in search of the famous Titanic. I hadn't forgotten about my dream to find the Titanic and recover her artifacts, but today, in Mexico, infected with "treasure fever," the Titanic would have to wait.

Doc Blanchard tied two gold coins to the end of his dowsing stick and held it up with one hand in front of him so he could feel the mysterious tug of Villa's gold hidden in the mountains. Then, like a modern day Pied Piper, holding his gold-laden dowsing stick in one hand and waving it before him, Doc led all of us back into the rough mountainous country outside La Cacita.

After two, long days of walking (almost all of it uphill), looking first into one canyon and then another, we finally found the canyon that Doc said he had discovered two years earlier. Our excitement climbed to a new level. All we had to do was follow Doc's dowsing stick to the secret hiding place of Pancho Villa's treasure. Treasure fever was rampant among all of us. Even the Mexican filmmakers were beginning to get excited.

The terrain was now extremely rocky, with stumpy oaks and boulders covering the landscape almost all the way to shear rock walls that rose majestically more than 500 feet above us. So when Doc pointed to an ordinary-looking rockslide on the north side of the canyon and stated, "The cave's in there!" I started having serious doubts he knew what he was doing.

On our slow trek into the mountains, I had noticed several other rockslides against the walls of other canyons. Those slides all appeared to have been caused by natural forces, not by dynamite. The slide Doc was pointing to didn't look any different. When I asked Eryl what he thought about Doc's treasure location, he looked a little surprised too, but shrugged and said, .With the big D8, it won't take us long to find out!. It had cost a lot of money to rent the bulldozer back in Chihuahua. Now it was time to get it up into the canyon and put it to work.

But there was one slight problem: the terrain was not only covered with boulders and stumpy trees, it was also very steep. For two days the heavy bulldozer had to cut its own path up into the canyon to where our expedition team waited with growing anticipation. The growl of the large metal contraption slowly working its way up the rugged mountain, getting closer and closer to where we waited, was literally music to our ears.

But on the third day, the racket suddenly stopped. Less than 100 yards from Doc's rockslide, the D8 bulldozer pulled to a stop and grew silent.

After a quick discussion with the operator, Bobby Blanco translated to me what the trouble was with the D8. Sadly, he said, the terrain was now too steep for its metal tread. Up where we were, close to the cliff face, there was very little dirt on the ground—only solid rock. It was impossible for the expensive digging machine to get any higher. It had simply lost all traction.

We discussed several different scenarios on how we might be able to get the D8 the last hundred yards to where we needed for it to dig. But in the end, we always came up with the same conclusion. Unfortunately, our ideas wouldn't work. Now there was no choice but to send the large digging machine back down the mountain and try to figure out how to dig through all that rock.

Treasure hunting was starting to feel a lot like hard work. We had one metal crow bar and a few meager pots and pans to dig with between us. We didn't have any real picks or shovels, but we did have our bare hands. Trying to be as enthusiastic as I could, I gathered my disillusioned expedition team around me and told them of my new plan.

"It might not be easy," I started, trying to put on a brave face, "but with a little pluck and perseverance we could dig out Pancho Villa's treasure with our bare hands." I continued, pleading, "Just think about it, Villa's treasure is just ten feet under the rocks we're sitting on!"

The looks on their faces told me I wasn't getting anywhere.

Trying again, I argued this time even more forcefully. "Doc's dowsing proves that Villa's gold is still in the cave! Don't give up! In just one short week we'll all be rich!"

No one bought it. Only Bobby Blanco, Dave Cory, Eryl Cummings and I agreed to stick it out. Everyone else headed back down the mountain to La Cacita. I'm sure they figured with summer coming, it was getting way too hot to do that much digging by hand.

Or maybe they just didn't have faith in Doc's dowsing. Either way, the bloom was now off the rose. Treasure hunting had become hard work with no guarantee that we would ever find Villa's cave and its treasure.

I kept a camera and tape deck with me, just to make an audio and film record of what we accomplished, good or bad. But the once large team of professional filmmakers and treasure hunters had now shrunk to just four.

When everyone left, following the D8 back down the mountain, our treasure site suddenly grew very quiet and seemed even more remote. As the four of us sat quietly together in the growing darkness, the enormity of the situation began to sink in. Here we were, in the middle of nowhere, sitting on a huge pile of rocks, that, somehow, we were now supposed to move with our bare hand.

Trying to remain enthusiastic, I told the guys we still had a little light left before it got completely dark and that the rocks weren't going to move themselves. I suggested we might as well start digging, slow and steady, one rock and one boulder at a time. So, that's exactly what we did, until it finally got so dark we couldn't see what we were doing.

We pitched a small tent at the bottom of the canyon, but actually ended up sleeping out under the stars. Without any city lights close by, the heavenly carpet above us stretched from horizon to horizon. For a city boy like me, the starry spectacle above was an unforgettable sight.

Early the next morning the four of us trudged back up the mountain and once again started moving rocks. Our metal crowbar helped us leverage a few of the largest boulders out of the pile. Gravity then rolled them on down the mountainside and away from the site.

The work was slow. The work was hard. And the work was hot! The ribs that I had broken the previous summer had healed, but my back still bothered me when we had to lift and push heavy boulders.

After about a week, we were able to dig down approximately six feet and were surprised to smell what appeared to be gunpowder. Eryl was quick to remind us that Pancho Villa's peons used dynamite to blow up the entrance to the cave. Maybe we smelled the residue from that blast.

With renewed vigor, all four of us started throwing rocks down the mountainside, until thirty minutes later we had dug our way down to bedrock. I don't mean we dug down to a cave that Doc and Eryl said we would find. I mean we dug down and found nothing but solid bedrock. There was no cave. No treasure. Nothing.

We were devastated. Not only were we devastated, we were physically and mentally exhausted. So much time and money had been spent looking for Pancho Villa's treasure, and we had come up empty. What had happened to Villa's treasure? Did one of the other "gringo" groups find the treasure and get away without letting anyone in La Cacita know? Or, was it all just a cruel hoax that had lured adventurers and treasure hunters into the mountains of old Mexico for years?

It was a long ride back home to Tampa, but I convinced myself that maybe I could make the best of it. For two years I had traveled throughout Mexico looking for treasure. Why wouldn't other people want to watch a film about our expedition and vicariously experience our great adventure? We may not have found any treasure, but we sure did have an adventure.

Mike Harris, Cesar Romero, Evelyn Harris

When I got back to Tampa with all the footage I had taken over the past two years, I decided I needed to feature a famous Hollywood actor in my adventure documentary. I found out that Cesar Romero was playing at a dinner theater in the area, so I immediately went to see him and asked if he would agree to be my on-camera host and narrator. Cesar said he would be more than happy to work with me and wanted to know when I wanted to get started.

I rented a bank boardroom in downtown Tampa, dressed it up to look like it could have been the offices of my company International Expeditions. Cesar was very cooperative and extremely professional. I couldn't have been more pleased with his on-camera sequences and narration of the film—that I distributed under the title Pancho Villa's Treasure.

Many people (including me) thought Cesar Romero was of Mexican descent. Actually, he was Cuban-American, born in New York City. His father was from Spain, but lived in Cuba and married his mother who was Cuban. In fact, Cuban liberator Jose Marti was Cesar's grandfather from his mother's side of the family.

Cuban or Mexican, it didn't matter. Cesar Romero made a terrific on-camera host and narrator for my second documentary feature. We didn't find the treasure, but we sure did have a wonderful adventure.

Pancho Villa's Treasure **Promo Sheet**

7 ALCOA SEAPROBE

As I was finishing up post-production work on Pancho Villa's Treasure. I received a phone call from Dick Greenwald, my friend at Deep Sea Ventures. He asked if I had heard the news about Bob Ballard. I told him I hadn't because I had been up to my ass moving rocks in Mexico. I then asked him, "Who's Bob Ballard?"

Dick told me Bob Ballard was an oceanographer at the Woods Hole Oceanographic Institution on the south coast of Massachusetts. He said Bob had an excellent reputation as an oceanographer, but also had a pretty big ego, which made it difficult for people to work with him. Having no idea what Dick was getting at, I asked another question: "What's Bob Ballard got to do with me?"

"You want to find the Titanic, don't you?" he asked sarcastically. I admitted that I did. "Well," Dick continued, "so does he!"

"Why are you calling me," I asked hoping to draw a little information out of him. I didn't know Bob Ballard. In fact, at the time, I had never heard of him. But if he was someone interested in searching for the Titanic, I figured I better find out something about him.

Dick went on to explain that Bob Ballard specialized in deep-ocean geology. Woods Hole owned a deep diving submersible called Alvin that could dive down to 6,000 feet. I reminded him that the Titanic was

Dr. Robert Ballard

sitting on the bottom in water that was at least 12,000 feet deep.

He acknowledged that was true and told me Bob Ballard was trying to find the Titanic using Seaprobe, Alcoa Aluminum's drilling ship. It has a large metal derrick built onto the main deck, with a hole cut through the middle of the ship, through which thousands of feet of metal pipe can be lowered.

Ballard convinced Alcoa to let him lease the Seaprobe so he could put a camera package at the end of all that string of pipe and go looking for the Titanic. He reportedly told Alcoa he could find the Titanic in just 10 to 12 days. All they had to do was let him attach his camera package to a string of pipe that was 12,000 feet long.

Alcoa agreed to Ballard's proposal, presumably in no small part because it would be good publicity for the company to be involved in finding the Titanic. During the expedition, however, the drill string broke and is now just a big pile of junk lying on the bottom.

Alcoa Seaprobe

I wondered if Bob Ballard's bad luck might turn out to be good luck for me. With Alcoa almost certainly upset with Ballard, and regretting their decision to help him look for the Titanic, I thought after things settle down a bit, I could talk Reynolds Aluminum into letting me use the Aluminaut to search for the Titanic. Dick agreed it might be worth a shot, but cautioned me to wait until the following year.

I told him he was probably right and let him know I had other fish to fry in the meantime. This got Dick's interest and wanted to know "What kind of goose chase are you off on this time?" I ignored his slight insult and without blinking an eye, told him I was looking for Noah's Ark on Mt. Ararat—and it wasn't a goose chase.

Dick was skeptical, but I didn't let him deter my enthusiasm. I told him about the trip Turkey the previous year. I went on to explain that it wasn't easy to get the necessary permissions, but fully expected things to be different this summer. Always well-versed in all things international and political, Dick reminded me that, as far as he knew, the situation in Eastern Turkey hadn't improved since the previous summer.

I allowed how that was true, but that there was a new development that would virtually guarantee the door being opened for our expedition. My partner in New Mexico, Eryl Cummings, had become friends with James Irwin, one the astronauts who drove a Land Rover on the moon. Jim had a religious experience during his moon mission. Upon returning, he formed a Foundation in Colorado Springs called High Flight and was spending a lot of his time traveling around the world talking to people about his moon flight experience and also telling them about his renewed belief in God.

Jim Irwin and Land Rover on Moon

I then told Dick that I planned to invite Jim Irwin to go to Turkey with Eryl and me when we returned on our second expedition later in the summer. Surprisingly, Dick said that sounded like a pretty good idea, but then cautioned, "You shouldn't forget about trying to find the Titanic. That could make you more famous than finding Noah's Ark!"

"I'm not putting together these expeditions to get famous," I responded indignantly. "I just want to find out the truth about what happened to two of the most famous ships of all time! If I can find the Titanic on the bottom of the ocean, or Noah's Ark on top of Mt. Ararat, the documentary films that I would produce would be of interest to everyone. All I want to do is solve great mysteries, not lead expeditions to get famous!"

"If you find the Titanic or Noah's Ark," Dick chided, "you're going to be famous, whether you want to be or not."

"That may be true," I conceded half-heartedly, "but it's not why I'm working on the two projects. They're just two of several interesting mysteries in this world that I'm curious about solving. Working on the research and trying to figure out what's really happened, historically, is what gets me up in the morning."

Dick must have been curious, because he asked me another pertinent question. "You just said the Titanic and Noah's Ark are two interesting mysteries that you'd like to solve. What's another one?"

Without hesitating, I responded quickly. "I'd like to find out what happened to Amelia Earhart".

Amelia Earhart on Lockheed Electra

Again, Dick was taken aback. "Amelia Earhart? I've never heard you say anything about her before. When did you get interested in finding Amelia? I lowered my voice slightly to make him think I was telling him a secret. "When I was in the Marshall Islands," I continued, "diving on ships at Bikini Atoll during atom bomb testing, I heard stories that Amelia Earhart the famous woman flier had crashed off Mili Atoll, was captured by the Japanese and then taken alive to Saipan. Wouldn't it be something to find out what really happened to Amelia Earhart?"

Dick had never heard anything like that before. And he encouraged me to let the Titanic situation sit for a year until the dust of Bob Ballard's Alcoa disaster settled. "If I were you," he said, "I'd go back to Turkey and see if you can get up on Mt. Ararat."

"You must be reading my mind," I told him cheerily, "because that's exactly what I intend to do. If you hear anything new about Titanic, I wish you'd please let me know. In the meantime, I'm going to contact Eryl's astronaut friend, Jim Irwin, and see if he would like to go with us to Mt. Ararat. Wish me luck!"

Dick countered prophetically, "You'll need more than luck, my friend. You'll need a full blown miracle!"

8   ARK OF THE COVENANT

When Eryl Cummings and I were in Turkey together in 1974 on our first trip to find Noah's Ark, we got some newspaper publicity back in America about our expedition. An elderly gentleman named Clinton Locey read about us and got in touch one day. He called out of the blue and said he knew the location of the Ark of the Covenant, the ancient container of the original tablets the Ten Commandments were written on. He wanted to know if we'd be interested. Eryl and I were speechless.

Who wouldn't be interested in finding such an important biblical relic? Eryl and I both knew that many people over the years had looked for the "Ark" that was said to contain the Ten Commandments Moses received directly from God on Mount Sinai. It's said the Israelites kept their holiest artifact in a very special place in the first temple built by King Solomon. The Bible states that when King Nebuchadnezzar of Babylonia attacked the Israelites in 1857 B.C., temple priests removed the holy relic and hid it so it wouldn't be captured.

Unfortunately, they seem to have hidden the ark so well, no one has ever been able to find it. To this date, no one knows for sure where it's hidden, or what happened to it. People from many faiths have been looking for the Ark of the Covent ever since.

When Mr. Locey called and asked if we would be interested in finding the ark, we immediately assured him that we would be. He said that if we would just pay his way over to Jordan, he would show us the location of a secret cave that he had been taken to fifty years before. He said the cave is on Mt. Nebo just outside the small town of Medaba, Jordan. Clinton went on to tell us that on one wall of the cave are written directions in ancient Hebrew that tell exactly where the Ark of the Covenant can be found.

Eryl and I couldn't believe that anyone in America would have access to such incredible information. Within two days we flew Clinton into Farmington, New Mexico, where Eryl Cummings lived and had all his Noah's Ark records. When he told us his story in person, Eryl and I knew that we had to get him over to Jordan as quickly as possible.

Suggested Ark of the Covenant Replica

Mt. Nebo sits on one side of the Jordan River. From the top of Mt. Nebo it's easy to look across the holy river into Israel and see the famous Biblical city of Jerusalem shimmering on a hill in the distance. The Bible clearly states that Moses led the children of Israel to Mt. Nebo where they could look down upon the river Jordan and into the land of Canaan on the other side. The Bible also states that God forbid Moses to enter Canaan. What happened to Moses? Did he die there on Mt. Nebo? Did he leave and go back to somewhere else, as God had instructed him not to enter Canaan. No one knows for sure.

Being aware of the legend, Eryl and I thought that Clinton Locey's story was completely plausible. What Clinton told us specifically was that fifty years ago he joined an expedition to Palestine that was led by Dr. A.T. Futterer, an explorer who had traveled extensively for many years throughout the area known as Palestine. Clinton said that Dr. Futterer took him to a spot on Mt. Nebo and told him there was a cave beneath their feet that had ancient Hebrew writing along one wall. The writing would describe the exact location of where the Ark of the Covenant could be found. Clinton said he was getting too old to mount an expedition himself, and knew from the article he had read about Eryl and me that we were both "God-fearing men" and we alone should be trusted with the information he had about the Ark of the Covenant.

Dr. A.T. Futterer

It didn't take us long to get over to Jordan with Clinton and take him to Mt. Nebo. But when we arrived, it soon became apparent the location he had visited fifty years earlier had undergone a number of significant changes. Consequently, he wasn't able to walk to the precise spot that Dr. Futterer had shown him.

Eryl and I walked him around, this way and that, but no matter which way we walked, things had changed so much since the last time he was there he couldn't find anything that looked familiar. This wasn't working out like we thought it would so I knew I'd have to do something different.

Often when I come to a roadblock of some kind, I pray. I realize there are some who would dispute the effectiveness of this, but I've learned over the years that praying to God for guidance or help isn't doing "nothing," it really is doing quite a lot! God knows what I need. All I have to do is quiet my thought so I can hear what He's telling me. Standing on top of Mt. Nebo with a well-intentioned, disoriented Clinton Locey, I once again sent up a prayer for guidance.

It wasn't long before an angel thought popped into my consciousness. I knew the closest town to Mt. Nebo was the ancient town of Medaba. If I could find an old-timer there who remembered how the top of Mt. Nebo looked fifty years earlier, maybe he could help Clinton get his bearings.

I went down to Medaba and found an elderly man who had been a tour guide on Mt. Nebo. When I told him what our problem was he agreed to go back up with us and point out to Clinton various things on Nebo that had changed over the past fifty years.

First he pointed out a parking lot where a row of trees had been. He then took Clinton over to one side of the mountain and showed him where a small stone building once stood. Also, there was now an excavation site where archaeologists were unearthing the remains of a first century church.

That was all it took. Clinton Locey's eyes lit up and he immediately got his bearings. Without hesitation, he walked fifty yards down the side of the mountain then announced happily there was a cave right below where he was standing. "This is the spot I was taken to fifty years ago by Dr. Futterer," he declared confidently. "I'm sure of it!"

Eryl and I stood there looking at each other in amazement. The rocky area Clinton pointed out looked absolutely no different from the rocky area that covered the whole top of the mountain. There was no grass or trees anywhere. How Locey Clinton could pick out that particularly spot from all the other rocky areas on top of Mt. Nebo was a mystery to me.

Early Tile Floor Map of Jerusalem in Medaba Church

But Clinton Locey would not be dissuaded. He was positive he had led us to the right spot, and that just below his feet was a cave with ancient writing that would tell us where we would find the Ark of the Covenant.

We had come this far, so I figured the only thing we could do was take Clinton at his word. But I knew that if we were going to dig on Mt. Nebo we would need permission from some government or church organization.

I discovered that the site was under the control of Franciscan Monks in Jerusalem. If we wanted to dig on Mt. Nebo, we were told we would have to go to Jerusalem and obtain permission from them.

We went to Jerusalem and found the Franciscan Monastery that housed the offices of important Franciscan Monks. When Eryl and I told them what we wanted to do they said that, unfortunately, they didn't have the proper authority. If we wanted to dig on Mt. Nebo in Jordan, we were required to make application with the Franciscan headquarters in Rome. This was beginning to remind me of the Navy Department back home.

We had no other choice but to put Clinton Locey on a plane for the states, while Eryl and I took an El Al flight to Rome. If we were going to organize a dig on Mt. Nebo, we needed to meet with the Franciscan leadership to get proper permission.

In Rome we were fortunate enough to meet Father Michele Piccirillo, a Franciscan archaeologist who was in charge of excavating the first century church on Mt. Nebo. The holy mountain, it turned out, was under Father Piccirillo's specific jurisdiction. When I explained why we wanted to dig on Mt. Nebo, he told us that he would be willing to meet us on the mountain and allow us to dig—but only

Father Michele Piccirillo

under his supervision. He said we would have to pay for all of his expenses to fly to Jordan and we would also have to pay the expenses of any diggers we might hire to help with the excavation. Eryl and I quickly agreed and made plans to meet with him back on Mt. Nebo in two months.

This was looking like it was going to be easier than I had hoped. With a little luck, two months would give us enough time to raise the money we would need to put together another film team and get in touch with Eryl's new astronaut friend Jim Irwin. If we could talk Jim Irwin into joining our expedition team, it would probably give us the credibility we needed to raise money from potential investors.

I wasn't too worried about talking Jim Irwin into joining us. I'd tell him that, first, we planned to stop in Jordan and go to Mt. Nebo so we could try and discover the location of the Ark of the Covenant. Then we would to Ankara, the capital of Turkey, and see if this summer we could get permission to climb on Mr. Ararat to find Noah's Ark. Who wouldn't want to be involved with an expedition that was going to search for the Ark of the Covenant and the Ark of Noah?

Everything worked out exactly as planned. Jim Irwin agreed to join our expedition team, and with the famous astronaut on board we were able to raise the funds we knew would be needed.

Two months later (right on schedule) I flew into Amman with our expedition team: Eryl Cummings, Dave Cory (who joined us on our expedition to Mexico), a four-man film team and U.S. astronaut Jim Irwin.

After a few phone calls, Jim was able to arrange for us to meet with the Chairman of Royal Jordanian Airlines. He was so impressed with meeting a famous astronaut, he arranged for us to be flown to Turkey in his private Lear Jet when we were ready to leave Jordan.

We thanked the airline Chairman for his generosity and were delighted that our trip to Amman had started out on such a successful note. Now if we could just dig in the spot Clinton Locey pointed out to us out to us—and actually find the cave he said he was shown fifty years earlier—we would really be in business.

The Franciscan archaeologist Michele Piccirillo was waiting for us in Medaba as planned. He said we would need about a dozen men to help us dig on the site. I nosed around and was able to hire twelve Bedouin tribesmen.

Astronaut Jim Irwin

When we got to the spot that Clinton Locey pointed out to us on our first trip to Mt. Nebo, the Bedouin men immediately started digging with their picks and shovels. I shot a little film footage of their activity, along with other members of our film team, then joined Dave Cory, Jim Irwin and Eryl Cummings off to one side and waited for the men to discover something. I was hopeful the Bedouins would find what we were looking for, but I must admit I was skeptical that they would find anything but rocks and dirt.

Suddenly, after about twenty minutes, one of the Bedouin diggers started shouting, "Mosaic! Mosaic!" I couldn't believe it. Could they have actually found something?

I asked Father Piccirillo what the Bedouin worker was shouting about. He told me in broken English the men were beginning to find ancient mosaic tiles. "It's very interesting," he told me with a smile. "It's very interesting indeed! There might be something here!"

Again I grabbed my trusty 16-mm Cannon Scoopic camera, tightened the battery belt at my waist, grabbed a camera light and moved closer to where the men were digging. Once again we started shooting just in case something important was found.

The Bedouin workers cleared away about twelve inches of topsoil from a floor that measured approximately eight feet wide by ten feet long. Within fifteen minutes all the dirt had been swept away. Excitedly, I shot everything that was happening, along with the rest of my film team. Curiously, the tiles were all uniformly white, about one-inch square, without any design on them whatsoever.

When the tile floor was cleaned off Father Piccirillo did an inspection and found a large round stone with a crack in it at one end of the floor. When he and four of the workers pulled the stone back they found that it covered the entrance to what looked like a hole in the ground that went down into a cave of some kind.

I couldn't believe it! Was Clinton Locey right? Were we about to discover the location of the Ark of the Covenant? Clinton Locey said that fifty years earlier Dr. Futerer had let himself down through a small entrance like the one we had just uncovered. He then told us that Futerer followed a short passageway until it opened into an underground cave where he found the ancient writing.

If this was the cave that Dr. Futerer entered fifty years ago, I wanted to be the first one inside so I could film the cave, completely undisturbed, for myself. So, after promising Father Piccirillo I wouldn't touch anything and would do nothing but film, I turned on my light, started my Cannon Scoopic and slowly began letting myself down into the dark entrance. With my camera in one hand and light in the other, I filmed continuously until I reached the bottom of the cave floor about fifteen feet away,

When I got to the bottom, the inside of the cave was pitch black. The only light was from the small amount that filtered in from the entrance and the motion picture light I held in my hand. Slowly and carefully I panned around the rough rock walls of the ancient cave.

When I finished I was terribly disappointed. No matter how hard I looked I could not find anything on the walls that could be described as writing of any kind. I wanted to find it. I prayed that I would find it. But I did not.

When I crawled back out of the cave, disappointed, I handed the light and battery belt to Father Piccirllio who wanted to have a look next. After about five minutes he retreated back into the sunlight and confirmed my observation. There was no writing.

True, we had made an archaeological discovery on Mt. Nebo. And Father Piccirillo was very grateful. But we had not found the writing that Clinton Locey said Dr. Futerer had witnessed fifty years earlier. But at least I got something on film. Maybe I could include it in the film I was going to

Picture of Mike on Mt. Nebo Taken by Jim Irwin

produce when we discovered Noah's Ark on Mt. Ararat in Turkey.

While we were wrapping up the filming on Mt. Nebo and getting ready to leave, I asked Father Piccirillo what he thought we had discovered. He said it was probably a home on Mt. Nebo that was built, possibly thousands of years ago. The cave beneath the home was probably used to store food and water. The plain white tiles indicated that the home belonged to a family who did not enjoy any particular wealth or stature. He was very happy that we had made the discovery, as it would add to the archaeological evidence he was finding in the excavation of the first century church close by.

Was there another cave on top of Mt. Nebo that Dr. Futerer spoke to Clinton Locey about? Did we discover the wrong cave? I have no idea, but have always thought I should return to Mt. Nebo someday and make a second attempt at finding the Holy Ark.

As we packed up our camera gear and headed toward our cars, one of the Bedouin tribesmen offered me a cool drink of water from a stone well not far from where we were filming. The water tasted terrific and was very much appreciated as the temperature was really hot and we were all getting dehydrated after the dusty morning of filming.

Within minutes of drinking the water I became sick. I don't mean I didn't feel very good, I mean I started vomiting like crazy and had to lie down on the ground beside the car. I've always prided myself on the fact that I never get sick when traveling in a foreign country.

My film team members have always said that I must have a stomach made of iron. But on Mt. Nebo in 1978, I got so sick I spent three days in an Amman hotel room lying in bed (when I wasn't otherwise engaged in the bathroom).

I didn't want the rest of the crew to just sit around and wait for me to get better, so I suggested they gather up our film gear and make a trip to the nearby ancient stone city of Petra.

Once again, the Chairman of Royal Jordanian Airlines provided our team with a government helicopter to the ancient site. Thankfully they were able to get some beautiful shots of the incredible stone city, but I wasn't able to join them because of my illness.

I learned—too late—that an outbreak of cholera was prevalent in Jordan when we were there, and that's most likely what made me so sick so quickly. I should never have taken a drink of water from an untreated well, especially a well in the remote area of Jordan.

Stone City of Petra in Jordan

After the fourth day, terribly weak and dehydrated, I crawled on board Royal Jordanian's Lear Jet, found a seat by a window and hoped that I'd start feeling better once we got to Turkey. As the sleek twin-engine aircraft rose from the runway I must have fallen asleep from exhaustion. I didn't wake up until Eryl Cummings and Jim Irwin gave me a shake and said we had arrived in Istanbul.

"That's great," I mumbled, putting on the best face I could muster. "Now if I can find the strength to get off this plane maybe we can go find Noah's Ark!"

9 BACK TO ARARAT

One nice thing about traveling with important people is you get to meet other important people. Our astronaut friend, Jim Irwin, made an appointment to meet President Fahri S. Korutürk of Turkey while we were in the country. Jim had a knack for opening doors using his celebrity as a famous astronaut who had walked on the moon.

When Jim was on the moon there were a lot of pictures taken of him at the controls of the Moon Rover, driving it across the stark landscape. The pictures of him in his astronaut suit driving the Land Rover are quite impressive indeed.

High Flight (Jim's Colorado Springs-based organization) would organize and schedule Jim's speaking engagements with a variety of audiences around the world. While he recounted his experiences on the moon, he would always manage to add comments about God and how his moon flight was such a meaningful religious experience.

Jim had a very clever idea when he blasted off for the moon. He took with him small flags from every nation on earth. He realized being an astronaut who drove a Land Rover on the moon would make him very famous. He also reasoned that if he wanted an introduction to any world leader, what better calling card could he have than a flag of the leader's country that had actually been on the moon.

Jim presented the president his picture driving the Land Rover on the moon. But he also presented him with a Turkish flag that Jim had with him when he was on the moon. Both the picture and the Turkish Flag were framed, mounted under glass and presented to the Turkish leader as a gift to the Turkish people.

This public relations routine worked wonders for Jim all around the world. He would get personal publicity, the country's leader would get publicity and Jim would be able to speak to each audience about his moon experiences, and (at least a little bit) explain how it impacted his faith.

President Koruturk

As far as our expedition was concerned, Jim was able to mention to the press that he was in Turkey with a group that was planning to go to Mt. Ararat and search of Noah's Ark.

After Jim's political duties in Turkey were completed, Eryl and I took our famous friend to meet Prof. Dr. Zinnur Rollas, the personal physician of President Korutürk. We hoped that Jim's recent meeting with the president would help us get permission to climb Mt. Ararat.

Unfortunately, it didn't work out that way. Jim's visit with President Koroturk didn't seem to garner us any more favor than we had

on our first trip when Jim wasn't even involved.

A lot of promises were made (just like the previous year). We were told to be patient as "these things take time" (just like the previous year). In the meantime, we were expected to cool our heels in a hotel room and just pray for the best—not something I am known for.

When we received our second, "please be patient, your permit will arrive very soon," I again became exasperated at the delays and told Eryl we needed to do something different. As I understood it, there was a problem between the U.S. and Russian governments. Since Mt. Ararat sits right on the Russian border, the Russians didn't like the idea of Americans climbing on the mountain and looking down into the Armenian capital of Yerevan.

But I couldn't see any reason why native Turkish climbers and filmmakers couldn't take our gear and film equipment up on Mt. Ararat. If we could find professional filmmakers who were Turks, who also had climbing experience, we could have them go up on Mt. Ararat and film the places we weren't allowed to go.

Eryl began to warm to my idea and suggested we could give our Turkish team a copy of the picture we had from Tom Crotzer of a boat-like object sticking out of the ice in the Ahora Gorge. If we couldn't get to the object ourselves to see if it really was Noah's Ark, maybe a Turkish film team could get there and film it for us. There really might be more than one way to skin a cat.

I hated the thought of not being able to climb Ararat ourselves, but we definitely needed some way to get to Crotzer's object and see if it was Noah's Ark. If politics wouldn't let Americans climb Ararat, maybe we could find some Turks who could.

We were able to locate Yucil Domniz, an ex-newspaper reporter who had climbed Mt. Ararat many times. Yucil not only had climbing experience, he also had personal friends who were professional filmmakers and climbers as well.

It took about a week to get everyone rounded up. When we did, Eryl and I gave each of them climbing equipment, camping equipment, motion picture cameras and all the film we thought they would need. We also gave them detailed maps and drawings that showed the exact location of Crotzer's object we wanted Yucil to film.

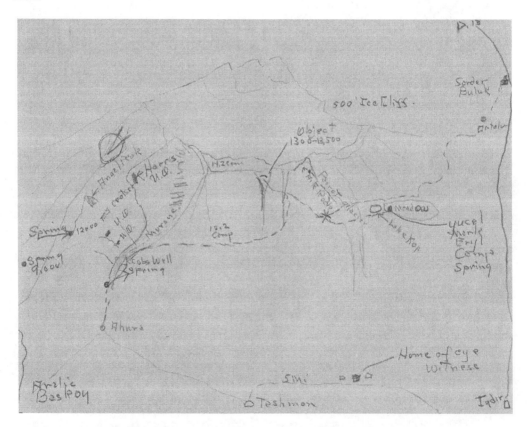

Eryl Cumming's Hand Drawn Map of Mt. Ararat

We all piled into a bus and headed east across the country toward Mr. Ararat on the border between Armenia and Iran. It took us about three days of non-stop bumping along their main east-west highway to get out to eastern Turkey.

Each dusty town looked pretty much like the one before, and each bus stop restaurant had a different way of serving eggplant. I never knew there were so many ways to fix eggplant. Don't get me wrong! I like eggplant, but too much of a good thing is, well, not a good thing.

After passing through towns like Yozgat, Erzincan and Erzurum, we finally arrived at the village of Igdir that seemed to be little more than a collection of rundown, one-story, weather-beaten buildings—and an equally rundown-looking two story hotel. Sometimes the hotel had water and sometimes it didn't. So much for modern conveniences.

Igdir Street Scene Features Horse Drawn Taxies

To make matters worse, the hotel was inhabited by Kurds who didn't seem happy to be around western Turks—much less a group of Americans. Almost immediately I began to have serious doubts about waiting at Igdir for our Turkish team to return from its excursion up the slopes of Mt. Ararat.

After Yucil and his Turkish team arranged to rent eight horses from the local Kurds (four for riding and four for carrying packs), we wished them well, checked out of our Igdir hotel and took the first bus back to Ankara.

The plan was for Yucil to lead his team up the slopes of the Ahora Gorge to locate the boat-like object Tom Crotzer had taken a picture of and claimed was Noah's

Yucil Domniz on Mt. Ararat

Ark. We asked Yucil to find the object, film it and take as many still photographs as he could so we could verify if Crotzer's object was, in fact, Noah's Ark. We told him that we would head back to Ankara and wait for him to return there.

We gave Yucil and his team about three weeks to get up the mountain and do everything we had asked him to do.

Climbing Partner on Ararat With Petrified Wood

Hopefully, he would return with film footage and photos of his discovery of Noah's Ark.

Waiting in our Ankara hotel room for three weeks seemed like an eternity. But eventually Yucil and his Turkish film team arrived back at our hotel right on schedule. We all gathered in my room to receive Yucil's highly anticipated report.

Yucil showed us slides of their climb up the slopes of Mt. Ararat into the Ahora Gorge. When they got to the boat-like-looking object that Tom Crotzer photographed sticking out of a glacier it was plain to see that the object Yucil filmed and photographed was nothing more than a rock. It was a protrusion—one of the natural geological features that are prevalent all along the walls on both sides of the Ahora Gorge. It was very disappointing to all of us, but at last we had learned the truth about Tom Crotzer's "ark".

Tom Crotzer's Fake Photograph   **Same Object as Solid Rock**

When I got back to the Florida, I eventually was able to locate Tom and call him on the phone. I asked him, point blank, why the photograph he showed everyone and said was Noah's Ark appeared to have lines drawn on it. I told him our Turkish film team took close up photos of the object and it is nothing but a rock with no lines anywhere to be seen.

Sheepishly, Tom admitted what he had done. He said he drew lines on the original photograph of the rock outcropping so it would make it easier for people to see wooden planks. That way, he said, the photo would look more like the original Ark. When I asked why he had committed such a blatantly fraudulent act, he boldly declared that Jesus had told him to draw the lines so others would believe there really was a Noah's Ark.

I suppose Tom was so convinced that the rock outcropping was actually Noah's Ark, he felt justified doing something that would make it easier for others to see the same "truth" he was seeing. Religious fervor is one thing, but intentional deception is quite another.

Speaking of which, shortly after I first got the picture from Tom Crotzer, I showed it to my friend Charles E. Sellier, Jr., film producer and author of *The Life and Times of Grizzly Adams*. Chuck looked at the picture and asked me what I thought of it. At the time, I told him I didn't know if it was Noah's Ark or not, but I told him that if I ever got to the object, I'd let him know after I could personally see it for myself.

Chuck apparently wasn't interested in waiting for the truth. He quickly produced a film he called *In Search of Noah's Ark*. Chuck didn't go to Turkey to shoot his film. He shot it entirely in the mountains of Utah, and included an enlarged version of

Two Donkeys on an Upper Meadow of the Ahora Gorge

the Crotzer photo (complete with Crotzer's fake lines) so he could make the startling claim that Noah's Ark had been discovered.

Chuck Sellier's incredible announcement received plenty of publicity around the world—especially by churches and preachers who wanted to promote the fact that the biblical ship had been found. The problem was—as I proved years later—it simply wasn't true. But Chuck wasn't concerned with such inconvenient details, as Chuck Sellier's film made more than thirty million dollars from the church faithful who wanted desperately to believe that Noah's Ark had been discovered.

I told Chuck at the time that he was going way out on a limb promoting the discovery of Noah's Ark when there was no actual proof Crotzer's photograph was true. But he didn't seem to care. He had made a tremendously successful film and that's all that seemed to matter.

I took the footage my Turkish film team shot on Mt. Ararat and combined it with the footage I had taken at various historical and biblical sites the previous summer. I then went to Hollywood and hired the veteran movie actor Joseph Cotten (Citizen Kane, The Magnificent Ambersons) to be my on-camera host and narrator.

I enjoyed working with Joseph Cotton in Hollywood. He told me wonderful stories about how he and Orson Welles began their acting careers together in New York. Neither of them knew anything about making or being in a movie. But back in the early 1940s, Orson was known throughout the nation as the boy wonder of radio and New York stage.

Consequently when RKO Radio Pictures invited Orson to come out to Hollywood and produce any film he wanted, he brought along his friend, Joseph Cotton.

In 1941 the 25-year-old Welles teamed up with Herman J. Mankiewicz to create the screen classic *Citizen Kane*. Orson not only helped write the film, he also directed and starred in it as well.

Joseph Cotton

The film I produced, *Expedition to Noah's Ark*, was never particularly successful—presumably because people weren't interested in finding out that what had previously been reported as Noah's Ark was nothing more than a piece of rock.

In subsequent years, Jim Irwin made numerous trips to Mt. Ararat and actually got permission several times to climb Ararat himself. But Jim never found Noah's Ark. Personally, I believe Noah's Ark is still up on Mt. Ararat waiting to be discovered. I believe this because the Bible clearly states that the Ark came to rest on the mountains of Ararat.

Others will search, and maybe someday I'll go back again. But in 1978, with three adventure documentaries under my belt, I figured I had enough credibility to convince a potential backer that I could lead more successful filming expeditions—maybe next time to the Titanic.

When I was saying goodbye to Doctor Zinnur Rollas back in Ankara, he asked if I knew a gentleman by the name of Jack Grimm. I told him I didn't. Dr. Rollas said that Mr. Grimm was from Abilene, Texas, and that he had come to Turkey a few years ago, also wanting to produce a film about Noah's Ark. He said that like me, Jack must have found out about his connection to President Korutürk and had come seeking help. Dr. Rollas said that he'd heard Jack Grimm had hired someone to produce a film on Noah's Ark, but that he hadn't seen it.

When I asked him what line of work Jack was in, Dr. Rollas said he was quite a colorful character who owned oil wells in Texas and liked to be known as "Cadillac.

Jack". He said he understood that Cadillac Jack not only looked for Noah's Ark, he had also looked for the infamous Loch Ness monster in Ireland. Dr. Rollas added that from what he understood, Cadillac Jack was rather famous in America. I smiled and said, "He might be famous, but I've never heard of him!"

Dr. Rollas then laughed and said that maybe I hadn't heard of him, .because you're not a card player!. He told me that a few years ago Cadillac Jack played Amarillo Slim in Las Vegas for the Poker Playing Championship of the World on national television. He finished by saying, "You ought to look him up. Cadillac Jack's a colorful character, just like you!" I wasn't sure if Dr. Rollas was giving me a compliment or not.

On the plane ride back to the States, all I could think about was how I was going to put a film together about finding Noah's Ark, when all I had been able to do was prove that Noah's Ark had not been found. I knew I didn't want to do a fabricated film like Chuck Sellier. I decided the only thing I could do was tell the truth and let the chips fall where they may.

Then I started thinking about the Titanic again. It hadn't been found either. The infamous ship was still sitting down there on the bottom of the ocean somewhere, waiting to be discovered. When I complete my film on searching for Noah's Ark, I told myself, I'm definitely going to concentrate on finding the Titanic. I'll put together the best oceanographic team I can find, then start looking for money.

Maybe I'll give Cadillac Jack a call. Dr. Zinnur Rollas thinks he might be just the guy who's crazy enough to fund my next expedition. Dr. Rollas said Cadillac Jack has looked for Noah's Ark and the Loch Ness monster. Maybe he'd like to search for the Titanic as well.

10 EXPEDITION TEAM

It was now 1979. Even though I had started out wanting to produce regular feature films, I had become sidetracked at the start and now found myself with three feature documentary films under my belt and anxious to produce a fourth.

I felt I had enough credibility and experience to successfully put together an expedition to find the most famous luxury liner in history. Titanic was the only expedition I had wanted to lead since completing my first expedition to Bikini Atoll in the Marshall Islands.

Finding sunken ships in the lagoon at Bikini Atoll was relatively easy because they were all sitting on the bottom in just 200 feet of water. The Titanic, I knew, sank in 1912 off the coast of Cape Race, Newfoundland, in water that was at least 12,000 feet deep (which also happens to be the average depth of the ocean).

When I began my Titanic research, my high school friend Dick Greenwald suggested I get in touch with Art Markel at Reynolds Aluminum. Reynolds' deep-diving submersible Aluminaut had been designed to dive to a depth of 15,000 feet, but had only been down to 6,500 feet when she helped successfully salvage the hydrogen bomb off Spain in 1966 and Woods Hole Oceanographic Institute's submersible Alvin in 1969. Unfortunately, Art's underwater baby had been sitting in storage in Green Cove Springs, Florida ever since the Alvin rescue. Art spent that time on the lookout for an opportunity to once again make the Aluminaut a working deep-diving submersible.

When I came along with my Titanic project Art hoped I would be his ticket to getting his Aluminaut back into the water. Unfortunately, having been in storage for several years, the submersible needed a million dollars worth of work before it could be put back into the water safely and declared operational.

The Aluninaut situation seemed a little risky to me. She had only been designed to operate at a maximum depth of 15,000 feet, which didn't leave a lot of room for error should the Titanic be found at a depth that was deeper than 12,000 feet.

Art Markel was basically trying to sell me on what Woods Hole's Bob Ballard was trying to accomplish with his camera system. Both wanted to get real time information from the bottom. Ballard's plan was to have his camera take pictures of the bottom, while Art wanted to put people in the Aluminaut on the ocean floor so they could see out and look around.

The problem with both of these methods was that below 2,000 feet, there's no detectable light. An underwater light source would need to be hooked to Ballard's camera system, or Markel's Aluminaut, but most light sources can only illuminate a ten-foot section of the bottom at any one time, which would make the search take a very long time.

When Titanic hit the iceberg in 1912, her radio-telegraph operator, Jack Phillips, sent out a CQD distress signal by Morse code. Phillips sent out the signal of where he was told Titanic was located at the time, but in 1912, there were no satellite positioning systems. Consequently, the Titanic's CQD position was an educated guess at best. It is from that position, that Titanic sent out signals for other ships in the area to come and help rescue passengers.

There are records of the speed and course the Titanic was traveling when she struck the iceberg. But her speed and course can only provide part of the equation. If there was an ocean current at the time, the speed of the current, plus its direction, also had to be calculated. A person trying to figure out where the Titanic landed on the bottom would also have to know the depth of the water where the Titanic sank.

If someone could determine exactly where the Titanic struck the iceberg, and how far (and in what direction) she might have drifted before she sank, they might be able to calculate a rough position where she could be found on the bottom. But unfortunately, there's yet another variable: time. As Titanic moved from east to west toward New York, she moved through a series of time zones. Did the Titanic's navigator know what time zone they were in when he calculated his last known position before striking the ice?

Taking into consideration all the known variables, I figured the area that would have to be searched in the North Atlantic was a box approximately thirty miles long by thirty miles wide. Nine hundred square miles. That was a tremendously large area to search—especially if you had to look at the bottom through a porthole or camera that could only light and take pictures of a 10-foot square area at a time.

Towing a camera sled or riding in a deep-diving submersible would be much too slow and consequently much too expensive. I decided that a much better, more efficient and cheaper way to find the Titanic would be side-scan sonar.

A sonar device could be towed through the water 50-100 feet from the bottom sending out an electronic signal that could record objects on the bottom within a three-mile swath—a far more efficacious and economical undertaking than searching 10-foot sections at a time. The side-scan sonar's signal is sent by electrical cable up to the ship and printed on continuously scrolling paper. Once the side-scan sonar device found a target that looked interesting, a magnetometer could be sent down to see if the object was made of metal or just a rock. If the target object seemed like it was worth investigating further, then a camera system or Aluminaut could be sent to investigate.

This could be accomplished by using a variety of camera systems available, such as the underwater Camera System designed by Bob Ballard, to take pictures of the object after it had been found. Or, it would be possible to put people inside a deep--diving submersible so they could get down on the bottom and positively identify the object and hopefully recover a few artifacts.

When I told Art Markel the Titanic should be found first by using side-scan sonar, then by confirming the find through a magnetometer, he enthusiastically pitched in to help. He quickly figured that he could attach a side-scan sonar and a magnetometer to the Aluninaut and kill several birds with one stone.

One of the first people Art suggested I contact was a friend of his named Tom Hilton, president of Colmek Systems Engineering in Salt Lake City. When I explained to Tom that I wanted to put together an oceanographic team that would help me locate the Titanic he was immediately interested. But the first question he asked was, "Do you plan to raise the Titanic after you've found her?".

I told him emphatically that I thought it was nothing but a crazy idea to raise the Titanic. What I did want to do, though, was find the Titanic using side-scan sonar then, at a later time, recover Titanic artifacts by using a deep diving submersible like the Aluminaut. I also told him my plan was to put the recovered Titanic artifacts on a world tour and produce a feature film documentary to help promote the expedition and tour.

I knew why Tom had asked me about raising the Titanic. For years, Douglas J. Faulkner-Woolley had gained publicity claiming that he was going to raise the Titanic. In 1976 author Clive Cussler published Raise the Titanic (which was made into a movie in 1980 starring Jason Robards and Alec Guinness). I'm sure the book and upcoming film release led Tom to ask me if I intended to raise the Titanic.

Tom also asked if I was going to get National Geographic involved. I told him I hoped so because having their name associated with any expedition added credibility. Tom's questions continued, which I took as an indication that he was genuinely interested.

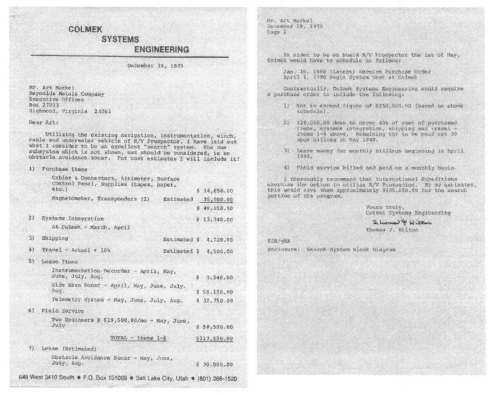

Colmek Systems Engineering Letter Signed by Thomas Hilton

Tom wanted to know if I knew a man named Emory Kristof. I'd never met him, but I knew he was a photographer for National Geographic. Tom told me Kristof had been doing experimental work on underwater lighting systems. He said if I planned to photograph the Titanic after she was found, Emory Kristof would certainly be the man to talk to about lighting the ship.

A week later I got to meet Emory Kristof at the National Geographic Headquarters in Washington, D.C. He was immediately interested in my Titanic project. He even took me to his home and showed me samples of his work and several sketches he had worked up which demonstrated how he thought a ship the size of the Titanic could be lit and photographed in its entirety on the bottom.

Emory explained to me that he was employed as a staff photographer for National Geographic, but that he was also Vice President of Seaonics International Limited. Seaonics developed specialized underwater equipment that could search for and film objects in the deep ocean. He said he would like for me to consider using Seaonics on my Titanic project.

Emory told me that Dr. Robert Ballard from Woods Hole was the president of Seaonics. A man named William H. Tantum IV from New York City headed the finances of the organization, and London attorney Alan Ravenscroft was Seaonics Executive VP. Bob Ballard and Emory Kristof were the main partners because they were the only members of Seaonics who actually had experience working in the ocean. Emory asked me if I heard of the Alcoa Seaprobe. He said the camera package that was lost at the end of the drill was a package that he and Ballard had developed. I told Emory I thought the publicity that Ballard got after the incident was less than favorable. He shrugged and acknowledged that Bob took a pretty big hit, but then added, "it's not always easy to work in the deep ocean".

Emory then started selling me again on the experience that he and Bob Ballard could bring to my Titanic expedition team. He believed he could bring in National Geographic magazine if he and Ballard were brought in as a major part of my expedition. I told Emory I would also need to include Tom Hilton at Colmek Systems (since he introduced Emory to me).

Emory said he figured that Tom would want to use a research vessel called the R/V Prospector on the expedition, and thought that might be a problem because it was small and not particularly sophisticated. He then added that he was sure Bob Ballard would want to work out a deal to use the Knorr.

Research Vessel Knorr

The Knorr was a large research vessel fully equipped with scientific instrumentation Ballard often used at Woods Hole. Emory said he would put together a written proposal for me to look at that would show all the costs for a 60-day expedition to find the Titanic. I said that sounded terrific and to please get it to me as soon as possible. I then asked him to also include a proposal from National Geographic magazine. He assured me it wouldn't be a problem and that he would.

True to his word, on December 4, 1979, I receive in the mail two letters. One from Emory on National Geographic magazine letterhead that stated Geographic was very interested in pursuing a story on "an expedition to find and photograph the TITANIC". The letter went on to explain that Geographic could also contribute to the expedition in additional ways, such as building special video equipment in association with RCA so the expedition would sail with the best possible camera equipment.

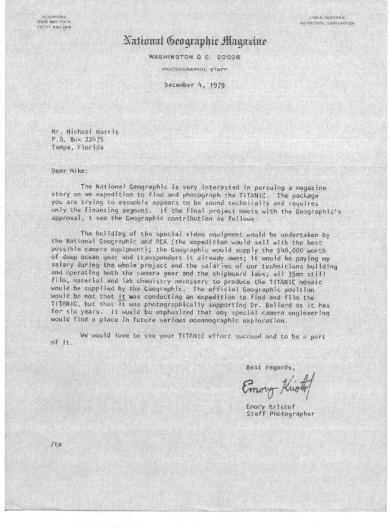

Emory Kristof's Letter to me from National Geographic

The letter stated that National Geographic would supply the $40,000 worth of deep ocean gear and transponders it already owned, and would be paying my salary during the whole project, as well as the salaries of our technicians building and operating both the camera gear and the shipboard labs. National Geographic would also supply all 35mm still film and materials needed to produce the Titanic mosaic.

The official Geographic position would be not that it was conducting an expedition to find and film the Titanic, but that it was photographically supporting Dr. Ballard as it had for six years. It would be emphasized that any special camera engineering would find a place in future serious oceanographic exploration. The letter ended with, "We would love to see your TITANIC effort succeed and to be a part of it".

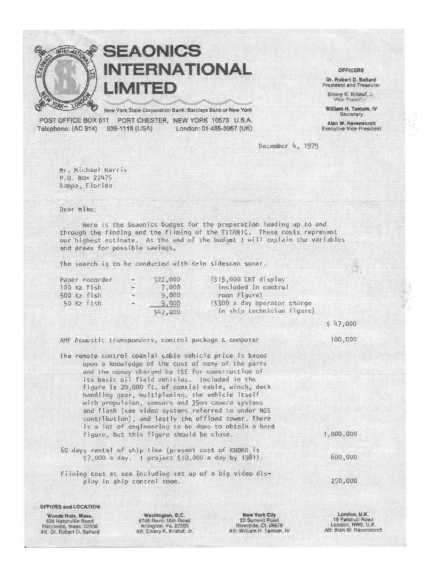

First Page of Seaonics International Letter to Mike Harris

The second letter in Emory Kristof's package was on Seaonics International Limited letterhead. It was the promised budget breakdown of costs associated with putting together an expedition to search for, discover and photograph the Titanic.

Michael Harris -2   December 4, 1979

Salaries for search and vehicle system technicians and
    computer operators at sea, special consulting engi-
    neering and operation of NY Seaonics office within
    Ben Kubasik's office. $150,000

Artist to do series of paintings at sea depicting ocean
    bottom activities (1977 agreement w/Pierre Mion).   25,000

Sea trial of KNORR with all systems to be tested.   60,000
                                                              $2,232,000

Bob Ballard and I would like to conduct the expedition from the R.V. KNORR and with Woods Hole's blessing. If Woods Hole can be convinced to participate and allow Bob to conduct the expedition as an engineering exercise, then Bob can gain access to his deep sea cameras, strobes, transponders, E-6 processing van, and shipboard computer. This would amount to about $250,000 in material that we would not need to acquire. Bob also feels that he can talk many of the suppliers into being helpful to our effort.

The remote vehicle is planned to produce 35mm color slides, low-light level real time B&W video, real time or recorded color video and high altitude strobe illuminated video stills.

The camera systems would be designed to be completely interchangeable between the main remote cable vehicle and the submarine. The small cable vehicles that would penetrate the TITANIC, I feel, would be based on a hardened ISE DART and would incur a cost of $200,000 above our budget.

Next November Bob and I have ALVIN dives scheduled for the Bahamas in order to test out the new camera gear we are building for the Easter Island dives (this will be the heart of the TITANIC camera system).

Next August I hope to get two weeks of ship time with Dr. Joe MacInnis in the Canadian arctic to continue the search for the BREADALBANE. This would be a good project on which to test the sonars and the DART vehicle.

Not only has the Seaonics group done a lot of planning and homework on the TITANIC project, but Bob and I work in the sea on a daily basis. The Geographic television show, "Dive to the Edge of Creation", will air in January. It is the first TV show ever done 9,000 ft. deep. We had to invent the camera systems and the filming techniques that made the show possible.

We have explored other means of financing the expedition as a total Seaonics project, but we have not committed ourselves. We would be happy to join forces with you and I feel we would have a stronger project as a result.

Best regards,

Emory Kristof

/ta

**Second Page of Seaonics International Limited Titanic Proposal
Letter to Mike Harris Signed by Emory Kristof**

Seaonics International Limited Titanic Budget included:

Klein side-scan sonar…………………………………………….. $ 47,000

AMF Acoustic transponders, control package and computer ….. $ 100,000

Remote control coaxial cable vehicle, including 20,000 feet
of coaxial cable, winch, deck-handling gear, multiplexing,
propulsion, sensors, 35mm camera systems, flash, and
offload tower…………………………………………………...$ 1,000,000

Sixty days rental and cost of ship time………………………..$ 600,000

Filming cost at sea including control room……………………. $ 250,000

Salaries for search and vehicle system technicians, computer
operators, special consulting, engineering and operation of
NY Seaonics office……………………………....………………$ 150,000

Artist to produce a series of paintings at sea depicting
ocean bottom activities (1977 agreement with Pierre Mion)…….$ 25,000

Sea trial of Knorr, with all systems to be tested………………....$ 60,000

Total cost for expedition…………………………………….....$ 2,232,000

Emory added that, "Bob Ballard and I would like to conduct the expedition from the R.V. Knorr with Woods Hole's blessing. If Woods Hole can be convinced to participate and allow Bob to conduct the expedition as an engineering exercise, then Bob can gain access to his deep-sea cameras, strobes, transponders, E-6 processing van, and shipboard computer. This would amount to about $250,000 in material that we would not need to acquire. Bob also feels that he can talk many of the suppliers into being helpful to our effort".

Emory also included, "The remote vehicle is planned to produce 35mm color slides, low-light level real time B&W video, real time or recorded color video and high altitude strobe illuminated video stills. The camera systems would be designed to be completely interchangeable between the main remote cable vehicle and the submarine. The small cable vehicles that would penetrate the TITANIC, I feel, would be based on a hardened ISE DART and would incur a cost of $200,000 above our budget".

Emory closed by saying he and Bob "have explored other means of financing the expedition as a total Seaonics project, but we have not committed ourselves. We would be happy to join forces with you and I feel we would have a stronger project as a result".

I felt I wouldn't find anyone stronger for my expedition team than Emory Kristof and Bob Ballard. Both brought the experience and credibility I needed to conduct a successful expedition to find and film the Titanic. Emory said he would find a way to include Thomas Hilton. I wasn't sure how I could include Art Markel and the Aluninaut, because Bob Ballard was so closely associated with Woods Hole and their submersible Alvin. But, with Kristof and Ballard as my main oceanographic scientists, I thought I had the best possible team to help me find the Titanic.

I created a Titanic Expedition proposal and sent it to several possible funding sources. It wasn't long before an interesting letter arrived in the mail from a Greek shipping magnate by the name of Spyridon Panayoteas. After a few phone calls he invited me to visit him in Athens. I did and during my meeting at his office he agreed to provide me with a minimum of $2,000,000.

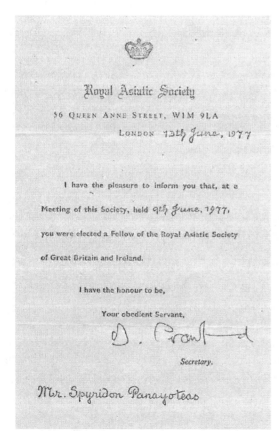

Spyridon Panayoteas Royal Asiatic Society

There was only one slight proviso. Spyridon said that it was expensive and time consuming for him to bring several of his lawyers and accountants to Tampa to close on our transaction. He was concerned about the expense of the trip, when weighed against the risk of me changing my mind before contracts were signed. I assured him that I would not change my mind, but he still wanted some type of guarantee.

Mr. Panayoteas indicated he wanted me to have my bank write a letter that would state on bank letterhead that should I change my mind and not sign a contact with his company when he got to Tampa, the bank would agree to reimburse all of Spyridon Panayoteas' expenses.

On the long flight back to Tampa

I was sure my bank in Tampa would write the letter the Greek shipping magnate requested. After all, there was no way I was not going to sign the contract with him when he and his people arrived in Tampa.

To my surprise, my bank said I was crazy and there was no way they would guarantee to pay all the expenses (who knew how much) for a group of Greek business people to travel from Athens to Tampa. I did everything I could to get my bank to reconsider, but it was to no avail. Crestfallen, I had no choice but to call Spyridon Panayoteas in Athens and tell him I couldn't arrange for his guarantee.

It was especially disappointing, because Mr. Panayoteas had given me documentation that showed he was a distinguished member of the Royal Asiatic Society in London and the Royal Institute of Navigation at The Royal Geographical Society in London. In addition, I was given letters that stated Mr. Panayoteas was personally known to British airline entreprenuer his Excellency Sir Freddy Laker, chairman of De Beers Consolidated Mines Harry Oppenheimer, former Vice President Nelson Rockefeller and other prominent businessmen.

Spyridon Panayoteas was definitely someone I should have been able to work out a business arrangement with, but unfortunately, I was not successful. To this day I don't know if he was the real deal or just someone trying to pull a fast one on me.

But I certainly didn't want to let go of my dream. Finding the Titanic was a worthy project and I had an expedition team that was second to none. Sitting in church a week later, I recalled Professor Doctor Zinnur Rollas' recommendation, "When you get back to the States you should look up Jack Grimm. I think he's someone who might be interested in funding one of your expeditions".

Cadillac Jack Grimm, a Texas oil man, was probably a much different type of person that Spyridon Panayoteas. Doctor Rollas said he liked both adventure and publicity. If I could talk Cadillac Jack into backing me on the Titanic, I was sure I could get him plenty of publicity.

Praise God for little angel thoughts. Throughout my life, whenever I've tried to figure something out, if the answer comes to me after I've turned the problem over in my mind searching for a solution, I've always attributed the solution as something I've cooked up myself. On the other hand, if an idea just suddenly pops into my mind about something I'm not necessarily thinking about or trying to figure out, I've always paid special attention, because to me, it's an angel thought from God trying to give me direction.

I now had direction. The next day, bright and early, I'd track down Cadillac Jack in Abilene and tell him about my dream to discover the Titanic.

11 CADILLAC JACK GRIMM

I called information and asked for the phone number of Grimm Oil Company in Abilene, Texas. When the secretary answered I asked for Jack Grimm and within minutes he was on the other end of the line. When I told him I got his name from Professor Doctor Zinnur Rollas in Ankara he laughed and asked why I was in Turkey.

I told Jack a little about my Noah's Ark expedition but let him know quickly that talking about Noah's Ark wasn't the reason I called. What I wanted to do was lead an expedition to find the Titanic in the North Atlantic. Jack wasn't interested in a lot of conversation and cut right to the chase.

In his easy Texas drawl he asked, "What makes you think you can find the Titanic?" I then told him as succinctly as I could about Emory Kristof, Bob Ballard, Thomas Hilton and Art Markel. I told Jack they were all top professionals and had extensive service working in the deep ocean.

Jack then asked, "Why are you calling me?" I told him that while I was in Turkey filming Expedition to Noah's Ark, Dr. Rollas told me several times I should give Cadillac Jack a call—and today that's what I was doing.

Jack laughed again then asked me to send him my Titanic expedition proposal and said he'd get back to me. Enthused that he hadn't told me to go jump in a lake, I put together a presentation of my work, and included information about Emory Kristof, Bob Ballard, Tom Hilton and Art Markel. I sent it off to Jack Grimm in care of Grimm Oil Company in Abilene, Texas.

About a week later I picked up the phone and heard a familiar Texas drawl. "Mike, I might be interested in putting a little money into your Titanic project. When do you think you could come over to Abilene and talk to me about it?"

After taking a deep breath I told Jack I could get to Abilene anytime he wanted. We set a date and he said he'd pick me up at the airport. Then, just before hanging up, he said he was going to hold a small lunch for a few of his friends at the Abilene Petroleum Club while I was in town. "If you don't mind," he said, "I'd like for you to explain to them how you plan to find the Titanic". I told him I wouldn't mind at all and that I was looking forward to meeting him.

When I went to Abilene, I took along a four-foot long plastic model of the Titanic that I had put together from a kit. I had it painted in all the right colors to match all the ship's original markings.

When Jack picked me up at the airport, I found out right away that he wasn't called Cadillac Jack for nothing. When I complimented him on his beautiful car he laughed and said he'd always driven a Cadillac. He then told me about being on ABC television once when he was playing Amarillo Slim for the poker championship of the world. "The TV producers wanted to jazz up their program," he said, "so they started calling me Cadillac Jack. I didn't complain. In fact I kind of like it! Guess I've been called Cadillac Jack ever since".

After Jack took me to his downtown Abilene office, we went over my plans to search for the Titanic, recover artifacts, put the artifacts on a world tour and produce a feature documentary film of the entire adventure. Figuring Jack liked publicity I told him I was sure he would get a lot of it if he backed my project.

Jack tried to pretend he didn't care about notoriety, but admitted he got more than his fair share. "People liked to write about the crazy things I get involved with," he laughed again, "especially with that moniker I got being called Cadillac Jack".

We took the Titanic model and headed to the Petroleum Club for the luncheon. When we got there, I discovered that Jack had rented a room much larger than I was expecting. At the front of the room was a long table where Jack and I would sit. He asked me to put my Titanic model on a stand in full view of his invited guests.

Titanic Model

I was stunned when about two hundred people started filing into the room for Jack's little luncheon. Before the fancy meal was served Jack introduced me as a filmmaker and expedition leader from Tampa. He then gave the guests a brief description of my film and expedition background and announced that I planned to lead an expedition to find the Titanic in the North Atlantic. Then much to my surprise, Cadillac Jack told everyone in attendance that he was putting up the money to fund the expedition to find the Titanic.

At the end of Jack's speech, the questions started coming—mostly to Jack, which he was eager to answer. With his good old boy Texas manner, Jack knew how to captivate an audience. What I didn't know was that a few of Jack's friends turned out to be the head of the AP news wire service in Texas and representatives of all the major newspapers and television stations throughout the state. Also in attendance were more than a few of his closest oil company buddies. From the get go, Cadillac Jack had all the bases covered.

The next morning, newspaper headlines across the country screamed the headline, CADILLAC JACK TO SEARCH FOR THE TITANIC. Long articles in all the major newspapers talked about how the colorful Texan was going to fund an expedition to find the

Dallas Newspaper Front Page

Titanic. Somewhere down near the bottom of each article, my name was mentioned as a filmmaker that Jack Grimm was going to hire to shoot a documentary film on Jack's great adventure.

Jack's great adventure? What happened to my great adventure? In one great poker-playing maneuver, Cadillac Jack grabbed all the headlines and from that day on it was no longer the Titanic expedition of Mike Harris it was the Titanic expedition of Jack Grimm—and so far he hadn't put up a dime.

I did manage to get a contract from Jack in which it was agreed his company, Grimm Oil Company, and my company, International Expeditions, would evenly split the profits from the Titanic project. I would have the official title as Expedition Leader and would be paid a salary to produce a feature-length documentary film.

That was it! Jack was not bashful about letting me know that he firmly believed in following his own version of the Golden Rule: "Whoever has the gold rules!"

This became evident the very first week. When word went out—not only throughout the United States, but also around the world—that Cadillac Jack Grimm was going to fund an expedition to search for the Titanic, inquiries and job applications began flooding into Jack's office in Abilene.

One of those who wrote Jack about a job was Dr. William B. Ryan from Columbia University's Lamont-Doherty Geological Observatory in Palisades, New York. Dr. Ryan stated in a January 10, 1980 letter to Jack, "I read in The New York Times of your project to locate and photograph the wreck of the TITANIC," and that Lamont has "been supported for many years by the Office of Naval Research, the National Science Foundation, and industry in tasks using deep submergence vehicles and state-of-the-art sonars to survey in detail small selected regions of the deep ocean floor. We have had direct hands-on experience with the Navy's SEACLIFF, TURTLE, TRIEST II, the Nuclear Research Submarine NR-1, as well as numerous expeditions with SDRV ALVIN operated by the Woods Hole Oceanographic Institution".

Dr. William Ryan

In his letter, Dr. Ryan went on to say, "We have developed and operate tethered robot camera and sonar devices specifically fabricated and field tested for deep-water missions (to depths of 6000 meters). At present we are improving the resolution of side-looking sonars using digital processing techniques that could permit the direct acoustic imaging of the hull of the TITANIC showing details of its outline to a resolution of a few meters".

Jack was hooked. There was no way Dr. William B. Ryan was going to let him off his line. Bill then told Jack that he was sure he could also bring in his good friend, Dr. Fred N. Spiess, director of the University of California's Marine Physical Laboratory at the Scripps Institution of Oceanography to direct the underwater survey at sea.

When Jack told me about the wonderful scientists he had arranged to help us find the Titanic, I reminded him that my team of scientists from National Geographic and Woods Hole were just as good and maybe better. Jack admitted they might very well be, but with all the publicity he was getting, it was better that he put his own personal stamp on who was going to be hired. And, he added shamelessly, if he were doing the hiring everyone would know who was in charge.

When I started to complain, Jack quickly reminded me about his Golden Rule adding, "Don't take it so hard. You're still going to get to produce a film on the expedition and you're still going to have a title as the official Expedition Leader!"

What he said was true. I did want to produce a film on finding the Titanic, and I did like the idea of having the title Expedition Leader. But being in charge of putting all aspects of an expedition together is one thing and just having the title is quite another.

But having the title, I reasoned, might help me become a member of The Explorers Club in New York. I had always wanted to be a member of the prestigious organization. Members of the Explorers Club included polar explorers Robert Peary and Richard Byrd, aviators Charles Lindbergh and James Doolittle, astronauts Neil Armstrong and John Glenn, anthropologist Louis Leakey, mountaineer Sir Edmund Hillary, President Theodore Roosevelt, explorer Thor Heyerdahl and journalist Lowell Thomas. Each had made giant contributions in science, exploration or government service.

I contacted The Explorers Club headquarters and found that membership requirements were more stringent than I had expected. Besides having proper experience, it was also necessary to obtain a personal recommendation from two Explorers Club members. I hoped that having led successful expeditions to dive on the ships at Bikini Atoll in the Marshall Islands, searched for Pancho Villa's gold in Mexico and Noah's Ark on Mount Ararat in Eastern Turkey would qualify me for membership. When I learned that The Explorers Club had a Chapter in Orlando I immediately got a representative on the phone and asked if I could attend their next meeting.

Dr. Fred Spiess

Several weeks later Evelyn and I eagerly drove to Orlando and found our way to the Officers Club at the Naval Reserve Training Center where the Central Florida chapter of The Explorers Club was holding its monthly meeting. I was immediately impressed with the interesting collection of people who were members of the Central Florida Chapter.

Capt. Glenn Doolittle, airline pilot and cousin of the famous aviator Jimmy Doolittle, stuck out his hand and was the first member to welcome us. Rear Admiral James R. Reedy, Jr., a pioneer in Naval Aviation who actually flew with Admiral Richard Byrd on his first flight to the North Pole was another member who quickly made us feel welcome. Col. Joseph W. Kittinger USAF (RET.), famous for riding a rocket sled in medical experiments prior to astronaut training was also an active member of the Central Florida Chapter and welcomed me warmly.

Evelyn Speaks with Bimini Wall Expert Dr. Mason Valentine

The list of famous explorers, scientists and government diplomats who were members of just the Central Florida chapter of The Explorers Club was truly remarkable. To say that I was humbled just to get to know them personally is a huge understatement.

When I told them of my background in exploration and my proposed expedition to search for the Titanic in the North Atlantic, I was quickly welcomed as a potential new member. I was truly honored when Rear Admiral James R. Reedy, Jr.

recommended me for membership—as did the chapter president Arnold Haverlee, a distinguished gentleman of Danish descent who was recognized for his remarkable career as a World War II OSS officer in London.

On March 11, 1980, I received my Certificate of Membership as a duly elected member of The Explorers Club and was truly thrilled. The membership certificate was signed by Dr. Charles F. Brush, president of The Explorer's Club in New York.

Mike Harris Explorers Club Certificate of Membership

Bill Ryan from Lamont Doherty did bring in Fred Spiess from Scripps Institution of Oceanography. Dr. Spiess's Marine Physical Laboratory at Scripps had developed a Deep-Towed Instrumentation System that had been successfully deployed for the military with the purpose of locating objects such as ship or plane wrecks. Unfortunately, Deep Tow was already committed for the spring and summer of 1980 to other funded research programs in the Pacific.

Dr. Ryan knew the experience and reputation of Dr. Spiess would greatly enhance his Titanic expedition scientific team. He also hoped the Scripps oceanographer would be able to help him develop a new search system that would incorporate the proven features of Deep-Tow, but would also increase the search width of the sonar signal across the ocean floor.

Lamont-Doherty and Scripps scientists drew up specifications for a high-resolution, mid-range, side-scan sonar system and sent the specifications out to four companies that built ocean survey equipment. The system chosen had to be fabricated in time for a 1980 summer expedition. The only company that would commit themselves to such an immediate engineering effort was IST (International Submarine Technology) in Redmond, Washington. The head of IST's scientific team was a theoretical physicist named James Kosalas. When Jim Kosalas and IST were added to the Ryan/Spiess team, the scientific portion of the 1980 Titanic expedition was basically set.

Jack Grimm picked his own scientific team and cast aside the one I had—partly because he demanded control. But he also did it for a more practical reason. I found out later that one main reason Jack Grimm hired Dr. Ryan and Dr. Spiess was because he wanted to save money. He talked the scientists into coming up with an expedition budget that was less than half of the budget that Emory Kristof and Bob Ballard had presented to me through their company Seaonics. I certainly didn't like the fact that my Seaonics team had been tossed aside, but Cadillac Jack was now pulling the strings and there wasn't anything I could do about it.

But Jack didn't want me to just sit around while he beat the bushes for money. He wanted me to also help him raise the money necessary to pay for our 1980 expedition. Although publicity went out around the world shouting the headlines that Texas millionaire Jack Grimm was going to fund the Titanic expedition Jack firmly believed in using OPM (Other Peoples' Money).

Consequently, the two of us started knocking on the doors of Jack's oil business friends. One of his more colorful associates was Bunker Hunt, a man who had tried to capture the silver-market back in the 1970s. Bunker was a big, heavyset, slightly disheveled man whose passion seemed to be not oil, but racehorses. The walls of his office were covered with pictures of racehorses he owned or admired.

Bunker Hunt

I put on my dog-and-pony show for Bunker, going over several of the Titanic's historical points. I also told him how our scientific team from Scripps and

Lamont-Doherty was going to find her. When I finished my pitch Jack quickly asked Bunker, "How much are you in for?" I'll always remember Bunker sticking his hand up with five fingers spread apart, which let Jack know he was in for five percent. There was no arguing. There was no negotiating. Cool as a cucumber, Bunker Hunt had just committed to deliver five percent of our expedition budget.

Prior to the 1980 expedition Jack and I were flown to New York City and featured on NBC's Today show. We were interviewed by Tom Brokaw who asked a lot of questions about how we were going to find the Titanic, which Jack and I managed to answer without embarrassing ourselves. Although Tom was friendly and supportive of our efforts to search for the Titanic, Today weatherman Willard Scott was even friendlier and more interested in the great adventure we were about to begin. Willard projects a very friendly disposition on television, and I can confirm that he is absolutely no different in person than he is on television.

Since I was now an official member of The Explorer's Club, I arranged for us to hold a big press conference at the Club's New York City headquarters to publicize the start of our great Titanic Expedition adventure. All the major radio, television, newspaper and news service organizations were present—including Lowell Thomas (Honorary President of the Explorers Club), who talked about how he reported on the sinking of the Titanic when he was a cub reporter in 1912. It was quite a memorable moment for me when Lowell Thomas concluded his remarks by saying, "Good luck to you Mike. Good luck to you Mr. Grimm. And so long until tomorrow!"

Lowell Thomas

October 1980

Smithsonian

Volume 11, Number 7

Bold men are still enticed by our world's frontiers

The Explorers Club celebrates its 75th birthday as the members uphold a grand tradition of brains, brawn—and pluck

Arctic mountaineer George Van B. Cochran and wife Caroline show the club flag atop Bylot Island peak.

A press conference was in progress at the Explorers Club on East 70th Street in Manhattan, an elegant six-story Tudor town house paneled with carved and fretted oak and filled with the memorabilia of a thousand explorations that have traversed ice, desert and jungle in scientific searches that often breached the limits of human endurance.

The conference had been called to announce an expedition that would combine bona fide science with science fiction, a union reminiscent of our voyages to the moon. Plans were to use the latest technological advances in a search for the hulk of the *Titanic*, which lies on the bottom of the North Atlantic in some 12,000 feet of water, 68 years after striking an iceberg. If the search ship should locate her—and indeed in mid-August it *would* locate an "object" of the right dimensions—next summer the deep-diving *Aluminaut* submarine would examine her; robot television cameras on long cables would creep into the hull to probe for her secrets.

The father of this project was Mike Harris, a 44-year-old expedition operator from Tampa, Florida, and a member—naturally—of the Explorers Club. Harris has searched for Noah's ark on Mt. Ararat and smashed his ribs going over a waterfall in Mexico while filming a quest for the legendary treasure of Pancho Villa. He took his *Titanic* idea to Jack Grimm, an Abilene, Texas, oilman, who put together a group to finance the venture. Next, scientists from Columbia University's Lamont-Doherty Observatory and from

the University of California's Scripps Institution of Oceanography formulated the experiments needed to locate a hulk that rests on the ocean floor and might be anywhere within a 300-square-mile area. A 180-foot vessel was engaged, Grimm began negotiating a book contract which, with Harris' documentary film, may or may not recover the costs, and the Explorers Club press conference was set.

Charles Brush (opposite), the club's energetic president, spoke first. Then Lowell Thomas, the 88-year-old honorary president and grand patron of the club, recalled reporting the original *Titanic* story in 1912, ending his remarks with a grin and a characteristic "Good luck Mike Harris, good luck Mr. Grimm—and so long until tomorrow!" Brush presented the 199th Explorers Club flag to the expedition, 198 already having been carried to almost every part of the Earth and to the moon. (The flag is lent—never *given*—to members engaged in original scientific exploration and must be returned to the club for the archives.)

Harris explained the *Titanic* venture and the scientists asserted their seriousness. The first press question was addressed to President Brush and it struck a sour note: "The Explorers Club has always been associated with serious exploratory endeavors. I wonder, in view of the media hype [for this one], second only to the jumping of the Snake River by Evel Knievel, if there isn't perhaps an overriding commercial consideration here that goes beyond the traditional feeling of the membership of the club?"

Smithsonian Magazine Article about Mike Harris as Father of Titanic Project

12 1980 TITANIC EXPEDITION

We left Port Everglades, Florida, on July 14, 1980, aboard the 175-foot chartered research vessel H.J.W. Fay. On her mast we proudly flew the American Flag, as well as the flag of The Explorers Club. The Explorers Club honored me by allowing me to carry one of their flags on my expedition. No flag can be kept. All must be returned to the Club at the conclusion of any expedition. The flag I was allowed to carry had already been on several adventures, including trips to the moon and the North Pole.

In order to test Jim Kosolas' newly designed long-range side-scan sonar device (which we dubbed the (Blue Fish.), we initially set a course for Bermuda that would take us over the site of the U.S. naval ship Briggs. The Briggs had been scuttled several years earlier in 15,000 feet of water in a known location that featured a smooth sandy bottom. The plan was to test the Blue Fish's sonar capabilities on a real ship-size object—even though the Briggs was not anywhere near the size of the Titanic.

If something can go wrong working in the deep ocean, it's a safe assumption that it will go wrong. A serious defect in the up-link digital telemetry was detected which was

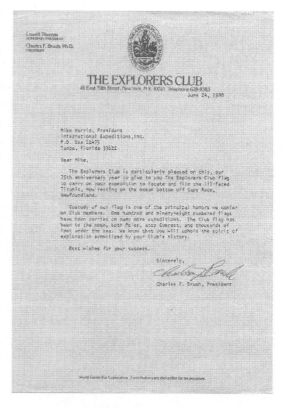

Letter Allowing Mike to Carry Explorers Club Flag on 1980 Titanic Expedition

solved by designing and building a separate clock circuit for the sonar vehicle. Bill Ryan and Jim Kosolas decided that it wasn't necessary to send ultra high frequency timing signals down the cable from the surface, but it would take at least twenty-four hours to make the necessary modifications.

While the Blue Fish was being modified, Lamont-Doherty's camera sled was placed at the end of the wire and lowered several thousand meters into the ocean.

Unfortunately it didn't work as planned either. The camera strobe had a faulty capacitor

Launching Blue Fish for Test

charging circuit. Murphy's Law seemed to be in full effect. All the scientists on board were working overtime to get the sonar gear and video equipment up and running. Jack Grimm was paying good money for the equipment to work correctly.

Lamont-Doherty's Camera Sled

To make matters worse he had scheduled a large press party in Bermuda for Saturday night, July 19, the date we were scheduled to arrive at the island port.

If we waited for modifications to be completed on the Blue Fish—and then have it tested on the Briggs—we would not be able to get to Bermuda in time for Grimm's publicity bash. Needless to say the scientists wanted to stay at the Briggs site and test the equipment while Jack Grimm didn't want to miss the opportunity for publicity the press party would bring. True to Jack's Golden Rule mentality, he ordered the H.J.W. Fay to head for Bermuda—much to the frustration of the scientific team.

I didn't argue with Jack's decision, mostly because I knew Louis Reynolds was waiting for us in Bermuda. Louis had followed the project closely ever since Art Markel and I met with him several years earlier. Through Art I had been able to keep Louis abreast of what was going on with Jack Grimm and our 1980 Titanic expedition. Louis was also aware that our initial plan was to find the

Louis Reynolds with Aluminaut Model

Titanic in 1980, then modify Reynolds' submersible Aluminaut to dive on the Titanic the following year and recover her artifacts.

We also needed to get to Bermuda to restock supplies and refuel the Fay for the long trip to the North Atlantic. And when some of our equipment had problems during our transit from Port Everglades, it became necessary to fly in replacement parts to Bermuda. Plus, the generator that supplied power to Fay's active rudders developed a serious problem during our transit from Florida to Bermuda. For low-speed maneuverability during launch and recovery and for towing in strong side-winds, dual auxiliary stern propulsion units were essential. Consequently it became necessary for an electrician to be flown in to Bermuda from Tracor Marine in Florida to make the necessary repairs.

After several days of scientific testing in deep water off Bermuda, Dr. Bill Ryan, Dr. Fred Spiess and Jim Kosolas agreed that the scientific equipment was finally working to their mutual satisfaction and declared they were "ready to go!" The H.J.W. Fay was topped with fuel and water, and on July 26 we left the picturesque harbor of St. George, Bermuda, and headed for that certain spot 400 miles off the coast of Cape Race, Newfoundland, where the Titanic was waiting to be discovered.

Jack Grimm did not sail with us to the Titanic site. After waving goodbye from the dock he flew back to his office in Abilene, having decided that it would be a lot easier to control worldwide publicity from Texas than from the middle of the North Atlantic.

Jack's decision turned out to be beneficial to me. The worldwide media didn't want to talk to someone in Texas. They wanted to talk to the expedition leader who was actually on site in the North Atlantic where the actual hunt for the Titanic was going on.

I received ship-to-shore telephone calls daily from media representatives all over the world. It was not unusual for me to be summoned to the Fay's bridge to take an incoming call from radio, television and newspaper people. I also received calls from school children in Japan, Australia and Europe. Everyone wanted to know what we were doing to find the Titanic, what type of equipment were we using, and most of all, how we planned to raise the Titanic?

I always responded to this question with the same answer: we definitely did not plan to raise the Titanic! It was a crazy idea. I also included in my reply that after the Titanic had been found, we intended to salvage some of her artifacts and put them on a world tour. I anticipated that people all over the world would be interested in seeing for themselves what had happened to the famous ship and what she looked like after so many years of sitting in 12,000 feet of water.

H.J.W. Fay First Day at Titanic Site

When we first arrived in the region of the Titanic's sinking, the North Atlantic was as calm as an inland lake. I had always heard about how rough the water was in the North Atlantic and was surprised to find the surface as smooth as glass. I said a prayer for the good weather and hoped it would continue.

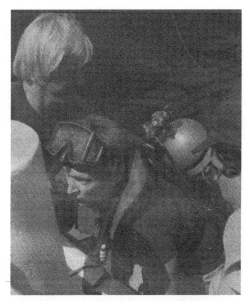

Mike Preparing to Dive at Titanic Site

The scientific team immediately went to work setting out three radio beacon transponders on the outside of the search area so they could navigate precisely within the area while searching for the Titanic. Their plan was to tow our Blue Fish side-scan sonar device back and forth within the target area in large three-kilometer swaths.

When Blue Fish was lowered toward the bottom, the team began towing it very slowly (one to two knots) from one end of the search area to the other. It was a very tedious process—not unlike mowing a very large yard.

"Blue Fish" Being Filmed While Being Lowered

Accuracy of navigation was critical as we didn't want to overlap any three-kilometer sonar swath that had previously been searched. Unfortunately the calm wind and smooth sea condition didn't last. On the second day, the weather began to change. As soon as we started making the slow thirty-mile-long search swaths across the ocean floor, the sea began to grow increasingly restless. Within days, winds increased to gale force causing the ocean to turn into a frothy mixture of boiling green and white liquid. Hanging on for dear life became a 24-hour objective.

Until then I never knew why shipboard bunks had wooden slats along each side. When we were rolling 45 degrees from one side to the other I no longer wondered why the bunk slats were necessary. The ship rolls were so violent at times that without the wooden slats a person lying in the bunk would be immediately thrown to the deck. Trying to sleep, trying to stay upright in the shower or just trying to brush your teeth became tiring tasks.

Mealtime was an adventure, as well. Anything and everything—plates, cups, bottles of catsup—would slide back and forth and even off the table if you weren't able to hold it down. I found it easier to eat when I could wedge myself against a wall, but not being able to adjust to the rolling of the ship made me more susceptible to getting sea sick.

What I would do after every meal was go up on the bridge, from which I could easily see the horizon spread out before me. By keeping an eye on the horizon I could more easily lean to counteract the constant movement of the ship. This is called getting your "sea legs". After you've been at sea for three or four days you get your sea legs and can more easily adjust to the

Dr. Fred Spiess Directing "Blue Fish" Recovery

continuous rolling and pitching of the ship.

Despite all the pitching and rolling, being out on the ocean searching for the Titanic was a tremendous adventure. But day after day having to fight the churning mountain of waves while the H.J.W. Fay plowed slowly forward on a ten-hour search leg quickly became very hard work.

Everyone on our science team had been on the ocean before and knew how difficult life on board a research vessel could be. But no matter how bad it got, they all stayed at their posts, night and day, in the lab or out on the Fay's fan tail (which usually was awash with ocean water from breaking waves).

Conversely, no one on my film team had ever been at sea before. Still, they made the best of a bad situation. Bobby Blanco—who had been with me on my Mexican expeditions—seemed to relish the rough seas and our daily struggle for survival. He eagerly pitched in to help me do whatever I asked.

My cinematographer Nik Petrik also did his best to persevere when the weather was particularly bad. But Nik wasn't quite as enthusiastic as Bobby about getting out into the worst parts of the ocean's violent display. On more than one occasion, I

Bobby Blanco at H.J.W. Fay Map Table

had to grab my 16mm Canon camera to get the shot I wanted when Nik balked about the weather being too bad or the shot too dangerous.

As we towed the Blue Fish about 100 feet from the ocean floor, its electronic signal would be sent up 20,000 feet of cable into the scientific lab on board the Fay. As the research vessel slowly moved the Blue Fish above the bottom, black and white marks were etched onto a continuous roll of white paper in the lab. The scientists were then able to get a graphic recording of the search areas white sandy bottom, interspersed with heavier marks and shades which clearly noted the presence of rocks, boulders, natural geological features and any man-made object.

Lamont-Doherty Scientists Working in H.J.W. Fay Lab

The trick was to interpret the black and white marks and shades of what each truly represented. Some large boulders or rock outcroppings left a white shadow on the paper, which made it difficult to figure out if the sonar had detected a large man-made object or just another natural ship-sized object that was nothing more than a large rock or geology in the form of a rock outcropping.

Bill Ryan, Fred Spiess and Jim Kosolas believed the Titanic's 900-foot-long hull would present a crisp white shadow on the tracing paper in the lab—which would clearly identify the target as the Titanic. But on our first runs through the laid out search area, no Titanic-size shadow was recorded. The search area was nine hundred square miles (roughly thirty miles on one side by thirty miles on the other).

Early in our search we discovered a fairly large geological cut that ran through most of our search area. We immediately named the large geological cut Titanic Canyon.

The first search leg we ran was through the precise area the Titanic said she was located when she hit the iceberg in 1912. Although none of us believed the Titanic was actually at that position when she sank, we would all feel pretty silly if we didn't search 41 degrees, 46 minutes North, by 50 degrees, 14 minutes West. After completing an initial reconnaissance of a 100 square mile patch of ocean north and east of the distress position, we began working several long transects through the region where theTitanic rescue operations took place in the days following the disaster.

Lamont Scientists Recovering "Blue Fish"

On August 10, 1980, we completed the western survey of the search area and retrieved the Blue Fish to move eastward. The recovery of the Blue Fish was successful despite the fantail once again being completely awash in high seas. Since the gale we had been fighting seemed to be worsening, we had no choice but to spend the next twenty-four hours riding it out without surveying.

When the wind was blowing too strong during a downwind search leg, it became impossible to control the necessary slow towing speed of the Fay. If gale force winds pushed our research vessel too fast through the water, the Blue Fish dangling at the end of the 20,000-foot cable would sail too high above the bottom (thereby negating the reliability of any sonar recording).

As soon as the weather abated slightly we re-launched the Blue Fish and made a long sonar track down our newly named Titanic Canyon—just in case the famous ship was hiding within the recesses of the deep geologic cut.

Mike in H.J.W. Fay Lab Discussing Canyon Discovery with Dr. Fred Spiess

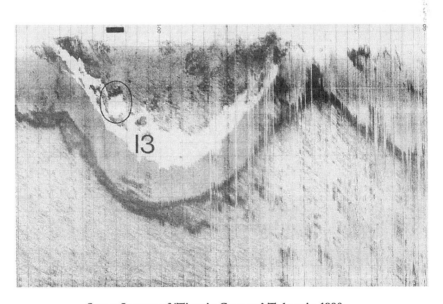

Sonar Image of 'Titanic Canyon' Taken in 1980

But, once again, there was nothing found in the canyon that appeared to be the size of the Titanic.

Since the Titanic's course in 1912 made a transverse through our search area from east to west, I reasoned that maybe we should be spending more of our time searching further to the east. Dr. Ryan and Dr. Spiess agreed. Consequently, we headed to the most eastern portion of our search area and within hours discovered two very interesting targets that we labeled "big banana" and "little banana" because both showed sonar shadows that could be identified as objects about the same size of the Titanic. Upon closer examination with our magnetometer, neither target appeared to register metal—which could only lead to the conclusion that the two objects were geological.

We began to seriously consider the possibility that the Titanic might not be in one piece as everyone thought, but may have in fact broken into several pieces upon sinking. If she did break, she may have been so camouflaged by the surrounding geology that it would be impossible to recognize her by a single broad shadow.

Several weeks into our survey we had completed more than 350 miles of linear track and had discovered a total of 14 acoustic targets but none of them represented the Titanic-sized sonar target we were looking for. With fuel and food beginning to run low, we felt we had no choice but to admit defeat, leave the Titanic search area and head back to Boston where Jack Grimm waited along with a large group of clamoring media.

When we arrived in Boston on the morning of August 21, 1980, Jack Grimm was waiting for us at the dock. As soon as he could get on board he headed straight for Dr. Ryan, Dr. Spiess and Jim Kosolas. He wanted to get their consent before announcing to the world that his 1980 expedition had made a discovery of the Titanic. But the scientists didn't want to make any such claim as their collective reputations were on the line. True, we had discovered Titanic Canyon and had made sonar records of several very interesting targets, but none of the targets could be identified conclusively as actually being the Titanic.

Jack was not a happy camper, but knew he couldn't force the scientists to claim something they didn't believe. Since I had been the one talking to the media during the expedition, all the reporters naturally sought me out when we docked. While Jack was on the ship talking with the scientists, I told the media I couldn't say anything until we held our official press conference a little later.

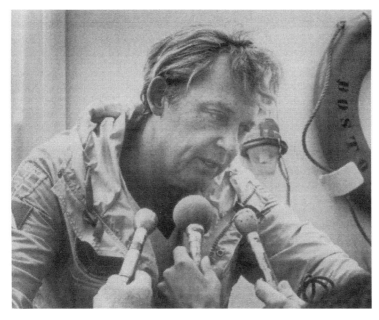

Expedition Leader Mike Harris Upon Arrival in Boston

A lot of pictures, however, were taken of me giving my impromptu mini press conference at the dock before our official press conference was held with Jack Grimm and members of our scientific team. Consequently, the picture of me at the dock as expedition leader ended up being sent around the world—thanks to the Associated Press who covered our arrival into Boston Harbor.

When Jack and I arrived back in New York, the successful billionaire /developer Sam LeFrak invited us, along with our wives, out for a cruise around Long Island Sound on his luxurious private yacht. Sam's yacht was almost as big as the H.J.W. Fay. During our afternoon cruise together, Sam asked me if Jack Grimm was a "man of means?" I told him that Jack owned several oil wells in Texas, but I didn't think he could be described as a man of means. Sam must have

Jack Grimm and Mike Harris Press Conference

liked my answer because he smiled and said, "Let's go have a little lunch".

Lunch turned out to be just as fancy and impressive as the rest of the outing. No creature comfort was overlooked. Sam even had a French chef on board who prepared exquisite dishes and desserts from scratch. All of the servant staff, both captain and crew, were dressed in their own special uniform.

Our cruise was scheduled to return to the dock at 5:00 p.m. The red-carpeted gangway was lowered and the uniformed staff assembled to say goodbye to Mr. LeFrak and his guests at precisely 5:00 p.m. I don't mean we left the yacht at 4:59 or 5:01. We departed precisely at 5:00 p.m. I was very impressed with what a real man of means can provide.

Jack Grimm and I made the round of network radio and television shows talking about our recent search for the Titanic and promoting the fact that we intended to go out again in 1981 on a second expedition. The reason we had not been successful on our first expedition, we explained, was partly because the new long-range side-scan sonar Blue Fish we developed specifically for the project had not worked as anticipated. It had not been sufficiently tested prior to leaving on our expedition. So while at sea its proper effectiveness was sporadic at best.

In addition, our scientists spent a lot of time either repairing or upgrading various components during the voyage. Plus, except for that first day, the weather had been exceptionally bad during our entire month at sea. Jack and I both believed that on a second expedition we wouldn't have so many factors working against us.

The prestigious William Morris Agency in New York had both Jack Grimm and I under contract, and had arranged with a publisher to pay us $1,000,000 for the rights to a book, which we expected to publish upon discovery of the Titanic. William Morris had contracted with Canadian author William Stevenson— who had been with us for the entire expedition—to write our book.

William Stevenson

John Davidson

Bill had previously published the bestseller *A Man Called Intrepid*. We roomed together on board the H.J.W. Fay. So when we came back to Boston he invited me to do an interview with him on the CBC television network in Toronto.

A few weeks later I was also invited to Los Angeles to appear on the John Davidson Show. Some of the guests who appeared with me included Fred Rogers, host of the popular children's show *Mister Rogers' Neighborhood*, and television star Jamie Farr of *M*A*S*H*. The Explorer's Club even invited me to be one of the featured speakers at the black-tie banquet they hold each year at the Waldorf Astoria in New York City.

My fifteen minutes of fame were fun, but giving interviews and appearing on radio and television shows wasn't really what I was interested in. My main focus was to lead an expedition to actually find the Titanic, not just look for it.

In the meantime, to honor the contract I had with Jack Grimm, I needed to get busy and produce a documentary feature of our summer 1980 expedition. I wanted to hire one of the best actors in Hollywood to be my on-camera host and narrator to help boost the project's credibility. I chose Orson Welles, partly because Joseph Cotton had told me so many interesting stories about the two of them making Citizen Kane. But mostly I chose Orson Welles because of the huge following he had maintained over the years as a serious film, radio and television

Orson Wells with Mike in Studio

talent.

I had been advised that I should arrange to film Orson at the small film studio on Orange Avenue in Hollywood he liked to use. I also made sure I hired the cinematographer and sound people Orson liked to use and was most comfortable working with. But it turned out the most important person I hired during the shoot was a man named Barney McNulty who was known as the "Cue Card King" throughout Hollywood.

Several of Hollywood's biggest stars had used Barney for years. He had worked with such famous film and television celebrities as Ed Wynn, Bob Hope, George Burns and Gracie Allen, Lucille Ball, Groucho Marx, Frank Sinatra, Jack Webb, Carol Burnett and scores of others.

Orson Welles and Barney McNulty on my Search for the Titanic Set in Hollywood

Thanks to the friendship I developed with Barney while working with him on my Titanic film I was able to meet with Bob Hope backstage during two television specials and talk to him about my Titanic expeditions. I also met Jack Lemon back stage after he appeared on The Tonight Show Starring Johnny Carson at NBC and had dinner several times with Burgess Meredith. Indeed, Barney McNulty knew everyone in Hollywood and everyone in Hollywood knew him.

I'll never forget the first day I met Orson Welles. He arrived at the studio in a long white limousine. His driver got out and opened the door for him while I waited nervously by the movie studio door. I was just a documentary film producer from Florida. Maybe he wouldn't like working with a documentary film producer. When he stuck out his hand and asked if I was Mike Harris I knew right away I didn't have to worry. I should have known. Everyone likes to talk about the Titanic—and Orson Welles was no exception. He immediately put me at ease by telling me stories about his grandfather who had been a ship's captain. I started telling him about last summer's adventure in the North Atlantic, during which we had to battle mountainous seas in our search for the elusive vessel. I don't know if he was just being polite, but he did seem genuinely interested in the stories I was telling him.

I showed Orson how I would like for him to position himself in front of the large Titanic model I had arranged to have on the set then move a few steps to where he could point to a map. Orson told me flatly, "Mike, I hate to admit it, but I'm much too heavy to move. All I am is a talking head. Just set me down on a stool somewhere and let me work with the camera".

So that's exactly what I did. And Orson Welles was the most wonderful and talented talking head I had ever worked with. His contribution to my *Search for the Titanic* film was all I could have hoped for and even more.

Two other film production experiences I enjoyed while producing *Search for the Titanic* was a trip I took to Greenland to film calving glaciers and the interview I conducted with Frank Goldsmith.

Orson Welles and Titanic Model

I flew with cinematographer Jack Cosgrove from Tampa to Reykjavik, Iceland. We then squeezed into two seats on a twin engine "Otter" equipped with snow skis that had been leased by an expedition team heading for Greenland. Since the expedition team planned to ski across the glacier ice cap that covers the Greenland landmass, they had most of the seats and isle space in between completely filled with tents, food and survival gear.

As we took the one-hour flight over to Ammassalik, Greenland, I remember looking out the window as the pilot flew about fifty feet above the ocean trying to find his way through the fog and around giant bergs that dotted the dark looking sea below. I pride myself on being an adventurer, but this adventure was a little too intense.

Giant Iceberg that Floated in the Water off the Coast of Greenland

After turning this way and that to miss the giant icebergs along out path, our little Otter was suddenly enveloped in a thick blanket of fog. Right away I knew this wasn't good. But about the same time the pilot shouted through the open door of his cockpit that he was going to give up and head back to Reykjavik. I found out later that such aborted flights trying to get to Greenland were considered almost routine. The weather was usually so bad and the communication so poor that landing at the small landing strip at Ammassalik really was hit and miss—often more miss than hit.

About 6:00 the next morning the phone jarred us awake in our hotel room in Reykjavik. Jack and I and the Greenland expedition team were told to get up now and get to the airport immediately. When we arrived twenty minutes later we found our twin-engine Otter waiting for us, her two engines warmed up and ready to go. The pilot said they had just received word the weather was supposed to be clearing on the Greenland coast. If we didn't leave right away we probably wouldn't make it.

Off we zoomed again in the direction of Greenland. When about twenty miles off the rocky coast once again the pilot let down through dense clouds and fog and began dodging the ever present icebergs. I personally couldn't see that the weather was any better than it was the day before when we had aborted the trip. But the pilot, seemingly undaunted, continued his zig-zag course toward the coast.

I couldn't see anything out of my window, and I prayed our fearless pilot could see more than I could. Suddenly, not two hundred feet away, a solid wall of rock zipped past my window. I tried to look around the equipment that was still tied down in the seats and aisle, hoping I could catch a glance out the window on the other side for a better look. No luck. But just about at the same time our two skis swooshed on ice and snow, two props were thrown into reverse and in a swirl of flying ice and snow we skidded to a bumpy stop. Somehow we were down and seemed to be in one piece.

The terminal was a one room wooden shack with a potbelly stove that thankfully threw off a little heat. There were a few maps tacked to one wall and a collection of radio gear stacked on a shelf.

While Jack and I waited for a helicopter to take us to our final destination at Kulusuk, we heard a huge roar outside. A large U.S. Air Force C-130 on skis had just landed right outside our door. A few minutes later an Air Force General bounded into the shack happy to shake hands with all of the few Americans present.

Jack and I flew over to Kulusuk, a small community on an island just off the coast of Greenland, to film calving icebergs. Each year, large pieces of Greenland's glaciers break loose when they hit the ocean and start floating into the shipping lanes of the North Atlantic. The iceberg the Titanic crashed into in 1912 had come from Greenland.

Mike Filming in Kulusuk, Greenland

When big ships like cruise ships or giant aircraft carriers travel through the ocean they bob up and down affected by the action of the wind and waves. When giant icebergs drift through the ocean, they are so massive that waves can be seen splashing at their edges—but the berg itself does not move. It drifts through the ocean slowly and steadily without ever bobbing up and down. No wonder the Titanic sank when she hit such a huge object.

Before the Titanic accident, the Coast Guard didn't track the building-size blocks of ice that so often float into the sea-lanes in the early part of each year. After the Titanic accident—and because of the Titanic accident—the location of major floating bergs began to be charted.

Jack and I rented a small boat along with a guide and went out to the base of several huge glaciers that continually break off and fall into the sea. We did get to shoot some spectacular footage of calving glaciers and I was able to use some of the footage in *Search for the Titanic.*

Guide in Small Seal-Skin Kayak Close to Kulusuk

After the Greenland trip, I took my cinematographer Nik Petrik with me to Orlando where we filmed an interview with a 77-year-old gentleman named Frank Goldsmith. Frankie, as he was called then, was nine years old when he traveled with his mother and father on Titanic's maiden voyage in 1912.

When Titanic hit the iceberg and was sinking, Frankie's father had to stay on the ship while he and his mother got into collapsible raft D. This was the last raft available. Frank related to me several stories about what it was like when the Titanic was sinking, but one of his more memorable stories involved the City of Detroit.

Frankie said that when he moved to Detroit many years after the Titanic disaster, he lived in a home not far from where the Detroit Tigers played baseball. On warm summer evenings whenever a ball player hit a home run the sudden roar from the fans at the stadium would drift softly across the neighborhood. He said that roar always reminded

Collapsible Raft "D"

him of the sudden screams the passengers left on the Titanic as it was sinking. Even in that raft with his mother about a half-mile away, he could hear the screams. Ever since I heard Frank Goldsmith's haunting story, stadium noise always makes me think of the Titanic and what it must have been like for that nine-year-old boy.

Tampa Newspaper Photo of Mike Harris Upon Return from 1980 Titanic Expedition

One other very talented person I brought into my 1980 Search for the Titanic film project was Ken Marschall, a talented artist I found working at an animation studio in Hollywood. Ken had a passion for anything that had to do with the Titanic. I hired him to create animation of how our side-scan sonar worked while we were looking for the Titanic in the deep ocean. I also hired him to create a promotional one-sheet of my *Search for the Titanic* film production.

I wanted to bring Ken along on the 1980 expedition, but unfortunately space was limited. With all the scientists and other film people on board, it just wasn't possible for me to have him join us. But Ken did the next best thing. He graciously presented me with a copy of one of his beautiful Titanic paintings that I took with me on the expedition. Then at the end of our adventure I had everyone on board the H.J.W. Fay, from the ship captain and crew to the scientists and film team, sign the back of Ken's painting as a historic trip memento.

When the film was completed Jack Grimm held a World Premiere at a theater in Abilene. It was well received but even the exceptional talent of Orson Wells couldn't hide the fact that during our 1980 expedition we didn't actually find the Titanic. Maybe our second expedition in 1981 would be different. The Titanic was still out there waiting to be found.

We'd give it another try next summer. Surely Titanic would not defeat us again. I was going to do everything I could to make certain it didn't!

1980 Titanic Expedition Logo

13 1981 TITANIC EXPEDITION

At the conclusion of the 1980 expedition Dr. Bill Ryan submitted a report to Jack Grimm and his corporation Titanic 1980, Inc. that described what we had accomplished during the summer's search for the Titanic. He listed the fourteen acoustic targets we discovered while at sea and recommended we revisit each target in 1981 with a deep-towed magnetometer at the beginning of next year's field season.

Dr. Ryan's report stated that we should be able to "fly the magnetometer within 2000 feet of each target without the need for bottom-moored acoustic navigation beacons and probably accomplish the target discrimination phase of the survey in less than 60 hours of station time. The survey should begin first with the high probability targets".

Bill went on to explain "as soon as an appropriate short wavelength magnetic anomaly is detected, the particular target causing the anomaly should be re-imaged with the sonar adjusted for the highest resolution scale".

Once the target was precisely defined Bill suggested we use "the photographic and television system already developed for the 1980 program. We envision making a few small and inexpensive modifications to reduce the electrical interference caused by the strobe charging circuit and to simplify the launch and recovery operation".

Bill suggested that "approximately eight to ten days of on-station time should be sufficient to locate the wreckage and complete an extensive photographic coverage. One should attempt where possible to construct overlapping mosaics of certain sections of the ship".

This last statement sounded like what Robert Ballard from Woods Hole and Emory Kristof from National Geographic suggested when I was planning to use their Seaonics team prior to getting involved with Jack Grimm. Emory showed me drawings he had created depicting how he envisioned lighting the entire length of the Titanic while the ship was sitting in the pitch black darkness on the bottom. But Bill Ryan's plan was not nearly as precise as Emory's proposal.

In Dr. Ryan's final report he recommended that in 1981 we should use both the mid-range sonar system developed in 1980 by Jim Kosolas and also bring along the Deep-Tow Instrumentation System belonging to the Marine Physical Laboratory of Scripps. Bill stated that "the Scripps sonar with its higher side-scan frequency and its higher resolution proton-procession magnetometer is better suited for the target discrimination phase".

Bill concluded his report by saying he had requested a charter for the 1981 field section on the Research Vessel Gyre that belonged to the Oceanographic Department of Texas A&M University. He said the Gyre was similar in size to the Fay, but that the Gyre had "greater slow speed maneuverability, more already existing, laboratory and shop space, somewhat better fuel economy and a greater range and endurance".

We could board the Gyre on the East Coast of the U.S., thereby reducing transit time to six days as opposed to the 17 days in transit in 1980. Twenty or more, fewer days of ship time would, of course, greatly reduce the cost for the 1981 expedition.

Jack definitely liked the sound of that. The investor group in 1980 wasn't particularly happy that we hadn't found the Titanic as Jack had enthusiastically tried to convince everyone we would.

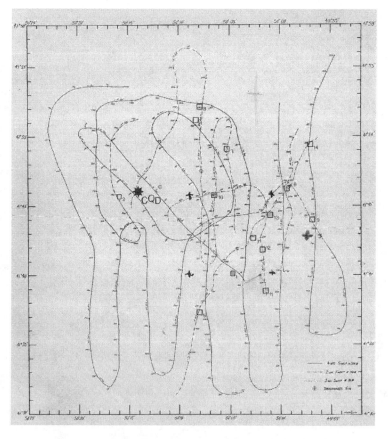

1980 Side-Scan Sonar Fish Tracks

They each knew Cadillac Jack was the consummate gambler, but weren't too happy he was gambling with their money.

Consequently, several of the original 1980 investors refused to ante up when Jack asked them to put up additional money in 1981. The total cost for the 1980 expedition and the production of *Search for the Titanic* was approximately $1.25 million. The William Morris Agency found a publishing house that advanced ten percent of a $1,000,000 contract to Titanic 1980, Inc. for the rights to the book that William Stevenson was hired to write. But when we didn't find the Titanic, Stevenson's contract was void and the balance of our contract was never paid.

Without finding the Titanic, even *Search for the Titanic* didn't get the distribution we had hoped. Everyone wanted to see a film that ended with the discovery of the Titanic. We didn't have that ending, but were determined to get it.

Research Vessel Gyre

During the summer of 1981, enthused as ever about finding the Titanic, our expedition and film teams got on board the R/V Gyre at Woods Hole Oceanographic Institute on the coast of Massachusetts and headed back out into the North Atlantic. The 1981 expedition differed from the 1980 trip in that we had basically the same scientific and film teams as we did the previous year, but in 1981 Jack Grimm got on board the ship with the rest of us. I'm sure he was determined to not miss out on all the free publicity that he did in 1980 when he stayed home in Abilene.

The other major change in the 1981 expedition was the addition of actor James Drury. Jim played the title role in "The Virginian" on television for about ten years and enjoyed quite an international following. Jack had met Jim at a social function and invited him to go on the expedition with us. Prior to the expedition, Jack did ask me if I would mind having "The Virginian" in the expedition film as my on-camera host and narrator. I told him I didn't think it would be a problem, especially since he had already been invited.

Jim turned out to be a wonderful talent and all-around great guy. He was quite friendly and certainly knew what he was doing around a camera. He delighted in writing many of his on-camera scenes for himself as he described what was going on during various phases of the expedition.

One humorous aspect of working with Jim was the fact that he wore a hairpiece. When it was properly in place on his head, he looked like a million bucks. But at sea, in the North Atlantic, it was not uncommon for the wind to blow constantly at 30 knots. Consequently, the compliance of his hairpiece was touch-and-go during many of the scenes. If the wind kicked up, Jim's rug would unceremoniously begin to go

Jack Grimm at Dock Prior to 1981 Expedition

flying off. Luckily for Jim he was always able to grab it before it sailed off into the ocean and was irretrievably lost.

On the way out to the site Jack Grimm was always anxious to take all of the incoming ship-to-shore telephone calls from the worldwide media. He loved to describe in his Texas drawl how, this year, Cadillac Jack was going to find the Titanic. Whenever someone called and wanted to talk to the expedition leader, Jack would tell me he was the one paying the bills so he was the one the media wanted to talk to.

I wasn't convinced that Jack was the one paying all the bills as he admitted often he liked to work with other peoples' money. In 1980, Jack took all the credit for funding our expedition to search for the Titanic.

James "The Virginian" Drury

Behind the scenes, more than one investor told me that it was really OPM that was funding 'his" expedition.

He may have put in a little of his own money for the 1981 expedition but many of the 1980 investors refused to back Cadillac Jack a second time. When I produced my film of the 1981 expedition, *Return to the Titanic*, with James Drury, the production budget was less than half of what it was in 1980. In fact the original musical score I had created for *Search for the Titanic* had to be reused in *Return to the Titanic*. I'm not sure anyone noticed, but it did enable me to complete a film of the expedition without spending nearly as much money.

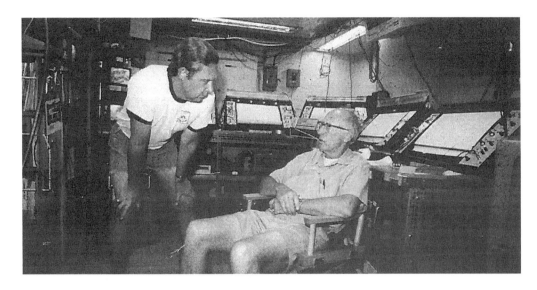

Mike Harris with Dr. Fred Spiess in Gyre Lab

When we arrived at the Titanic site in 1981, we again dropped transponders over the side to mark the edges of our projected search area. Just as Dr. Bill Ryan suggested in his report, we began going back over the targets discovered in 1980.

When that didn't work and no metal was detected on any of the previously discovered targets, the scientists began second guessing themselves as to why we had not been able to find such a huge vessel. We knew we were in the right area—even if it was an area approximately thirty miles wide by thirty miles long. But where was she? Had she fallen into Titanic canyon? Had a giant underwater landslide completely covered her as she lay on the bottom? Plenty of theories were floated, but no obvious answer presented itself.

Launching Deep Tow Sonar System

When we didn't find the Titanic within the search area, our scientists decided that she must be hidden within the jagged walls of Titanic Canyon. Consequently Dr. Fred Spiess' high-resolution sonar vehicle Deep Tow was dropped to the bottom at the end of our 20,000-feet of wire and carefully navigated within the canyon's walls. Unfortunately Deep Tow's expensive magnetometer didn't detect the presence of metal on any target and her sonar sweeps found nothing but geological features. Once again our expensive equipment and professional scientists did not come up with any target that we could identify as the Titanic.

In 1980 when I was about to lead the first expedition to search for the Titanic a lady contacted me and said she wanted to give me a note that her family had kept for more than sixty years. She said her mother found the note in a bottle while she was walking along the coast of Maine several months after the Titanic sank in 1912.

The lady gave me the note, along with a picture of her mother (who found the note) wearing her long Victorian dress that was stylish in 1912. The note which was actually scribbled on a small piece of notepaper stated simply "Our ship is lost...all hope of being saved is abandoned...Jack Steward...ill fated Titanic".

I looked in some of the Titanic history books and discovered that John 'Jack' Stewart, 27, was on the Titanic's maiden voyage and was employed a Verandah Steward. The note states "Jack Steward...ill fated Titanic".

Lady Who Found the Note

In the old days, especially in Europe, people were often called by their profession — such as George the Butcher, or Tom the Painter. So it's entirely plausible that John Stewart who was known on board the Titanic as "Jack the Steward" wrote "Jack Steward"

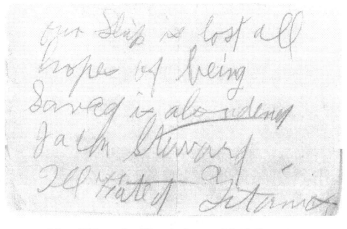

Note Written by Titanic Steward Jack Stewart

on the note when the ship was sinking.

With charter time on the Gyre coming to a close, we had no choice but to once again head back to port without being able to announce to the world that we had discovered the Titanic. With only bad news to report, Cadillac Jack was no longer interested in talking to the media. He turned our communication duties back over to the Expedition Leader: me. There was no getting around the fact that Cadillac Jack liked talking to the media when everything was positive an upbeat, but when things didn't turn out as planned, he didn't have the stomach to report only bad news.

Mike Filming Deep Tow Launch in 1981

I chided him for his unreasonable behavior—which he freely admitted wasn't particularly fair. But then, smiling broadly, Jack reminded me again of his Golden Rule. "It may not be particularly fair," he gushed, "but that's how I play the game. Now go out there and put a good spin on what we accomplished. I know you can do it!"

Wanting to be a good soldier, I did just that. I always enjoyed talking to the media and putting the best spin I could on what was happening, but I sure wished we had accomplished more during that summer's expedition.

Preparing to Launch Dr. Ryan's Camera Sled

As we started to head back across our search area one last time on the way home, Dr. Ryan decided it would be a good time to test his underwater camera system. He attached the system to the end of our 20,000-foot wire and started recording whatever was on the bottom as we exited our search area.

After about four hours we hauled in the wire with Bill Ryan's camera system, took the videotape to the recreation area on board the Gyre and started replaying what had been captured.

Most of the videotape was pretty boring as we watched several hours of the flat sandy bottom drifting past the camera—highlighted every now and then with scenes of deep ocean fish or crabs scurrying out of the way of the device. Occasionally great plumes of silt filled the screen like a giant cloud whenever the camera sled unexpectedly banged into the bottom.

All the scientists—as well as the ship and film crews—were there in the recreation room that afternoon watching the bottom footage that Bill Ryan's camera sled had recorded. Suddenly the camera passed over an object that looked like a barnacle-encrusted ship propeller. Everyone in the room sat up and shouted at once, "Did you see that?!?" We couldn't believe what we had all just seen on the video monitor.

"Play that again," Jack ordered. "I think we just found the Titanic's propeller!"

Propeller-Shaped Object from Dr. Bill Ryan's Camera Sled

One of the guys on the science team sprang into action. He rewound the footage about thirty seconds as everyone in the room waited—holding their breath—for that propeller-like image to again cross before our eyes.

I immediately shouted to my film team to start filming as the ghostly image of what looked hauntingly like a huge propeller once again drifted before the camera. "There it is, men!" Jack crowed triumphantly. "That's the Titanic's propeller!"

Dr. Ryan and Dr. Spiess looked at the image repeatedly, but were not as sure as Jack. They were reluctant to rush to any type of unscientific conclusion until it could be conclusively proven.

The image did look interesting, but even I wasn't sure it looked like a propeller from the Titanic. As we replayed the scene over and over there was a lot of debate about whether it was a propeller encrusted with sea life or just a propeller-shaped rock formation. There was no clear consensus among any of us.

Still, the next time someone from the world media called the Gyre, there was no question as to who would take the call. Cadillac Jack immediately stepped up to answer the phone. Somehow he had forgotten his instruction six hours earlier for me to talk with the media. Frankly being more than a little skeptical, I didn't mind at all that Jack wanted to reclaim his position as communications director.

Jack had a wonderful time telling anyone who would listen, that he had discovered part of the Titanic. I would have been delighted if we had known it was actually true. But "Jack's propeller" (as everyone began calling it) looked to me like nothing more than a rock outcropping.

Jim Drury and I developed a nice friendship during the expedition and post-production of *Return to the Titanic*. One day when we were working together looking again at the footage of Jack's propeller, I asked him what he really thought about it. He admitted he didn't know for sure, but that it was "certainly better than a poke in the eye with a sharp stick!"

We featured Jack's propeller in *Return to the Titanic* and played it up quite heavily in the conclusion of the film—mainly because Jack was still the driving force behind getting my expeditions and films funded. If Jack Grimm said he had found the Titanic's propeller, then we had found the Titanic's propeller.

Jack Grimm with Dr. Ryan and his Camera Sled

On the strength of that vexing video image, Jack vowed to go back again in 1982 on a third expedition to find the Titanic. The propeller image was enough proof for Cadillac Jack, but whether it would convince additional investors was quite another matter. Jack had several professional photo companies enhance the video image and had it analyzed thoroughly. But even though the image remained interesting test results could never determine conclusively the object was made of metal—or that it actually was a propeller blade from the Titanic.

The crew of the *Gyre:*
Left-to-right, along the bulkhead: Mark Olsson, Skip Gleason, Mary Linzer, Jack Cosgrove, James Drury, Bobby Blanco, Bill Hoffman, John Farre, Wayne Wardlow, Michael Harris, Fred Spiess
Right-to-left, inside the bulkhead: Nik Petrik, Anita Brosius, Dale Chayes, Jack Grimm, Tony Boegeman, Bill Ryan, Jack Bechtold, Carl Lowenstein, John Jain

William Hoffman *Beyond Reach* Book Photo of 1981 Titanic Expedition Team

There was plenty of conversation and speculation about Jack's propeller. Some speculated that when the Titanic scraped against the iceberg, her starboard propeller must have been knocked off and fallen to the bottom. The Titanic then would have drifted for several hours before finally sinking to the bottom herself. Jack claimed that the propeller blade he was sure he found was the blade that some speculated had been knocked off when the Titanic brushed past the iceberg.

Since I was officially the Expedition Leader of the expedition in 1981, I would love to have believed that my expedition had indeed been the first to find part of the Titanic. But I couldn't bring myself to make such a claim. I didn't want to publicly come out and say that my friend and benefactor Jack Grimm didn't know what he was talking about. But I also didn't want to stick my neck out on something that I wasn't absolutely sure was correct.

Jack's propeller image was something we could talk about when trying to raise money for a third expedition. But I also was becoming to believe more strongly that the best way to find the Titanic was to reactivate Louis Reynolds' deep diving submersible Aluminaut. Maybe by modifying the Aluminaut we could get down to the bottom, find Jack's infamous propeller and prove to everyone one way or the other that we had indeed found an important piece of the infamous ship.

We had now been out to the Titanic site on two different expeditions with some of the world's best underwater scientists, but still had not found the Titanic. I could only guess that Robert Ballard and Emory Kristof were surprised, but probably delighted. In their mind I'm quite sure they believed we got what we deserved, as I was only a documentary filmmaker and Jack Grimm an oil promoter from Texas. Neither of us were professional oceanographers. Neither of us had the proper credentials, nor were we worthy enough to make such an important contribution to underwater archaeology as the discovery of the Titanic.

I had heard from friends of Bob Ballard that he kept himself busy during our expeditions in 1980 and 1981 working at Woods Hole and diving in the submersible Alvin. I was also told that Bob had great respect for Dr. Ryan and Dr. Spiess and really didn't think the expeditions of Harris and Grimm would fail. But if by some miracle they did fail, Bob speculated, only then would he have a chance to keep his own dream alive of finding the Titanic.

I don't like to wish anyone bad luck, but I certainly did want to keep my own Titanic dreams alive. Disappointed at having led two expeditions that failed to find the Titanic, I began trying to figure out how we could do something different.

I didn't think searching on the bottom with a camera sled like Bob Ballard originally proposed and tried to prove during his ill-fated Alcoa Seaprobe expedition in the 1970s was an efficient way to search for anything on the ocean bottom. If you can only illuminate and photograph a small ten-foot by ten-foot portion of the ocean bottom at any one time, I reasoned, it would take forever to search an area thirty miles wide by thirty miles long.

But so far, side-scan sonar hadn't found us anything—not even Jack's questionable propeller, which Dr. Ryan found with his own camera sled. Hoping to come up with something different, I began thinking about placing Jim Kosolas's long-range Blue Fish or Dr. Spiess' short-range Deep Tow onto the sides of the Aluminaut.

Maybe then we would have the best of both worlds. We could not only search a wide swath of the ocean bottom we could also have people inside the Aluminaut looking at the bottom through portholes for any ship wreckage that might be missed by the sonar.

I began working closely with Art Markel to figure out exactly what it would cost to make the necessary modifications to the Aluminaut so she could successfully operate at a depth of 15,000 feet.

The Aluminaut's length was slightly more than 51 feet. She displaced 81 tons and the diameter of her hull was eight feet. She could cruise along the bottom at three knots for 32 hours (72 hours with emergency life support). She was large enough to carry a crew of six: one pilot, two engineers and three scientists.

Art Markell Showing Mike Aluminaut's View Port

One feature of the Aluminaut that really interested me was its two manipulator arms that enabled an operator inside to pick up and collect objects from off the sea floor. The collected items could be placed into exterior bins and safely returned to the surface. Once we found the Titanic, my goal had always been to recover whatever items we could, then preserve them and put the artifacts on a world tour. I always wanted to make a movie of the discovery but recovering the Titanic's artifacts and conducting the world tour had always been my main interest in trying to find the historic ship.

Art Markel worked up a list of what would have to be accomplished in order to get the Aluminaut ready to work again in the deep ocean. She was originally designed to operate at 15,000 feet, but had never been deeper than 6,000 feet. Unfortunately that was back in the early 1970s. Since then she had been sitting out of the water in storage at an industrial park located in Green Cove Springs, Florida. Almost all of the submersible's seals, wiring, cables, connectors, lights and electric motors had deteriorated significantly so needed to be either refurbished or replaced.

When Art gave me an initial estimate for the Aluminaut's overhaul, the total came to $750,000. I didn't think that was too bad, but then he gave me another estimate for $400,000 which included even more items he believed would have to replaced. The total amount now added up to $1.15 million, which to me was significant. I told Art I would try to set up a meeting with Jack Grimm back in Abilene and see if I could sell him on the idea of backing our new plan.

I went to Abilene and met with Jack Grimm. But when I told him how much it would cost to get the Aluminaut operational he hit the roof. "Them damn Arabs are killing me with the price of oil," he shouted. "I got me a few oil wells, but when they keep the price of oil so low I can't make a thing! What's wrong with Louis Reynolds putting up money?" he shouted at me again. "He owns the Aluminaut. It's his submersible. Go talk with him. Tell him to put up the money to fix his submarine. I'll put up the money for the expedition." Jack then pointed his finger at me and said forcefully, "Tell him Cadillac Jack gives his word on that!" I told Jack I'd see what I could do and headed for Richmond.

Jack Grimm always talked about all the money he was spending on trying to find the Titanic, but the truth as far as I could tell was that he had actually taken comparatively little money out of his own pocket. I was fairly certain that our 1980 expedition was funded entirely by Jack's oil field buddies, including Bunker Hunt who I saw hold up five fingers to let Jack know he was in for five percent of the expedition costs. I had heard from several others that Jack never spends any money himself. The general consensus among his friends was that Jack likes to grab all the publicity, but always does his best to use other people's money.

I'm quite sure that our 1981 expedition was no exception. I'm also quite sure we spent less than half the money on our second expedition than we did for our first. Jack was apparently only able to talk half his buddies into sticking with him for a second year—which is also why we had a shorter second expedition and I had to pay for a lot of the film costs myself.

When Art Markel and I sat down in Louis Reynolds' big corporate office in Richmond, we went through all the targets that had been discovered in our 1980 and 1981 expeditions. I tried to sell Mr. Reynolds on the idea that what we really needed to find the Titanic was use of his Aluminaut. I also told him as Jack had instructed that Jack Grimm is prepared to pay for all expedition costs. "Cadallac Jack gives his word on that."

Unfortunately, Mr. Reynolds was not persuaded. He said he would be more than happy to make the Aluminaut available if Jack Grimm would pay for the modifications. "He's the one who wants to find the Titanic," Louis exclaimed softly from behind his beautiful corporate desk, "Not me!"

"That may be true," I countered quickly, "but think of all the publicity Reynolds Metals Company will receive when it's announced the Titanic has been found by your Aluminaut."

Louis was ready with a counter of his own. "I'm sure Art Markel would be delighted," he told me with a smile, "but not my stockholders. We're in business to make and sell aluminum products, not find the Titanic." When Louis saw the disappointment on my face he added softly, "I'm sure it would be a grand thing to do and I'm sure it would be nice to find the Titanic. But please tell Jack Grimm that if he wants to use the Aluminaut he'll have to come up with the money himself."

I flew back to Abilene to tell Jack what Louis Reynolds had said in our meeting. I knew he wouldn't be happy, but I also knew he wouldn't want to throw in the towel on a third expedition. Jack had received too big a boost to his reputation to admit that he had failed at anything.

Before I left his office he asked me to see if I could come up with some money to fund a third expedition. In the meantime he said he'd continue to beat the bushes among his oil friends in Texas. "If I can't get the money together for an expedition in '82," he said, "I'll try to get us out there in '83. I know that propeller we found last year came off the Titanic. We've just got to get back one more time so we can prove it!"

14 EARHART AND ZHENG HE

Before returning home to Tampa from Abilene I received a call from a man named Buddy Brennan in Houston. I had met Buddy in Abilene the year before at the premiere for *Search for the Titanic*.

But Buddy didn't want to talk about Titanic. He wanted to talk about Amelia Earhart. He reminded me of a conversation we had together over dinner the previous year when I told him about shooting *Deadly Fathoms* in the Marshall Islands. I told Buddy about several stories I'd heard from various Marshallese officials who told me about what really happened to Amelia Earhart. Buddy said he had always been intrigued by the woman aviator and asked if I would lead an expedition back to the Marshall Islands to search for the famous flyer. He asked if I would be interested in shooting a feature documentary just like I had done about the Titanic.

Since Jack Grimm wasn't sure how he could find the money for a third expedition to find the Titanic in 1982 it didn't take me long to tell Buddy that leading an expedition to look for Amelia Earhart sounded like a good idea.

Amelia Earhart was a famous female pilot who disappeared in 1937 while flying her twin-engine Lockheed Electra on a flight around the world. When she and her navigator Fred Noonan didn't arrive on Howland Island as anticipated, President Franklin Roosevelt sent out several U.S.

Amelia Earhart

Navy search parties to look for her, but to no avail.

One problem at the time was that the Japanese had declared war against China just three weeks before Earhart's fateful flight. Consequently with Japan on a war footing there were areas in that part of the Pacific that were off limits to the U.S.—even if it was for the humanitarian purpose of searching for the famous pilot.

As soon as I could get a small film team together, we flew with Buddy to Honolulu, then took Air Micronesia down to Majuro—just as I had done years earlier when I was putting together my expedition to Bikini. When we arrived, I took Buddy to meet my good friend Oscar DeBrum who was First Secretary of the Marshall Islands back in the 1970s. Back then the Marshall Islands were part of the United States Trust Territory and Oscar was the man in charge.

When Buddy and I arrived in 1982 the islands were no longer part of a Trust Territory. They had gained independence and were known officially as the Republic of the Marshall Islands.   Former court judge Kabua Kabua was the elected president. Oscar DeBrum now had the title Vice President (but still ran everything as usual).

When I introduced Vice President DeBrum to Buddy Brennan I explained that I had returned to Majuro to talk to people who had stories about Amelia Earhart. Before explaining further, Oscar surprised me when he said he had a story about Amelia Earhart he would be happy to tell me. This was working out better than I could have hoped. I quickly assured Oscar that I'd love to hear his story and asked if he would mind if I filmed him while he told me what he knew about the famous aviator. Again Oscar was very cooperative and said he wouldn't mind, but that I'd have to film him sometime in the evening after he finished his government work.

When the Vice President arrived at our hotel that evening I seated him in a small wooden chair under a tall coconut palm by the beach. When he was comfortable I had my cinematographer Nik Petrik start the camera then asked Oscar to please tell me his story. Oscar was a well-educated and highly positioned individual. I considered it a great honor for him to take time out of his busy schedule to tell me his Amelia Earhart story. This is the transcript of what Oscar said while he was being filmed:

> "My name is Oscar DeBrum. I'm with the government of the
> Marshall Islands…as the First Secretary. I remember distinctly
> …when I used to go to school in Jaluit…Marshall Islands…
> about 1937…when my father came home and informed us that
> an American lady pilot had been captured…and that she was
> being taken to the Japanese office…and that people were not
> permitted to go close to her…or even come anywhere near to
> where she was being captured…and taken into office. He did

not say how long she was…whether he saw her or not…but the information he passed along to the family was that…and I recall that distinctly…that an American lady had been captured…and that she was taken to the high commands office in Jaluit…and this was in 1937."

I thanked Oscar for telling us his story, and asked if he had any ideas about what I should do to let people in the Marshalls know I was in the area. The next day he picked up the phone and called the U.S. Information Agency that had an office in Majuro. When they learned that I was on the atoll looking for people who had information about Amelia Earhart they asked if I wanted to broadcast an appeal to all Marshallese living in the islands. I thought that was a wonderful idea, so the Information Agency representative sat me down in front of a microphone and interviewed me for about thirty minutes.

Mike Giving Radio Interview on Majuro

The interview was broadcast live throughout all the islands. I talked about my background leading expeditions around the world and also about our quest to find out what happened to Amelia Earhart and her navigator Fred Noonan. I ended my talk with an appeal for any Marshallese with stories about Amelia Earhart to please come talk to me at my hotel on Majuro.

A few nights later I found an elderly gentleman named Lotan Jack crouched beneath one of the tall coconut trees outside my hotel. Mr. Jack said he heard my radio broadcast and that he had a story about Amelia Earhart.

I never ask a lot of questions while I'm filming an eyewitness because it's too easy to lead people into giving me an answer I want to hear. I believe it's more honest and informative if I just set up my camera, point it at the subject and ask them to tell me their story in their own words. This is the transcript of what Lotan Jack told me on Majuro Atoll that evening while Nik Petrik filmed what he had to say:

> "My name is Lotan Jack. I was working with the Japanese people on
> Jaluit Island as a coffee maker for the high ranking officer on Nemit
> Island…it's about eight miles from Jaluit Japanese headquarters.
> During that time we heard stories about…Amelia…Earhart…from
> Japanese Navy officer. They said she was…airplane was shot down
> … between Mili and Jaluit. It's about thirty miles from Mili. And one
> Japanese ship found her and pick her up…and took her to Mili Atoll
> …and from Mili Atoll…they took her to Jaluit…after Jaluit…they took
> her to Kwajalein. And last time…they sent her to Saipan. And the
> Japanese Navy officer told all the Marshallese…not to talk about her
> … because there were…kind of…secret words about her. They said
> she was flying…around the world…they said she was…spying for the
> American people."

Lotan Jack Being Film on Majuro Atoll

This is the transcript of what Mrs. Blas granddaughter translated as I filmed what she and her grandmother were saying:

> "She said she saw Amelia riding in a motorcycle with a
> blindfold…and a handcuffs on her hands…and these
> two guards on the side of Amelia…and they take her
> down to the place where they are going to kill her…
> and they shot her right straight in the chest…and then
> she fell on her back…to the grave."

The granddaughter was a little shaken at what her grandmother had just told her and had to stop for a few minutes to compose herself. After she gathered herself we continued filming as she again translated for her grandmother:

> "She says she knows the place where they kill Amelia…
> because she left the place…and then she went back to make
> sure they buried the body there…and she went back and
> checked on it…she found they buried her under that
> breadfruit tree…that was her mark."

I certainly wanted to dig under that breadfruit tree that Mrs. Blas was talking about so I quickly asked her if the tree was still standing and if she thought she could take us to it. Her granddaughter translated my question and when she received the answer told me, "She said she was sure she could."

Mrs. Blas with Granddaughter on Saipan

I knew from talking with Saipanese officials that the Japanese had a large seaplane base on Saipan in 1937. I was worried that if Amelia was shot and buried somewhere on the military base especially during wartime I didn't see how Mrs. Blas could have been an eyewitness to the execution. I was a little embarrassed to question what Mrs.Blas had just told me but needed to hear her answer so I could decide for myself if what she told me on camera was true.

Mike Harris, Mrs. Blas & Mrs. Blas Husband on Saipan

I asked the granddaughter to ask Mrs. Blas how she could have seen Amelia being shot if the area was a Japanese seaplane base in 1937 and most probably a restricted area. After getting the granddaughter's reply I decided that what she had told me could very well be true.

Mrs. Blas confirmed that there was a large Japanese seaplane base located at Garapan during World War II. I knew that the Japanese flew their large Kawanishi flying boat out of Saipan during World War II because when I led my first expedition to Bikini Atoll in the early 1970s, I dove on a Kawanishi flying boat on the bottom of Wotje Lagoon in 50 feet of water. I did a little research at the time and found out that the main Japanese seaplane base during World War II was at Saipan.

Mrs. Blas related that her parents owned farmland on a hillside that abutted the Japanese seaplane base. She said the Japanese would allow some of the Saipanese landowners to tend their fields from time to time on the hillside that ran along one side of the restricted military enclosure.

Mrs. Blas said that she was with her parent's one day on the hillside when she looked down into the base and saw several motorcycles drive up and park just below them. She said one of the motorcycles was carrying an American woman in a sidecar. She said there was a dump area at the edge of the seaplane base close to where she and her family were watching and that's where she saw Amelia being shot and buried under the breadfruit tree.

Buddy Brennan and I returned to Saipan two months later after we obtained permission to dig where Mrs. Blas told us she saw Amelia being shot and buried. We dug down five or six feet and found things like parts of World War II Japanese planes, medical supplies, bullet shells and a few animal bones—just the kind of trash you would expect to find in a dump at the edge of a Japanese military base.

But we also unearthed an old blindfold that Mrs. Blas said she saw Amelia wearing when she was shot. It was very tattered looking from being buried for forty years but it was very clearly a Japanese military blindfold.

Unfortunately there wasn't any way to prove that it once really did cover the eyes of Amelia Earhart.

Mike Digging Under Breadfruit Tree on Saipan

On adventure expeditions it's not unusual to come up empty. Proving what happened to Amelia Earhart still needs more work. But in my mind there's no reason to believe that someone as educated and professional as Oscar DeBrum,

Vice-President of the Marshall Islands, was lying to me about the story he heard from his father in 1937.

The same goes for Lotan Jack who as a young coffee maker for the Japanese during the war only repeated to me what he heard the Japanese officers talking about before WII. I'm not sure what to think of Manny Munoz' stories on Saipan. Maybe the Japanese ship captain shot down a silver twin engine aircraft at the beginning of the war in 1937 but who knows if it was the plane being flown by Amelia Earhart as Manny was later told?

I also don't know what to think of Mrs. Blas story. I now think that Buddy Brennan and I may have dug in the wrong spot when we dug under the breadfruit tree that Mrs. Blas pointed out. We carefully dug right where Mrs. Blas told us the tree stood during the war and we did uncover the rotting remains of the breadfruit's large roots. But common sense now tells me we probably should have dug further away from the massive trunk and not right under it. If Mrs. Blas' story is true, Amelia would have been buried some distance away and obviously not right under the trunk. I'd like to go back some day and give it another shot but when the search expedition ended I didn't want to produce a completed documentary film until we had absolute proof of what really happened to Amelia. I had already produced two documentary feature films on not finding the Titanic. I didn't want to produce another on not finding Amelia.

Mike Harris, Buddy Brennan, Nik Petrik on Saipan

When I got back to Florida, my wife Evelyn and I drove over to the Naval Base in Orlando so I could attend the monthly meeting of The Explorer's Club. I gave a report on my two expeditions to search for the Titanic and also on my most recent expedition to search for Amelia Earhart. After the meeting Bradley Hahn, a naval historian and one of the members of The Explorer Club, asked me a simple question. "Mike, you lead expeditions around the world and make movies of your expeditions, why don't you make a movie on the greatest explorer who ever lived?"

I told him breezily that it sounded like a terrific idea but I didn't have the slightest idea about who he was talking about. Being a naval historian it was Bradley's business to know about naval explorers all around the world. When he told me who he was talking about I still had never heard of him.

"The Chinese explorer, Zheng He," he sang out happily. I was completely dumbfounded. I had never heard of any great Chinese explorer, much less one named Zheng He.

Bradley knew he had my attention and launched into a history lesson about Chinese exploration during the early Ming period from 1400 to 1430. Right away I knew that was before Columbus and was curious as to why I had never heard anything about Chinese exploring foreign lands before Columbus discovered America. I asked Bradley what kind of ships Zheng He sailed.

"Baochuan treasure ships," Bradley responded firmly. "Each was 430 feet long, 92 feet wide, with nine masts 12 sails and a three tower

Admiral Zheng He

Ming Pagoda." I couldn't believe that anyone in the 1400's was building ships that were 430 feet long, 80 years before Columbus discovered America. "How many of these big ships did Zheng He command?" I wondered aloud. Bradley Hahn was ready with an even more astounding answer. "Zheng He had 60 of these huge ships," he told me confidently, "plus hundreds of others."

Hundreds of others? I couldn't believe it. Columbus only had three ships. I think one was about 40 feet long, another 50 feet and his main flagship the Santa Maria was still less than 100 feet in length. "Are you telling me," I ventured cautiously, "this Chinese explorer had 60 huge ships 430 feet long, sixty years before Columbus discovered America?"

Baochuan Treasure Ship

"That's exactly what I'm saying," Bradley stated flatly. "And that's why I think you should produce a film on the life and exploits of this incredible Asian explorer."

"But why haven't I ever heard of this Chinese explorer?" I asked incredulously. "It sounds to me like what he accomplished was pretty astounding."

"It was more than pretty astounding," Bradley agreed, "and that's why someone like you should produce a film on his incredible exploits."

I was hooked. Before long Bradley introduced me to Dr. Daniel Lee, an instructor at the U.S. Naval Academy in Maryland. Danny Lee turned out to be an "Ambassador without portfolio" and had been involved for many years as a liaison between the U.S. and Chinese governments. An "Ambassador without portfolio" is someone who does not have the official title as "Ambassador" but does, in fact, do unofficial work for the United States government. With Dr. Lee's help I was able to obtain permission to travel to China and meet with Chinese historians who were specialists in the Ming Period in general and the voyages of Admiral Zheng He in particular.

Over the next three years I ended up going back and forth to China meeting with these Chinese experts each time getting another piece of the Zheng He puzzle in place. Eventually I presented a 100-page report to the Chinese government. The report contained information on the research I had accumulated, the story I wanted to tell and how I planned to interest film people in the United States in producing a feature film about China's great unknown explorer Zheng He.

The first thing I did was sign a contract in Hollywood with Brookfield Productions. Fern Field had produced the television series Maude and The Baxters in the 1970s. Fern and her husband, Norman Brooks, had a very good reputation around Hollywood. Both became quite excited about representing me to various media outlets both in California and New York. Their plan was to produce a television mini-series on Zheng He and his incredible treasure ship voyages.

Although they personally were interested and enthusiastically pitched my China project to several of their Los Angeles and New York contacts, they were not able to get a network studio to go forward. Both NBC and CBS were initially interested (especially CBS), but eventually—because of other Chinese projects they already had in development—turned the project down with the suggestion that we "Keep in touch!"

The only person who did keep in touch was Jack Grimm. He had decided to fund a third Titanic expedition—this time mostly out of his own pocket. He didn't want another summer to pass without taking another shot at proving his "propeller" really did come from the Titanic. He said that if I wanted to film the expedition I could, "But we're on a shoestring budget this year," he whined. "Only bring yourself along and one cameraman. Is it a deal?"

The idea of only having one cameraman with me was a real downgrade from the professional group I had assembled for our expeditions in 1980 and 1981. But now that Jack was going to try and put the expedition together out of his own pocket it was going to be a very scaled down expedition from top to bottom.

But I figured a scaled down expedition was better than no expedition at all. And who knows, maybe Cadillac Jack's propeller actually did come off the famous ship. I didn't think so, but I also didn't want to take the chance of missing out on the discovery of the Titanic. Without skipping a beat I told Jack that he had a deal. "When do we sail?"

15 1983 TITANIC EXPEDITION

With no money to modify the Aluminaut, our only hope of finding the Titanic was to go back to the site and search further to the east of our search area. In 1981 we had searched Titanic Canyon thoroughly and didn't find her, so we didn't want to waste any more time there.

The scientist team reasoned that if we hadn't found Titanic close to her historic SOS site, she must be located in water that was farther to the east. We had discovered some interesting sonar hits on the eastern portion of our search area back in 1980 but nothing that seemed to be the length or size of the Titanic.

Nik Petrik, Mike, Bobby Blanco Leaving Tampa 1983

We left Halifax, Nova Scotia, this time on board Lamont Doherty's Research Vessel Conrad and headed for our search area off Cape Race, Newfoundland. After again laying out a network of transponders on each edge of our search area, we made a careful sonar/magnetometer pass over the site of Jack Grimm's Titanic "propeller."

Needless to say, Jack was not a happy camper when his Titanic "propeller" turned out to be nothing more than a geological formation as the scientists had expected. It might have looked somewhat like one blade from a large propeller, sticking up off the sea floor, but it definitely wasn't made of metal. It couldn't possibly have been anything that came from the Titanic.

Research Vessel Conrad

With that necessary bit of business concluded we headed the Conrad toward the eastern side of our search area and prepared to make several long sonar sweeps through what now seemed to be the most likely spot where the Titanic might be hiding.

The science team did their best to remain positive, believing an object as large as the Titanic just couldn't disappear or cease to exist. It had to be somewhere in the area we were searching. We had covered all the search area further to the West and

Titanic definitely wasn't there. Consequently the only place she could realistically be was on the eastern portion of the area. The team told Jack they could cover the area they needed to search in just ten days. The Titanic had to be in the area they wanted to search, and they were quite sure we would be able to make a discovery.

On this third expedition we began to believe we would find the Titanic and be able to celebrate the discovery for the rest of our lives. Cadillac Jack and I could both shout from the rooftops that we had indeed gone against all odds and found the world's most famous shipwreck.

But, alas, during our third night at sea—while combing the eastern edge of our search area—a signal was detected in the science lab that indicated there had been a malfunction in our towed sonar array. When the scientists hauled in the 20,000 feet of cable and hoisted the device on deck, it was quickly discovered the side-scan sonar instrument had completely destroyed itself.

I don't know what the problem was with the equipment that it could not be repaired. I had complete confidence in our scientific team as extremely intelligent and resourceful men. But if they said the equipment couldn't be fixed, there was no question in my mind that nothing could be done.

Side-Scan Sonar Being Retrieved from Stern of Ship

On our 1980 expedition the weather was so bad it broke loose the large yellow fin on the back of the Blue Fish. Attached to the yellow fin was an expensive proton magnetometer. Jim Kosalas and several members of his sonar team put their heads together and created a proton magnetometer made entirely of spare parts they found around the ship. I couldn't believe the creative ingenuity it took for them to make such a complicated device out of common shipboard objects.

Unfortunately there was no Jim Kosolas on board during our third expedition, and maybe there was just so much damage to the electronics this time that it wouldn't have made any difference if there had been. The 1983 expedition came to an abrupt and unexpected halt after just a few days at sea.

The film footage we shot on our way out to the search area was put into storage and never used. Since the expedition had been cut short no attempt was made to complete a film of our aborted expedition.

1983 Expedition Members with Explorers Club Flag

I imagine Bob Ballard was delighted when he heard the news that the third Harris-Grimm expedition had again ended in failure. Bob was probably as surprised as us that Bill Ryan and Fred Spiess had been unable to find the Titanic. Both men were held in very high regard as credible scientists—not only by Bob, but also within the entire oceanographic community.

With renewed vigor, Bob Ballard began to quietly gather funding for his own Titanic search. I met him briefly in Los Angeles where he was giving a press conference on his recent discovery of another underwater vent while diving in the Woods Hole submersible Alvin. He never missed an opportunity to publicize whatever underwater work he was doing. I'm quite sure he knew the publicity would come in handy one day when talking with potential investors about funding his own expedition to find the Titanic.

Prior to meeting Bob Ballard in Los Angeles, I had only communicated indirectly with him in the late 1970s when I was meeting with Emory Kristof at National Geographic trying to put together a scientific team for my first Titanic expedition. When we met, he was cordial to me, but not overly friendly. And why should he be? I represented direct competition to what he wanted to accomplish for himself.

When I initially talked Jack Grimm into funding my search for the Titanic, Bob Ballard, Emory Kristof and their company Seaonics International Limited was an integral part of my expedition team. I often wondered if things would have turned out differently if Jack Grimm had accepted my expedition team of Ballard and Kristof, rather than substituting Ryan and Spiess.

When the three Harris-Grimm expeditions failed, it did provide the opportunity Bob Ballard was hoping for.

Undaunted, I had not given up on my own quest to find the Titanic. If Jack Grimm wouldn't—or couldn't—come up with any more money, maybe I could find someone else who would. Maybe I could work some kind of deal with the French. I knew they had an oceanographic organization called Center National for the Exploration of the Oceans (CNEXO). Maybe I could interest them in helping me find the Titanic.

I flew to Paris and made arrangements to meet with several members of the CNEXO management. When I told them I would like to get CNEXO involved in my search for the Titanic, they were immediately interested and arranged for me to meet with two French gentlemen named Robert Chappaz and Yves Cornet. Robert and Yves were owners of Taurus International, a company CNEXO had contracted with to drum up business for their work in the oceans around the world.

During my meeting with Robert and Yves I told them of what Jack Grimm and I had accomplished during our three expeditions to find the Titanic. I also told them that I was beginning to believe we had been unsuccessful because side-scan sonar alone couldn't see enough of what was really on the bottom in the Titanic search area. I explained to them that if we could get a deep diving submersible in the Titanic search area with people on board they might be able to make a visual check for wreck debris on the bottom that possibly was being missed by the sonar.

I explained to them that I was not a scientist and that I'd only been out on four oceanographic expeditions. On my first expedition I took divers and filmmakers to Bikini Atoll in the Pacific to look for ships that were sunk by atom bomb testing. My three recent expeditions were in the Atlantic to search for the Titanic. I let them know I realized I had limited deep ocean experience, but that the experience I did have seemed to indicate to me that sonar alone couldn't tell the difference between pieces of ship wreckage and natural rock formations. I explained that since we covered the search area thoroughly and still hadn't found the Titanic, I was afraid we might have gone right over the wreck on my previous expeditions and not known it!

Robert and Yves didn't disagree with what I was telling them. They told me that CNEXO had one submersible available that they used in relatively shallow water. But they also had one submersible, the Nautile, on the drawing board that was being designed to dive down to 20,000 feet, but unfortunately it wouldn't be available to lease for another two years. When I told them I didn't want to wait for two years, they came up with another suggestion.

"Maybe we could arrange for you to meet with the French Navy," Robert said carefully. "They own a bathyscaphe deep-diving submersible they call Archimede. It will go down to the very bottom of the ocean and it's available now." I told them that sounded like a good idea and asked what I needed to do to arrange for an appointment.

Deep-Diving Submersible Archimede

Within three days I was ushered into the headquarters of a French Navy Admiral who was curious as to why I had been told I should meet with him. When I gave him my film and exploration experience, he seemed slightly amused but maintained a haughty air of French indifference. I thought to myself that I was just wasting my time trying to convince a French Admiral that he should do anything with me.

But au contraire, I was wrong. After quick consultation with a colleague, the Admiral told me that as a matter of fact they would be happy to sell me their submersible Archimede (plus all of her spare parts) lock, stock and barrel for one million U.S. dollars. Needless to say I was surprised. Cautiously I asked if I could see their submersible Archimede. The Admiral replied in his heavily accented French, "But of course!"

So off we went to inspect their famous deep-diving submersible Archimede that had been to 31,164 feet at the bottom of the Marianna Trench. But one look at the record-setting vessel told me immediately she wouldn't do—at least in trying to find and dive on a wreck like the Titanic.

Having worked at a depth of 31,164 feet there would be absolutely no problem for Archimede to get down to 12,000 feet where we expected to find the Titanic. But like the Swiss-U.S Navy bathyscaphe Triest, Archimede relied on a soft envelope filled with gasoline to obtain its lift. As my friend Dick Greenwald explained to me years ago, gasoline is lighter than seawater, which enables submersibles to obtain the lift they need to rise from the bottom to the surface.

Should a protruding piece of metal from the Titanic wreckage accidentally pierce the soft envelope of gasoline the Archimede depended upon for lift, there would be no way to get the submersible and its crew back to the surface. It didn't take a brain surgeon to figure out that using Archimede around a sunken wreck would be just too dangerous.

I thanked the French Naval representative for showing me his historic submersible but told him as politely as I could that I didn't think Archimede was the right research vehicle to help me find the Titanic.

I returned to Paris and got back in touch with Robert Chappaz and Yves Cornet. I told them why I didn't think the Archimede would work for finding the Titanic. Both reluctantly agreed. I then asked if they had any other suggestions. Robert and Yves huddled together for a minute then said they might have a solution. After a quick phone call I was introduced to a gentleman by the name of George Grosz. George was president of Corporate Development in Paris and had a pretty impressive resume of working with major companies and individuals throughout Europe. Robert and Yves believed George might be able to help me raise the money to secure a submarine to search for Titanic.

Before long I found myself having lunch with George Grosz, who thankfully spoke excellent English and my new French friend, Robert Chappaz. George was born in

Austria, but was taken by his family in the late 1930s to London to escape the persecution of Jews during World War II. He said his family planned to take the last ship out of London for Shanghai but for some reason, which I don't remember, George and his family missed the boat. Consequently George was raised in London and eventually graduated from the prestigious London School of Economics in 1957 and the Institute of Chartered Accountants in 1960.

George related to me how he joined Cooper Brothers & Co. in London on his first job as an auditor and worked particularly with international groups. Since George was fluent in English, French and German, Cooper Brothers regarded George as a real asset.

George Grosz, Mike Harris, Robert Chappaz

When Cooper Brothers merged with Lybrand, George was sent to Paris as a Senior Manager responsible for audit and advisory services to foreign subsidiaries in France. While in France he met his wife Michelin. Michelin had her own Ann Franke-like experience growing up during the war in Paris. She and her family had to hide from the Germans in an abandoned attic until Paris was liberated by allied forces in 1944. The childhood experience affected Michelin for the rest of her life. She never wanted to stand out in a crowd nor did she ever want to identify herself as being Jewish to anyone but her closest and most intimate friends.

George, on the other hand, liked to stand out. He was a very gregarious fellow by nature, which served him well when working in the international business community. In 1967 George left Cooper Brothers to become Financial Controller, then Financial Director of Schlumberger. In 1975 he took a position as Financial Director of United Technologies, Otis Elevator Group. Then in 1978 he founded his own company, Corporate Development International, which specialized in international company search throughout Europe. This was his position when Robert Chappaz and Yves Cornet set up my meeting with him in 1984.

If Jack Grimm was no longer in a position to provide the funds I needed to fulfill my dream, maybe George Grosz was. Here was a businessman who could tell my story to qualified investors throughout Europe. If I couldn't raise funds in America, maybe George could help me find wealthy individuals I could talk to from his circle of associates throughout Europe.

In the meantime, we agreed that I would go home and continue my search for a proper deep diving submersible. I had lost faith in finding the Titanic strictly through the use of side-scan sonar. I was now convinced that it could only be done through the use of a submersible.

I knew activating a submersible would be more expensive but rationalized the money difference was actually inconsequential when measured against the success or failure of the mission. If the Titanic could be found using a submersible, the resulting financial benefits from producing films and putting recovered Titanic artifacts on a world tour would be profound. What I needed was a new beginning—a new beginning that would finally allow me to grab my dream and make the discovery of the Titanic.

16   A NEW BEGINNING

I left Paris and headed straight for San Diego knowing the U.S. Navy owned a submersible called Turtle that I hoped could be used to help me find the Titanic. From my previous research on submersibles, I knew the Deep Submergence Vehicle Turtle (DSV-3) had been built for deep-sea search and recovery missions, oceanographic research and underwater archaeology missions for the U.S. Navy. She had a seven-foot diameter spherical pressure hull that could support a crew of three people for up to 72 hours. She was launched on December 11, 1968 and was accepted by the U.S. Navy in 1970.

The Turtle was initially rated to dive to a depth of 6,500 feet, which wouldn't be deep enough to get down to the Titanic at 12,000 feet. But she had received several upgrades in the early 1980s that enabled her to get down to 10,000 feet. That still wasn't quite deep enough to reach the Titanic, but maybe there were other upgrades that I hadn't found out about in my research.

The main reason I wanted to use the Turtle was because she had solid construction, which meant her lift capabilities weren't compromised by a soft envelope of gasoline like the Archimede. Maybe additional modifications could be made that would allow Turtle to get down to 12,000 feet.

I arrived in San Diego and made a beeline for the harbor where I knew the Turtle was being held in storage. Surprisingly, it wasn't difficult to gain entrance to the facility. When I explained what I was hoping to accomplish in using Turtle to find the Titanic, the officers overseeing the Turtle said they would like to help but realistically didn't think they could. The Turtle recently had several modifications that enabled her to get down to 10,000 feet, but with current budget constraints they saw little or no chance the Navy would give a civilian permission to get the Turtle involved in a treasure hunt. They explained that it sounded like an exciting project and they would certainly like the Titanic to be found some day, but there was just no way the public would be happy about the Navy spending government money to help a private citizen find the Titanic.

Deep Submergence Vehicle Turtle

Seeing clearly that I was dejected, they suggested that I talk with Don Walsh, the Navy lieutenant who dove with Swiss scientist Jacques Piccard in 1960 to the deepest part of the ocean. They even helped set my appointment with him.

Don Walsh and Jacques Piccard received worldwide attention when they took the deep diving submersible Triest to a record depth of 35,800 feet in the deepest part of the Marianna Trench in 1960. I was truly honored to get to meet such a giant in underwater exploration—and hoped that someday I would also be able to meet his Swiss associate, Jacques Piccard.

Jacques Piccard (left) with Don Walsh

I told Don about the expeditions I led with Jack Grimm in 1980, 1981 and 1983 to find the Titanic and the reasons I thought we had been unsuccessful. I told him I didn't think Jack Grimm was going to be able to come up with any more money to fund Titanic searches in the future. I also told him I was disappointed that our side-scan sonar technology hadn't been more successful and why I was trying to find a deep diving submersible that I could use to help me continue my search in the future.

Don said he had followed our expeditions with great interest because he knew Dr. Fred Spiess and his many accomplishments at Scripps. He was a little surprised that we hadn't been more successful with our side-scan sonar operations but didn't disagree with my theory that getting human eyeballs on the bottom in a submersible might be the difference between success and failure.

He said that since submersibles don't move very fast and are able to light up only a small portion of the seabed at any one time, using a submersible could become expensive. I told him that sonar could definitely "see" much further at any one time but it couldn't distinguish very well between man-made objects and the natural rock or sand geography on the bottom.

I told Don that going out on three oceanographic expeditions with scientists and all the equipment they needed without any positive results to show for it had also been quite expensive. I reasoned that if I could find a submersible that wouldn't cost too much for modifications, that might be the most cost-effective way to search for and find the Titanic.

Don Walsh was a retired Naval Captain and had a Ph.D. in Physical Oceanography from Texas A&M University. He was also Dean and Founder of the University of Southern California's Institute of Marine and Coastal Services. He didn't think I'd be able to use the Turtle since it belonged to the U.S. Navy. He also agreed with me that the Triest and Archimede submersibles could easily dive to 12,000 feet, but definitely wouldn't be safe to use as a working platform around a wreck on the bottom.

He then asked me about the Reynolds Aluminaut. I told him I had met several times with the Reynolds brothers in Richmond, and had even invited Art Markel out on my first Titanic expedition. But, like Turtle, the Aluminaut needed extensive modifications to get down to Titainc's depth.

Don was supportive of what I was trying to do, and told me that I should "Never give up! The sea never gives up her secretes without a struggle." I was sure he was right about that and let him know I had no intentions of giving up on my Titanic dream.

Not knowing exactly where to turn next to raise money for my Titanic project, I flew home to Florida and within a few days received an unexpected phone call from Jack Grimm in Texas. He asked me if I wanted to go to Stuttgart, Germany and appear in a television program about our expeditions to find the Titanic. I told him I would love to, and asked him if they would pay me anything for giving the interview. He said they had agreed to pay $10,000 if the Expedition Leader would appear personally on their German television program and let them use up to ten minutes of our expedition footage. I asked Jack if he would be on the program with me. He said he was too busy trying to run Grimm Oil Company in Abilene, but if I wanted to go over and do the show for the publicity, he'd set it up.

On October 17, 1983 I received a letter from Rainer Wagner of Suddeutscher Rundfunk Stuttgart inviting me come over to appear in their Titanic Project television program—and to please bring along 16 mm footage of my expeditions. They said specifically that I was not to bring videotape as "we cannot transform the NTSC standard into our PAL standard for transmission."

I flew to Stuttgart and discovered the German program was a very elaborate production. The television station designed sets, hired actors and scientists and several people who were actually on the Titanic when she sank. The survivors were asked to appear on the program so they could talk

Letter from German TV Stuttgart

about how the Titanic sank and why she sank. I was on the program to talk about the expeditions that had been conducted trying to find her. The production was broadcast, of course, in German, and unfortunately I was able to speak only a little German.

The program director gave me a small earplug that enabled me to hear a translation of the program. When the host came to me and asked in German about my expeditions I knew immediately what he was asking so I could give him, at least in English, an answer to his question. My English was then translated into German for the nationwide television audience.

The broadcast turned out to be one of the highest rated programs on German television ever. Whether I ever received publicity from it, at least in America, I'm not sure. But it was a good experience and gave me a chance to meet again with my friend George Grosz in Paris—who I hoped was still trying to raise funds for another Titanic expedition.

George said he saw me on the German Titanic TV program, which also had been broadcast in France. He said he was certain that a program on the Titanic would have received a very good audience all over Europe. I told him I hoped we could both use the program to help publicize my efforts to find the Titanic. He assured me that it would and said he would now double his efforts to try and find funds for the project.

George had several connections all over Europe, and was very active in clubs and business organizations. He was very proud of the fact that he had graduated from the prestigious London School of Economics. Consequently now that he was a permanent resident of Paris, he became quite active in club affairs in Paris and was eventually elected LSE's club president in France.

I made plans to fly back to the States to pursue my fundraising efforts there. My hope was that by the time I raised the money for another Titanic expedition, I could come back to Paris and work out something with CNEXO to lease their new submersible. Hopefully the French would be pleased to have their new submersible involved in finding Titanic.

As soon as I got home I called Jack Grimm and thanked him for helping me get on the Titanic television program in Stuttgart. I told him the production value of the program was very good. He thanked me for agreeing to be on the program, and said he needed the $10,000 to help pay back some of the expedition costs he had incurred earlier in the year.

This was a surprise to me. I thought I was going to get at least some of the $10,000 for appearing on the program. But it wasn't to be. Jack made certain the money was wired directly to him, once again citing his adage, "Whoever's got the gold, rules!" None of it came to me. Being a good soldier, I bit my lip and said nothing.

Jack asked me about the Titanic survivors on the program with me. One was an English lady named Eva Hart who I had met previously at a gathering of Titanic survivors in Philadelphia. I suspected

Eva Hart

Eva's life mission was to show up on any program or gathering that had anything to do about the sinking of the Titanic so she could tell her personal story.

Eva loved to tell of how her father went down with the ship, but she and her mother were saved. She would tell the same story at every survivor gathering. To Eva, the Titanic is a gravesite where her father was buried and it shouldn't be disturbed by anyone. She, of course, had her opinion, but I also had mine. Most of the other survivors I spoke to, however, didn't have a problem with anyone searching for the Titanic.

I also told Jack about my meeting with CNEXO and their Nautile project. I told him I thought the only way we were going to find the Titanic was with a deep submersible—and I was going to raise the money to get one for my next expedition.

Jack asked me about the Aluminaut and Art Markel. I told him I was still in touch with Art, but was disappointed the Aluminaut was old and now needed a lot of expensive modifications to get her back into the water. I let Jack know the Aluminaut was still in the mix, but I was exploring the availability of other U.S. and French Navy submersibles as well.

He wished me well and asked me to stay in touch. I told him I would and immediately began making plans to head back to California. There was movie money out there. Maybe I could interest someone in backing me on a fourth expedition, this time using a deep submersible as a search tool, rather than just relying on side-scan sonar.

Don Walsh was right when he told me, "Don't give up! Trying to find something in the deep ocean is never easy!" I wasn't about to give up on trying to find the Titanic. But Don never mentioned that raising the money for an expedition was probably the hardest part of all. Without money it's impossible to search for anything.

17 Discovery

I was in California seeking financial backing in 1985 when I received word that Bob Ballard was preparing to mount his own expedition to locate the Titanic. It didn't come as a shock because I knew Ballard wanted to find the Titanic as much as I did. I was curious, though, about how he was going to raise the money. Bob's connection to Woods Hole Oceanographic greatly increased his credibility. He was also a close friend of Emory Kristof at National Geographic, but I didn't think the National Geographic magazine would fully back an oceanographic expedition—even to find the Titanic.

I knew National Geographic would pay for rights to film the discovery and publish a big spread in their magazine. They had agreed to pay me $300,000 for a television film on my first Titanic expedition back in 1980, but that wasn't enough money to launch the type of deep-ocean search I knew it would take to make the discovery.

Secretary of the Navy, John Lehman

My good friend Dick Greenwald at Deep Sea Ventures in Virginia had direct contacts with members of the U.S. congress. Dick also knew what was going on behind the scenes in the oceanographic community. He told me that Bob Ballard was a personal friend of the Secretary of the Navy, John Lehman. Dick had heard that Bob convinced Secretary Lehman that the deep ocean camera sled he developed at Woods Hole could be of great value to the U.S. Navy. He also told the Secretary that if the Navy would allow him to use a vessel from Woods Hole on his proposed Titanic expedition to test his sled in the deep ocean, the U.S. Navy could benefit greatly from his deep ocean research.

Bob still had a problem though. It's pretty hard to search for a ship on the bottom of the ocean by just dropping a camera over the side. You still need to get a sonar device to cover a larger area, or at least get a submersible on the bottom with people inside who can look for manmade wreckage. That's why I was pushing so hard to find someone who would help me fund an expedition so I could dive on the wreck with a manned submersible.

Once John Lehman told Bob he could use the U.S. Navy's Research Vessel Knorr, Bob went to Paris and met with the French government folks at the Institute Francois de Research pour L'Exploration de la Mer (IFREMER), hoping to talk them into joining forces with him. In June 1984 CNEXO had changed its name to IFREMER. Bob had worked with the French on other oceanographic projects in the past and was fairly confident they would join with him to search for the Titanic—especially since he had already obtained a portion of his financial backing from the U.S. Navy.

Bob knew that IFREMER's Jean-Louis Michel had developed a side-scan sonar device called SAR (sonar-acousteque remarque) that was supposed to be as good as, or better than, Fred Spiess' Deep Tow device we used in 1981.

I later learned that prior to Bob's expedition in 1995 Dr. Bill Ryan at Lamont-Doherty let him look at all of our Sea Marc side-scan sonar records from our 1980 Titanic expedition. Interestingly, Fred Spiess wouldn't share his Titanic records with Bob from our 1981 expedition. Because of the bad weather we encountered in 1980 many of Sea Marc's sonar records were blurred. When Dr. Spiess refused to share his Deep Tow sonar records from 1981 Bob and Jean-Louis decided they had no choice but to go over the entire Titanic search area again with the French sonar device SAR.

The plan was for Jean-Louis Michel and his French team to find the Titanic using his high-resolution sonar device SAR during a 4-week search in July. Then Bob Ballard would bring his scientific team, which included Ralph White and Emory Kristof, to the site and use his Argo/Angus underwater photography system to document Titanic's discovery. Then, when the expedition was completed at the end of August, the French and American oceanographic teams would make a joint announcement of the Titanic's discovery.

Things, however, didn't work out as agreed. Jean-Louis Michel ran into some bad weather—just as Jack Grimm and I had experienced during our expeditions—and was only able to cover 70-80 percent of the intended search area. In that area, though, his SAR sonar device didn't find a target that could be identified as the Titanic. In other words, SAR didn't find a Titanic-sized sonar target any better than had Kosalas' Blue Fish or Dr. Spiess' Deep Tow.

Consequently when Bob Ballard and his American expedition team, along with Jean-Louis Michel from IFREMER, left the Azores on board the Research Vessel Knorr they did not have a specific sonar target of the Titanic that they could go to and photograph with Bob's Argo/Angus system.

Jean-Louis told Bob he was confident the Titanic wasn't in the portion of the search area his SAR had covered. They had searched the same area my three expeditions had covered and came up with basically the same geological formations. If they were going to search anywhere for the Titanic the only choice they had now was to start photographing the ocean bottom with Bob's camera system in the 20 percent of the area Jean-Louis said they had not been able to cover with SAR. Bob Ballard knew it wasn't a good way to search for a wreck in such a large ocean but now he had no other choice!

Bob ordered the Knorr to sail into the eastern portion of the search area the French SAR system did not cover. When Bob dropped his camera over the side, all he was able to photograph was a flat sandy bottom along with occasional fish, crabs and rocks. But then, with his charter time on Knorr running out, just before heading for home, Argo accidentally flew over one of the Titanic's boilers sitting on the bottom.

Finding that boiler with Bob's camera system made it possible for his scientific team to follow other pieces of the Titanic's wreckage to where the bow and stern sections lay waiting to be discovered on the ocean floor. The Titanic's discovery was definitely because of the tremendous technology that Robert Ballard and his Argo/Angus system provided, but is was also due to a very large dose of good old-fashioned luck. Just one day before Bob Ballard was scheduled to return back to Woods Hole defeated—just like the expeditions of Harris and Grimm—that man-made object from one of Titanic's boilers slid into view.

Word leaked to the press that Bob Ballard had found the Titanic and immediately spread around the world. There was no mention of the French and their joint-expedition with the Americans contrary to their signed contract. Only that the American oceanographer from Woods Hole had discovered the Titanic.

Bob, of course, was delighted and thrilled that his dream of finding the Titanic was fulfilled. But what Bob didn't want was for anyone else to learn the location of where the Titanic had been found. He especially didn't want someone like Mike Harris or Jack Grimm to horn in on what he now considered to be his own private gold mine of wealth and fame.

Bob knew that Jack and I wanted to find the Titanic, film the famous ship on the bottom, recover some of her artifacts and put the artifacts on exhibition around the world. If we were able to find out where the Titanic was, we could launch our own expedition.

Consequently, Bob concocted a story to protect "his" Titanic by claiming the Titanic was a sacred graveyard. He intimated strongly that if anyone attempted to salvage anything from the historic ship they would be desecrating the very souls of those who went down with the vessel in 1912.

When Bob returned to the States amid a huge hero's welcome, he talked Rep. Walter B. Jones into introducing legislation before the U.S. Congress to "encourage international efforts to designate the shipwreck a permanent memorial." Further, the legislation directed that U.S. Secretary of State George P. Shultz enter into negotiations with the U.K., France, Canada and others to develop an agreement that would keep others from salvaging the Titanic. Congress then suggested that "pending the agreement, the R.M.S. Titanic should rest in peace."

The U.S. Congress almost went along with Ballard's folly but stopped short of passing laws that would protect the Titanic from future salvagers. It was ultimately decided the ship was in international waters. Consequently, neither the U.S. Congress nor any other country had jurisdiction over the wreck site.

I tried to contact Bob when he returned from his expedition to congratulate him on his historic discovery. Maybe he was too busy or maybe he never got my message but in any case he never responded to my personal offer of congratulations.

When I heard that Bob was planning to dive on the Titanic again during the summer of 1986 using the deep submersible Alvin at Woods Hole, I thought that with a little luck I could beat him to it. I had heard—again, from my good friend Dick Greenwald—that IFREMER was suing Bob Ballard. Their 1985 expedition was to be a joint expedition whereby they would together announce the discovery of the Titanic. Instead the world media announced that Bob Ballard had discovered the Titanic with very little mention of his expedition partner IFREMER.

I didn't know where the Titanic was located but I was pretty sure that IFREMER certainly did. If they were not happy with Bob Ballard, maybe they would join with me to help promote their new deep diving submersible Nautile, which had recently been added to their submersible fleet. Maybe I could be the first to dive on the Titanic and recover some of its artifacts working together with the friends I'd met at IFREMER back when it was known as CNEXO.

French Deep Submersible Nautile

I jumped on a plane and flew over to Paris. Within a day Robert Chappaz and Yves Cornet from Taurus International arranged for me to meet with IFREMER's senior manager Yves Sillard, who joined IFREMER after a successful career in the French space program. During our meeting Sillard expressed his displeasure with the way things had worked out the previous summer with Bob Ballard, and was more than willing to listen to what I had to say. Prior to our meeting, Robert Chappaz and Yves Cornet had briefed Yves Sillard on my first three Titanic expeditions and two subsequent documentary films.

Yves Cornet signed a contract with me which stated I would agree to pay IFREMER $1,000,000 for the lease of their new deep-diving submersible Nautile, their oceanographic ship Nadir and their remotely-operated photographic vehicle they called Robin. Our joint expedition would involve staying on-site for 45-days and making at least ten dives to the Titanic for filming and collecting artifacts. Most important, my contract stated our joint expedition would be completed before Bob Ballard's proposed expedition in August.

It was now January 1986. I knew there wasn't much time for me to raise the $1,000,000 I needed to pay the French for lease of the Nautile and organize a major expedition to dive, film and recover artifacts from the Titanic all before Bob Ballard got out to the site in August with the newly modified Woods Hole submersible.

I had great confidence though that I could approach major television networks in California and offer them the exclusive rights to obtain the first-ever pictures of the Titanic and the dramatic recovery of a portion of its artifacts. I was positive that any television station would be able to make a lot of money on such a major scoop.

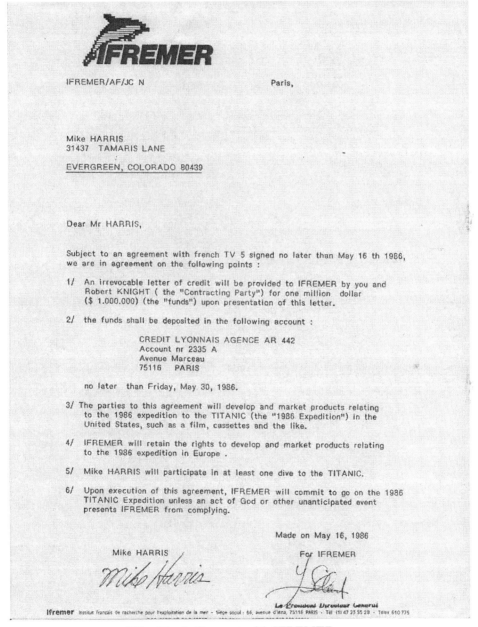

Mike Harris Contract with IFREMER

One caveat to my agreement with IFREMER was that we would never sell any of the Titanic artifacts we recovered. We were both aware of Ballard's continuous complaining in the newspapers that people who wanted to go out and recover

Titanic artifacts were nothing but grave robbers. To negate the complaints we knew would be coming our way, both IFREMER and I made a point of making sure our contract stated specifically that 'Titanic artifacts could be recovered, filmed, catalogued and preserved, but none of them would ever be sold."

I flew to California from Paris and immediately began making plans to meet with the management of three of the largest television networks at the time—NBC, CBS and FOX. It was now February and I knew I didn't have much time to put a deal together. But with my IFREMER contract in hand I was sure that getting financial backing would not be a problem.

Prior to meeting with network representatives I received a telex message from France that outlined the following expedition schedule:

1.   ALL PARTICIPANTS TO THE CRUISE ON BOARD NADIR
     29 JUNE AT LA CORANA, SPAIN.

2.   NADIR LEAVES FOR DIVNG ZONE ON JUNE 30 MORNING.

3.   DIVES CAN BEGIN JULY 7 OR 8.

4.   AFTER 2 OR 3 DIVES YOU AND ME GO BY HELICOPTER
     ON FRENCH NAVY SHIP AT SAINT-PIERRE FOR PRESS
     CONFERENCE AND BACK TO NADIR IMMEDIATELY.

5.   DIVES CONTINUE UNTIL 16 IN EVENING.

6.   REFUELING AT SAINT JOHN OR SAINT- PIERRE 18
     AND 19.

7.   BACK TO THE DIVING ZONE 20 MORNING.

8.   DIVES CONTINUE UNTIL 31 JULY.

9.   NADIR ARRIVES ST JOHN OR ST PIERRE AUGUST 2
     END OF OPERATION.

10. PLEASE CONFIRM IT IS OK FOR YOU.

     CLAUDE RIFFAUD.

I immediately sent a confirmation to Claude Riffaud at IFREMER, and set up a meeting with officials at NBC. I showed them my IFREMER contract and offered them the exclusive rights to be the first to dive on the Titanic. They politely informed me that they had already purchased the exclusive television rights from Bob Ballard to dive on the Titanic in Woods Hole's submersible Alvin. I was surprised, but not completely shocked. I thanked them for their time and immediately began setting up a meeting with officials at CBS.

At CBS I again pulled out my contract with IFREMER and offered them the exclusive rights to dive on the Titanic using the Nautile. After a few minutes of listening to my pitch they smugly announced that they had already purchased the exclusive rights to dive on the Titanic from Bob Ballard, later that summer, in Woods Hole's submersible Alvin.

"Excuse me?" I asked, not quite believing what they had just told me. When they reiterated that they had purchased the exclusive rights from Bob Ballard to dive on the Titanic in August I told them I was afraid that I might have a little bad news.

Now it was the CBS executives who were shocked. When I told them what the NBC executives had told me two days before, they couldn't believe it. As I left, the executives at CBS were making frantic calls to their legal department.

I certainly didn't want to get involved in any legal disputes between Bob Ballard and the two television networks, so I quickly arranged to visit the top management at FOX—the new kid on the block in 1986. Wanting to associate themselves with such an important project as recovering Titanic artifacts, they said they were interested and told me they saw clearly the potential of televising and promoting my salvage expedition.

They didn't argue over the $1,000,000 I told them I had to pay to IFREMIR for use of their Nautile. Their only concern was having enough time to sell the program and block the time at enough of their television affiliates around the country so they could make the venture profitable. Clearing stations was a time consuming process that couldn't be done overnight. It was now the end of February so truthfully they didn't have much time.

I told them I needed to be out on the Titanic during a June-July window before Ballard went out on his own expedition in August. This meant there was less than 60 days for FOX to clear the necessary stations. Before the end of May I needed to have my money in hand so IFREMER could make the necessary preparations for an expedition.

Over the next two weeks, FOX's initial jubilation sank like the Titanic. It didn't take them long to come to the realization that there just wasn't enough time to clear the necessary stations.

Terribly disappointed that I couldn't honor my contract with IFREMER and Yves Sillard, I had no choice but to fly back to Paris and report to him in person that I had failed. When I told Yves about NBC and CBS both purchasing the exclusive rights from Bob Ballard to dive on the Titanic, he muttered something in French about Ballard's character. He also let me know in no uncertain terms (in English) that they were in the process of suing him themselves for his failure to honor their joint venture agreement the previous summer.

With that bit of disappointing business concluded, I flew back to Tampa with my tail between my legs and watched quietly while Bob Ballard dove on the Titanic that August in Alvin on NBC and other networks which were given the feed second-hand. He had not only shattered my dream of finding the Titanic he had also shattered my dream of being the first person to dive on the historic wreck.

Even though I was terribly disappointed, I knew Bob Ballard would not dare recover any artifacts from the wreck. He had put his reputation on the line by telling everyone who would listen—including the U.S. Congress—the Titanic was a sacred memorial. Anyone who tried to recover her artifacts would be desecrating the very souls of those who lost their lives on the famous wreck.

This, of course, was a lot of bull. Ballard had absolutely no such qualms about recovering artifacts from the Titanic back in the 1970s when he and Emory Kristof and his other Seaonic compatriots were trying to raise money to find the Titanic. Now that he had found the Titanic, unfortunately for him, it was not with private money. His backing had come from the U.S. Navy. I imagine Bob figured that the only way he could keep the Titanic as his own private domain was to play up the angle that the Titanic was a gravesite and shouldn't be disturbed by anyone.

Now that Ballard had discovered the Titanic in 1985 and was the first to dive on her in 1986, I hoped that maybe I could raise the money needed to salvage her artifacts and put them on a world tour. I contacted Jack Grimm and told him what I was planning to do and asked him if he wanted to be a part of it. I told him about IFREMER and their deep-diving submersible Nautile that could dive to 20,000 feet and didn't need to be modified like Louis Reynold's Aluminaut. The Nautile, I assured him, would be the perfect vehicle to use to recover artifacts from the Titanic site and put them on a world tour. Jack said he wished he could help but his oil business at the time wasn't in the best of shape and he'd just about "blown his wad" on our three unsuccessful expeditions.

We talked about how Bill Ryan offered Ballard our sonar search records from 1980, which we figured must have helped a little. Jack said the "son of a bitch is a traitor!" But I told him that Bill was a good guy and was only trying to provide help from one oceanographer to another. I told Jack I didn't think our sonar records were much help in Ballard finding the Titanic. "He just got lucky".

What I sincerely believe helped Bob find the Titanic was the fact that IFREMER's sophisticated sonar system SAR didn't find Titanic any better than we did. That convinced Bob the Titanic wasn't located anywhere within that original search area. Luckily for Bob the only area that Jean-Louis Michel's SAR system had not been able to search—mainly because of the weather—was the one area in the ocean where Bob's ARGO camera system could find her.

I told Jack that technology is certainly good but having a little luck, especially when you're looking for something in the deep ocean, is sometimes better. We had come close but no cigar.

Actually we had come very close. When we eventually found out where the Titanic was located, Dr. Bill Ryan went over all of the sonar records we collected from our 1980 expedition. To his great surprise he discovered that our own Blue Fish had flown right over the Titanic as she lay on the bottom. Unfortunately our scientists were looking for a full-sized Titanic in one piece. They weren't looking for a sonar signature of a ship that had broken in two with the bow and stern sections more than a mile apart.

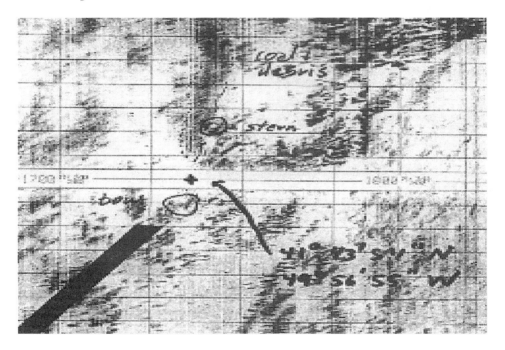

Sonar Record of Bow and Stern Sections of Titanic Taken During 1980 Titanic Expedition

Even though our scientists used Seamarc and Deep Tow, the sophisticated sonar devices couldn't tell the difference between manmade objects on the bottom and natural geological features. In the end it took Bob Ballard's camera system and old-fashioned luck to discover the Titanic.

Now that it had been successfully accomplished I switched gears and decided that even if I hadn't been able to find the Titanic, that didn't mean I couldn't form a company to salvage her artifacts. I still had my contacts in Paris with Robert Chappaz and Yves Cornet at Taurus International. I also had my contacts at IFREMER. I knew their deep-diving submersible Nautile would work just fine to help me salvage artifacts. I also had my good friend George Grosz whom I was sure would be interested in helping me raise money for my new dream. I knew I had been knocked down, but I definitely was not out! Bob Ballard had found the Titanic and received all due publicity for his exceptional accomplishment. But he had also painted himself into a corner. All of his holier-than-thou pronouncements about the Titanic being a graveyard that shouldn't be desecrated made it impossible for him to ever go out and salvage her artifacts.

It may have been too bad for him, but it wasn't going to stop me from trying to make something positive out of my long-standing dream. I knew Titanic was like a time capsule. First Class, Second Class and Third Class passengers were traveling on the Titanic to America but they were not traveling with equal creature comforts. I thought people all over the world would be very interested in seeing what life was like for the different classes on board the Titanic when she sank in 1912.

Grimentz, Switzerland

Buoyed by my perpetual glass-half-full optimism, I quickly put together a business plan which would show that money could be made by salvaging Titanic artifacts. I now had several years experience leading expeditions at sea, and could put together a reasonable prospectus that would include recovering artifacts, producing a film of the expedition, preserving the artifacts, and putting them on display around the world. I had produced successful films of previous expeditions. My research on deep diving submersibles enabled me to have, at least, a basic knowledge of how they operated and what their capabilities might be in recovering artifacts. I contacted a long time friend of mine, Carlos Piaget, who through his family in Neuchâtel, Switzerland, was one of the heirs to the Piaget watch fortune. Carlos and I had known each other for years. In fact the first time I ever went to Europe back in the 1960s it was to spend time with Carlos and his family in Switzerland. The Piaget family had a wonderful home that overlooked Lake Neuchâtel, but they also had a beautiful chalet at Grimentz, which was located high in the Swiss Alps. Carlos arranged for my wife Evelyn and me to spend a week at his family's chalet in Grimentz during our honeymoon in 1970.

When I got out of the Marine Corps in 1960 and began distributing films in Europe it was Carlos who drove me more than once to the Cannes Film Festival in his super-fast, super-impressive Lamborghini. Those were the days we had many happy times together working and playing around Europe. So I knew quite well just whom I was dealing with when I asked Carlos to help me raise money to salvage artifacts from the Titanic.

Mike at Piaget Chalet in Grimentz

My wife Evelyn had also gotten to know Carlos through the previous business dealings I'd had with him over the years. She reminded me that Carlos didn't enjoy a particularly good reputation. He had gone through a lot of his family's money in the early 1960s trying to develop a 'Watchaus of Switzerland' business selling Swiss watches and jewelry in and around Lansing, Michigan. His business ended up in several lawsuits, as did his effort to manufacture MG convertibles in Switzerland and sell them to select dealers in the United States.

But it was through this MG manufacturing effort that I met George Tulloch a successful car dealer in Stamford, Connecticut. When Carlos shipped two MG's over to New Jersey from Switzerland he and I picked them up when they cleared customs and drove them to George Tulloch's dealership in Stamford. I didn't know it then, but both George Tulloch and Carlos Piaget would become key figures in my Titanic story in the years to come.

Mike and Carlos in the Swiss Alps

18 Forming ORE, Inc.

Prior to my marriage to Evelyn I married Barbara Burton and had two children, John Michael and Lisa Gael. Michael is now a doctor in Sarasota, and Lisa teaches school and lives in St. Petersburg. In 1987 my other two children, Gerald Michael and Stephen Herschel lived with their mother, Renee, in Clearwater. When Gerald (G. Michael) was growing up I always called him Jerry, as did his mother, brothers and sisters, but by 1982 he thought it sounded too childish for business, so started going by his middle name Michael. I really don't care what name he goes by, but as his Father, I still call him Jerry. Madalene Elizabeth, the child that Evelyn and I have together, lived with us at our home in Tampa, along with two of Evelyn's three children, Todd and Robin. By 1987 Evelyn's oldest child, Carrie, had moved out and was married with two children.

Hoping to fortify my home-team, I went to see my son Jerry (G. Michael), who was very successful in making his living booking comedians into comedy clubs and television shows around Florida and the Southeastern United States. He was actually pretty good at it. One of his friends, Mike Robinson, booked Musical Acts and Bands, mostly into hotels and night clubs in the Southeast as well. My son would find clubs for Robinson and his bands while Robinson found clubs for my son's comedians. It was a very symbiotic relationship.

Jerry had always been interested in my expeditions when he was growing up. In fact, I planned to take him with me on my first Titanic expedition in 1980 when he was 15 years old. But just before it was time to leave he had a terrible motorcycle accident that put him in the hospital. Having to stay home probably hurt Jerry more than his broken bones, but there wasn't anything I could do about it.

Now that he was 22 years old and successful in the entertainment industry, I figured it was a good time to see if he still wanted to get involved in one of my great adventures.

I knew he had a comedy club in Tampa, so Carlos Piaget and I decided to go and see him. When we got there, Jerry asked if I planned to do anything else with the Titanic? I told him that Bob Ballard had made the discovery, but that didn't mean I had giving up on my dream. I let him know I was disappointed I hadn't been able to make the discovery myself, but wouldn't let that stop me from trying to salvage her artifacts and put them on a world tour. I figured if anyone would understand touring artifacts, my son would, since he had over 50 night clubs from Shreveport, Louisiana to Key West, Florida and had to move his comics around to a different location 7 nights a week. I was sure it was a logistical nightmare, but fortunately, he was really good at it. Not to mention getting all those club owners to hire him, I figured he could sell ice to an Eskimo. No doubt my boy had a real gift. He was a regular chip off the old block.

G. Michael (Jerry) Harris

I explained to Jerry that all the publicity Bob Ballard was getting, telling everyone that salvaging artifacts was wrong, made it difficult to raise money in the U.S. I told him that Carlos could raise money through his friends in Europe. I suggested that it probably wouldn't be a bad idea if we formed a corporation in Switzerland and used that for trying to raise money to salvage the Titanic. That way I may be able to keep my own name out of the papers and away from all the bad publicity that might arise. I could see Jerry was interested in what I was selling and anxious to get involved with me in my new Titanic project even though he had his own business which continued to be successful.

I told him the first thing I needed to do was raise a little money so that Carlos and I could travel to Switzerland for a month to get things started. He said he thought that he and his Joint Venture partner, Mike Robinson, could put up the initial money which sounded encouraging. After a quick phone call to Robinson in Orlando, Jerry set up a meeting for the three of us to go meet with him.

The next day Jerry, Carlos and I drove to Orlando and had a meeting with Mike Robinson. I showed him my background on leading expeditions and producing feature documentary films of the adventures. I also told him about my new plan to recover artifacts from the Titanic and put them on a world tour.

Carlos then told Mike about his personal business connections in Europe and how he was sure we could form a Swiss corporation in Geneve and use that to raise money for a Titanic artifact recovery expedition. Carlos and I told Jerry and his friend we could not guarantee we would be successful, but if we were, the venture should generate a lot of money for all of us.

Mike Robinson and Jerry agreed to provide Carlos and me with the necessary traveling money we needed to spend a month or two in Europe in exchange for ownership in the project and the exclusive rights to book and tour Titanic artifacts around the world. It was also agreed that my son would go along with us on the trip so he could get up to speed on the deal as well as keep track of how Carlos and I were spending their investment. Robinson, it was decided, would stay in the States and start putting the Titanic Artifact Tour together.

Once Carlos and I got back to Tampa we immediately began planning our trip to Europe. It was now January 1987 and I didn't want to waste any time in getting my new Titanic project started.

Strangely, though, what began with great hope and excitement almost ended tragically in disaster. On January 27, 1987 when Jerry, Carlos and I took off from Miami on board a 747 I noticed two long sheets of flame belching out from our inboard port (left) engine just as our wheels left the ground. I have spent enough time flying airplanes myself and riding in commercial airliners to know that, long sheets of flame coming out of an engine, is not considered normal. A few minutes later the Captain came on the intercom and told everyone that we had lost an engine on takeoff and that we were going to circle over the ocean for 30-minutes and dump fuel. He then said we would return to Miami for repairs. What a way to start our new adventure. But after spending the night in Miami we were all put onto another flight and finally made it safely to Paris via Madrid, Spain.

The first thing I did upon arrival was contact George Grosz so I could introduce him to Carlos and Jerry. Carlos told George that our plans were to go to Geneve and form a Swiss corporation then use the Swiss entity to raise the money we'd need to salvage artifacts from the Titanic.

George Grosz

George was pleased to meet my son Jerry (he still wished I would call him Michael, or at least G. Michael, but as his father he was still Jerry to me), but he was especially pleased to meet Carlos. George was sure that his Piaget name would make it easier for him to help us raise money for the project. He suggested that if we were going to form a Swiss Corporation we should use an attorney in Geneve that he was familiar with and had used successfully in the past. Carlos didn't see any problem with that, so Carlos, Jerry and I bid George a friendly goodbye and headed straight for Geneve.

The law firm George suggested was Fidinam Fiduciaire S.A., Geneve. George had previous commitments in Paris so wasn't able to travel with us to Switzerland. We were introduced to William Balzli, a senior attorney who worked for Groupe Fidinam. When we told him that we wanted to form a Swiss corporation, William suggested the quickest way to do that was to purchase a shell corporation. He said he was sure he could find a shell for us that required little money down.

While William Balzli started his search for a shell corporation we retreated to the Swiss Alps where the Piaget family owned a wonderful chalet. It was the same chalet where Evelyn and I spent part of our honeymoon in the early 1970s.

Swiss Alps in Winter

While we waited for William Balzli to get back in touch with us with news about his search for a Swiss shell, I worked almost full time on my Titanic artifact recovery project Business Plan. While I was working on the Business Plan, Carlos got in touch with M. F. Cardis at Sef Société Fiduciaire S.A., in Lausanne.

M.F. Cardis was a long time friend of the Piaget family. Carlos knew he had a lot of good financial contacts in Europe so was anxious to get in touch with him and ask for his help in raising money for our salvage project.

Once Carlos, Jerry and I met with M.F. Cardis, I was delighted that Carlos had selected him to help us raise the money we needed for the project. M.F. Cardis had a European business savvy that I was confident would help us immensely in meeting and, hopefully, securing the right financial contacts.

Unfortunately all was not sweetness and light in dealing with Carlos. He and I had been friends for quite a long time. Consequently, I was not unaware that he had a serious drinking problem. I had cautioned Carlos more than once that his continued drinking would only lead to serious problems for both of us. His response was that he could handle it and not to worry. In the middle of January in the Swiss Alps there was plenty of deep snow on the ground outside our Swiss chalet. Each day Carlos complained mightily about his liver hurting and that all he needed was a little drink to make him feel better. Jerry and I both tried to watch him closely to see where he was getting all the booze he was drinking that was making him "feel better."

Every day we would search the chalet for Carlos' hidden stash of alcohol. Whenever Jerry or I would find a bottle we'd open a chalet window and throw it out into the snow, without telling our friend what we had done. We finally surmised that Carlos must have been sneaking down to the local grocery store in Grimentz every morning and charging the whisky, gin, wine or vodka (it never seemed to matter) to his Piaget family account.

I wasn't about to buy Carlos any alcohol on the money we had received from Jerry(G. Michael) and Mike Robinson. I was delighted we were able to stay for free in the Piaget chalet as it did help what little money we had go further. But buying Carlos alcohol to feed his growing addiction was completely out of the question.

While we waited, we knew we had to come up with a name for our proposed corporate entity. Carlos, three sheets to the wind, suggested we use a name like Oceanic Research and Exploration Limited, or ORE for short. I thought it was pretty long and convoluted but if Carlos was going to raise the money we needed to get my dream funded I wasn't going to argue with the name he came up with and seemed to like.

When we got back to Geneve and met again with William Balzli, he said he had located the perfect shell corporation for us. Actually it was George Grosz who located the shell. While vacationing in Gibraltar, George nosed around and found a company that happened to be available called Gulf Energy Ltd. He called his friend William Balzli and told him he was sure that Gulf Energy would work just fine for the shell that we were looking for.

William Balzli knew we would want to change the name so when he asked us what name we wanted to use we told him about Oceanic Research and Exploration. He then asked which one of us wanted to be president. I told him I wanted Carlos to be president because we were forming a Swiss corporation and Carlos was a Swiss citizen. I also told William what Bob Ballard had to say about Americans who wanted to go out and salvage artifacts from the Titanic. When publicity comes out about ORE having an expedition to salvage Titanic artifacts, I thought the criticism might not be as bad if a Swiss company was doing the salvage.

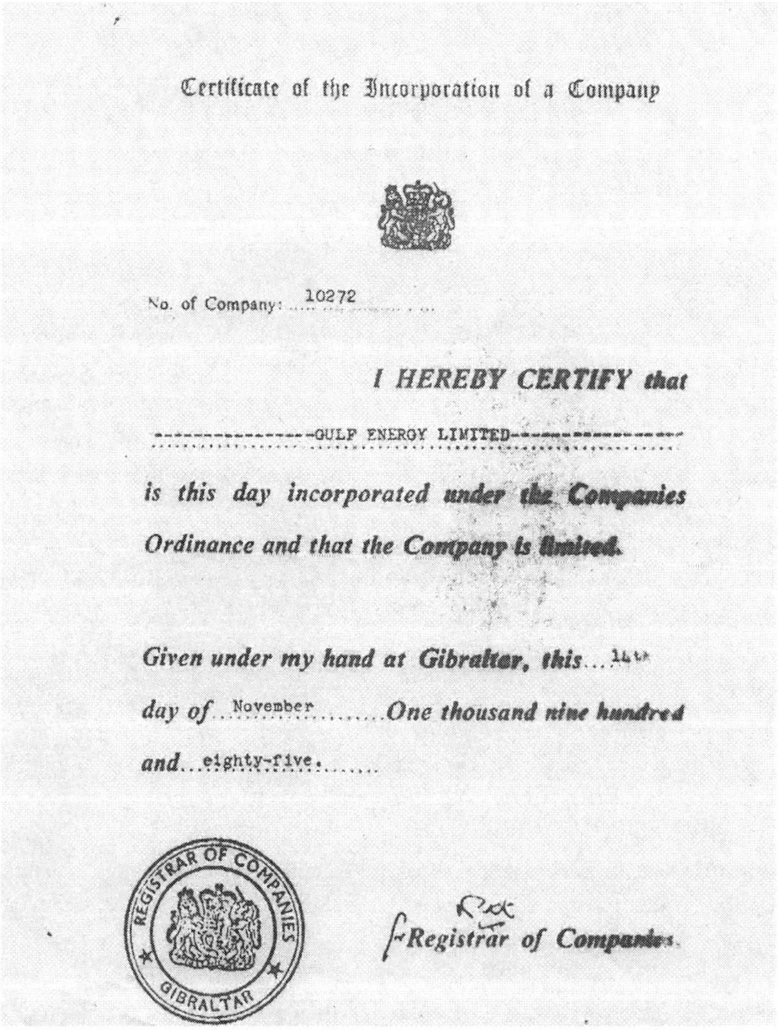

Certificate of the Incorporation of a Company

No. of Company: 10272

I HEREBY CERTIFY that

--------------GULF ENERGY LIMITED--------------

is this day incorporated under the Companies Ordinance and that the Company is limited.

Given under my hand at Gibraltar, this 14th day of November One thousand nine hundred and eighty-five.

Registrar of Companies.

Original Gulf Energy Document

William then said he had one hundred shares of Bearer Stock. He said it was divided into two stock certificates, each representing fifty shares. He handed one 50-share certificate to me and one 50-share certificate to Carlos.

I had no idea what Bearer Stock was. To me one type of stock was no different than any other type of stock. Stock was stock. I told William that since Carlos was in charge of the financial side of ORE, and I was in charge of the expedition, movie and salvage side, I thought it would be best if Carlos held on to both shares of stock for safekeeping. So I handed Carlos my fifty shares of Bearer Stock and he put them in his briefcase along with his own fifty shares of Bearer Stock.

That turned out to be the most stupid decision I had ever made in my life. To this day, I don't know why William Balzli didn't explain to me that Bearer Stock is called Bearer Stock because it belongs to the person who 'bears' the stock—meaning, whoever has possession of the certificate. If a stranger found Bearer shares of stock lying on the ground and picked them up that stranger would then "own" the bearer shares he had just found.

I had just named Carlos Piaget president of our new Swiss corporation—and I had put him in possession of one hundred percent of the company's stock. That night Carlos, Jerry and I went back to the chalet in the mountains, sat down before a warm, roaring fire and celebrated the successful formation of ORE. As usual Carlos had one too many but this time I didn't complain. I thought he deserved it. Maybe what I didn't know was that he was actually celebrating the fact that I didn't know anything about Bearer Stock.

But he didn't know anything about organizing an expedition to salvage artifacts from the Titanic. He also didn't know anything about producing a film of the adventure. We both needed each other to get ORE off the ground. I promised Carlos I would make sure we received a favorable contract from IFREMER. He promised me he would obtain the money we needed to carry out a successful expedition.

The next day we drove back to Paris and asked George Grosz to find a hotel for us that was close to his office, and not too expensive. George called the Hotel Cambaceres and reserved one room for Carlos and another for Jerry

Hotel Cambaceres Card

and me.

We told George we had been successful in getting a Swiss corporation set up and asked if he would please call his two friends, Robert Chappaz and Yves Cornet, to let them know we were back in Paris and would like to meet with them as soon as possible.

Early the next morning, George, Jerry, Carlos and I, met with Robert and Yves at Taurus International. I introduced them to Carlos Piaget and told them how he, through his family connections, was going to help me raise the money we needed to conduct an expedition to salvage artifacts from the Titanic. Robert and Yves looked at each other, obviously surprised then sheepishly told us we were too late. "Too late?" I blurted out. "What are you talking about?" Chappaz then pulled out a contract that had been signed on November 18th, 1986 between Yves Sillard of IFREMER, Robert Chappaz of Taurus International, John Joslyn of The Westgate Group and Jack Grimm of Grimm Oil Company in Abilene.

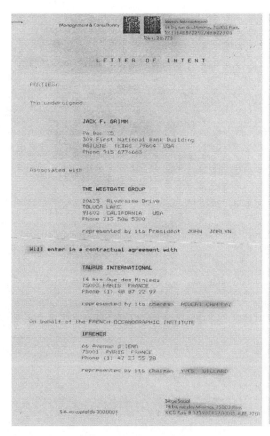

Page 1 of Contract

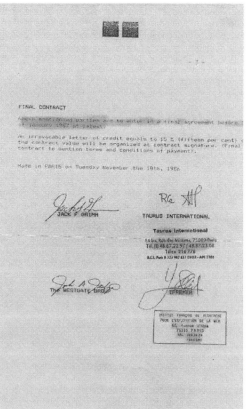

Page 2 of Contract

"Jack Grimm was here?" I asked, obviously astonished that my former Titanic partner had come over to Paris, used my personal contacts and signed a contract behind my back without telling me.

"Yes," he answered with a shrug, probably a little surprised that Monsieur Grimm had come to Paris without me but also figured it was none of his business or concern just as long as he got someone to sign a contract with IFREMER.

I then asked Robert, "Who the hell is John Joslyn?" He calmly told me that Joslyn was a television producer from Burbank, California who had joined forces with Jack Grimm to help him come up with the money they needed to pay for their expedition to salvage artifacts from the Titanic.

I couldn't believe it. IFREMER had signed a contract with Jack Grimm behind my back and I didn't know anything about it. Jack Grimm had never even heard of IFREMER until I told him. All the time and money I had spent over the years trying to educate myself on how a submersible works and how it could be used to locate and salvage artifacts from the Titanic seemed to be going down the tubes. I was indignant and understandably angry.

When Bob Ballard found the Titanic in 1995, I went on my own to Paris and met with IFREMER to see if together we couldn't be the first to dive on the Titanic using their new submersible Nautile. All the while I kept Jack Grimm fully informed of what I was doing and expected him to be a part of it when I was able to put something together. He never said a word to me about contacting IFREMER himself and bringing a television producer into the mix to help him raise money and produce a film of the expedition.

While these negative thoughts whirled around in my head Robert Chappaz threw me a bone. "The contract we have with Grimm and Joslyn is scheduled to run out in one week on January 31st, 1987. If they don't come up with an Irrevocable Letter of Credit for 15% of the expedition costs by that date their contract will be canceled."

"How much is that?" I demanded. "Similar to what we negotiated with you when you wanted to be the first to dive on the Titanic last year," Robert hedged, hesitant to divulge the exact amount while he was still under contract to someone else.

I figured their contract would be something over $1,000,000. Not a huge amount of money, but I hadn't been able to come up with such a sum the year before. But Jack Grimm and John Joslyn were only supposed to come up with 15% of that amount. They didn't need an Irrevocable Letter of Credit for the whole amount. Whether they came up with the money or not, there wasn't anything I could do about it. I told Robert and Yves that Carlos Piaget, through his family connections, could definitely come up with the money. If I got the chance I wouldn't leave them in the lurch a second time.

Obviously Robert and Yves were well aware of the Piaget name and seemed genuinely impressed that I was bringing to the table a member of the famous Piaget family to help in my fund raising efforts.

Robert Chappaz then threw me another bone. He said he didn't think that Grimm and Joslyn would be able to come up with the money. They had been given three months to get the money and so far hadn't come up with anything but excuses. I told Robert that we were going to go back to the Piaget chalet in the Swiss Alps and wait for his call. If IFREMER didn't receive the Irrevocable Letter of Credit for 15% of the contract by the end of the week, I let him know that Carlos and I were ready to step up to the plate and take their place.

Before leaving Paris I called George Grosz and let him know what had just taken place. He assured me that with a contract in hand from IFREMER he would have no trouble raising money for the expedition. I thanked him for his support, then Carlos, Jerry and I retreated back to the Piaget chalet in the Alps to wait for the very important phone call from Robert Chappaz and Yves Cornet.

While we were waiting, we didn't just sit around and watch snow fall. Carlos got back in touch with M.F. Cardis in Lausanne and informed him of our opportunity to conduct an expedition with IFREMER. I busied myself putting together the strongest Business Plan I could on how to salvage artifacts from the Titanic and film the historic expedition. I even designed what I thought a land-based Titanic artifact exhibition should look like, as well as a commemorative coin that could be produced from metal salvaged from the Titanic and sold as a souvenir to Titanic enthusiasts around the world.

Carlos continued to find bottles of alcohol he'd stashed away to satisfy his growing addiction. At the same time Jerry and I, both non-drinkers, did all we could to find his hidden bottles of alcohol then throw them out the window into the snow. We hoped we'd be able to keep Carlos sober long enough for him to interact satisfactorily with M.F. Cardis in Lausanne. If Jack Grimm and John Joslyn didn't perform—as we hoped and prayed they wouldn't—I wanted to be ready to re-negotiate a salvage contract with IFREMER immediately and get the money together to back it up.

Our prayers must have worked. Robert Chappaz called us, as promised, at the Piaget chalet in Grimentz to tell us that Jack Grimm and John Joslyn hadn't come up with the Irrevocable Letter of Credit by their deadline.

Careful not to let Carlos celebrate too much that night, we left the next morning for Paris confident that M.F. Cardis in Lausanne or George Grosz in Paris would be able to come up with the investor we needed to finance our proposed salvage expedition.

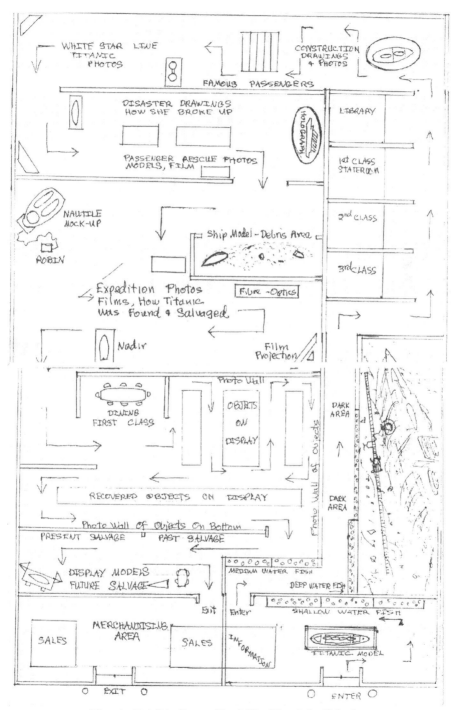

Titanic Exhibit Created by Mike Harris in Grimintz

It was now late February 1987. We were given 90 days by Taurus International and IFREMER to fund an expedition which we identified as "TITANIC 1987". An estimated budget in French francs (FF) for the use of IFREMER's deep diving equipment was negotiated as follows:

Oceanographic ship Nadir .;...................................... 54,000 FF/day

Deep diving submersible Nautile……........................ 83,500 FF/day

Use of remotely operated vehicle Robin.................... 14,500 FF/day

Total daily rate………………………………….. 152,000 FF

The extra cost for each dive was estimated at 10,500 FF daily. Consequently the estimated expedition cost for 45 days at 152,000 FF, plus extra cost for 10 dives at 10,500 per day came to 6,945,000 FF—or rounded off to 7,000,000 FF. Consumables such as fuel, oil and harbor fees, plus taxes, raised IFREMER's estimated expedition costs to 8,000,000 FF.

Since IFREMER didn't reap the benefit they had hoped for in their contract with Bob Ballard in 1995 they added an additional 2,000,000 FF for divulging to us the location of the Titanic and taking us to the wreck site. Bob Ballard was keeping the exact location secret because he still didn't want anyone else to dive on what he considered to be "his" wreck.

But IFREMER knew the location and decided that it was only fair that we should pay them an extra 2,000,000 FF for that knowledge. I couldn't say that I blamed them.

Then Taurus International and Corporate Development added another 1,000,000 FF for work they perceived they spent with me in 1986 in my aborted attempt to fund a diving expedition to the

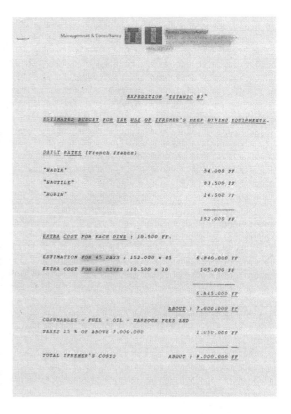

Contract with IFREMER

Titanic with Nautile. Plus, they included additional costs they figured they would have in helping to manage and organize technical developments for our new expedition.

The total estimate for IFREMER, Taurus International and Corporate Development for all expedition costs, expenses and special fees came to 11,000,000 FF which, at an exchange rate of approximately six francs to the dollar, came to a little over $1.83 million. Tentatively the expedition was scheduled to take place sometime between June 15 and August 15, 1987.

Our expedition contract was set. Now all we needed was the money.

19 DOUBLECROSSED

Jerry and I and Carlos took up residence at Hotel Cambaceres, a modest looking hotel at 16 Rue Cambaceres in Paris. George Grosz made the reservation for us since it was only about a block down the street from his Corporate Development office.

I loved the time we spent in the Swiss Alps and especially at Grimentz, one of the most beautiful Alpine villages I had ever seen. But secretly I was hoping our move to Paris would cut down on the amount of drinking that Carlos did everyday—no longer having access to "free" bottles of alcohol at the local grocery store. I hated the fact that my friend was an alcoholic, and that keeping him sober was becoming a full time job.

In Grimentz Carlos could sneak off to the local food store and charge bottles of alcohol to his family's account. I wouldn't give him money for anything but food. I wasn't about to waste what little money we had on booze for Carlos.

Now that we were at Hotel Cambaceres, I hoped that Carlos' drinking would begin to taper off. I was very wrong. Jerry and I shared one small hotel room while Carlos had a room all to himself. In each room there was a small refrigerator that contained small bottles of juice, soft drinks and water. I was afraid to even open the refrigerator door for fear I would be charged for drinking a bottle of juice or water.

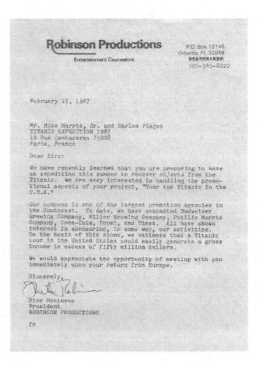

Letter from Mike Robinson

216

Consequently I didn't know that inside the refrigerator were also four rows of small bottles that were filled with all types of alcohol, like wine, gin, vodka, whiskey, bourbon and scotch.

Each day Jerry, Carlos and I would walk down to George's office and organize our fundraising efforts. Carlos stayed in close touch with M. F. Cardis at Sef Société Fiduciaire in Lausanne while I did my best to drum up interest from different contacts I had back in the states.

One contact that expressed interest in salvaging the Titanic was Sonny Anderson, Vice-President of Operations for Disney worldwide. Another was Joseph F. Prevratil, President of Wrather Port Properties. Wrather was interested in exhibiting recovered Titanic artifacts on board the famous ocean liner Queen Mary—now docked permanently as a hotel and tourist attraction at Long Beach, California.

Mike Robinson in Orlando was also busy drumming up support for Titanic Expedition 1987. He received letters of interest from several major corporations. One was from Ralph Cline, Director of Public Relations for Walt Disney World that stated, "We are very interested in your June First Expedition. Send us immediate up-to-date information on this venture. The possibilities are unlimited."

In 1987 Royal Crown Cola executives were launching a new promotional campaign with a new slogan: "People go out of their way for the taste of RC." They told Mike Robinson they wanted us to put a can of RC Cola on the bottom of the ocean and have the Nautile pick it up.

Jack MacDonough of Anheuser-Busch requested "information regarding the Titanic Expedition 1987 and possible Anheuser-Busch participation." Mike also talked with Coca Cola and PepsiCo about expedition sponsorships. Pepsi wanted to out-bid Coke for a sponsorship and also talked about purchasing network television time in our proposed 1987 expedition film.

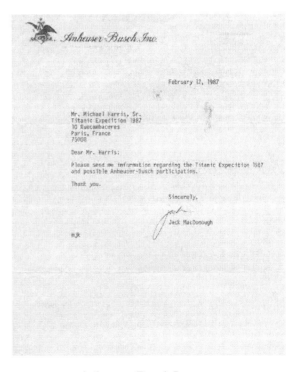

Anheuser-Busch Letter

Budweiser Beer agreed to pay $1,000,000 if expedition members would wear Budweiser caps while salvaging artifacts from the Titanic. Miller Beer stepped up to the plate and said they were willing to pay us $2,000,000 if expedition members would wear Miller caps instead.

Busch Gardens owned by Busch-Budweiser had entertainment centers around the U.S. that were similar to, and competed with Disneyland and Walt Disney World. Busch told Mike Robinson that they wanted to out-bid Disney for the artifact display rights. Timex watch wanted to develop a special "Expedition Watch" and also purchase a sponsorship.

The interest in our Titanic Expedition 1987 was growing. Almost daily, a new offer would come in from a U.S. or European company looking to participate in expedition sponsorships, display Titanic artifacts, publish a book or somehow get connected to the expedition. As the list grew I passed the information on to Carlos who gave it to M.F. Cardis in Lausanne.

We were on a 90-day clock to get the expedition funded and the clock was definitely ticking. I thought about Jack Grimm and John Joslyn losing their contract with Taurus and IFREMER and wondered if John Joslyn would join forces with me now that his deal with Jack had crumbled. I got his number from Robert Chappaz and gave him a call at his office in Los Angeles.

Joslyn was surprised to hear from me, but was also interested in talking about leaving Jack Grimm's team and joining mine. Not wanting to look a gift horse in the mouth, he agreed to fly over to Paris and have dinner with Carlos, Jerry and me.

Joslyn let us know quickly that he had no particular loyalty to Jack Grimm and was emphatic that he could raise television money from his contacts in Hollywood. He said he was on the verge of closing a television deal when he and Jack's contract with IFREMER ran out. I agreed to add John to our team on the proviso that he continued his efforts to put together a television deal for us.

When Joslyn went back to Los Angeles, Carlos, Jerry and I put together a final presentation which included all the companies that I had contacted, Mike Robinson had contacted and several that George Grosz had been in touch with in Europe. The presentation included the written and verbal interest we had received from the various companies, plus the estimated amount of money each would pay for sponsorship, merchandise and television rights for Titanic Expedition 1987.

M.F. Cardis took our presentation with its optimistic financial projections and began following up on phone calls to prospective investors with whom he had previously been in touch.

With our organizational work completed, Carlos, Jerry and I went back to the Hotel Cambaceres and waited for Carlos's Swiss friend in Lausanne to work his magic. After several days the hotel manager pulled me aside and asked if Carlos was all right. I was caught off guard by his question and cautiously asked him why he was asking.

He lowered his voice and looked around to make certain no one was listening then said that since we had been at the hotel the room maids had noticed that every night Carlos removed and drank each small bottle of liquor in the refrigerator. The manager wanted me to know that Carlos might have a drinking problem. He also politely let me know that I was financially responsible for his expensive drinking habit.

The first thing I did was thank him for letting me know what was going on and expressly told him to not restock the room refrigerator with any alcohol whatsoever. I also told him to give specific instructions to his hospitality staff to not serve Carlos any alcohol in the hotel restaurant and bar.

I then went to Carlos and told him what the hotel manager had told me. He sheepishly confessed and admitted that he might have a small problem, but promised that he wasn't going to let it get the better of him.

I didn't believe him, but he was my friend—and had been my friend for many years. I told him I would do whatever I could to help him get over his drinking habit but it was something that he would have to want to do himself. Nobody could really do it for him. Deep down I wasn't sure what, if anything, I could do.

Within a week we received the good news we were waiting for from M.F. Cardis. He informed us that two brothers named Pardo owned a very large insurance company in London and that he was flying into Geneva to meet with us at his office in two days. We drove back down to Mr. Cardis' office and met with David Pardo. We offered Pardo a 50/50 split on everything Titanic. Pardo was very excited and after a 45 minute meeting he decided to fund the expedition!

We still had a problem. We explained to Pardo that we needed to give IFREMER a deposit of $500,000.00 to lock up the deal and didn't have time to reduce our deal in writing. He said "Let's wire the money today to IFREMER so we can lock up your deal. We can meet at my lawyers office next week in New York City and do the paperwork!" Mr. Cardis left the room and came back 30 minutes later with the wire confirmation that $500,000.00 was sent to IFREMER on our behalf.

Finally, we were funded and ready to roll. What could go wrong? As Carlos Piaget used to say, "almost everything!"

We immediately called Robert Chappaz at Taurus International and happily told him that Carlos's family connections had come through as expected. We told him about the insurance company in London and asked him to please inform Yves Sillard of the good news. Robert assured me that he would and congratulated me on a job well done. The only thing left to do was get back to Paris so we could fly home and prepare for our meeting in New York.

On March 17, 1987 George Grosz drove Jerry, Carlos and me to Charles De Gaulle Airport and wished us well in our upcoming negotiations with the Pardo brothers in New York. Finally it looked like we were going to have success and obtain the remaining funds for Titanic Expedition 1987.

We flew back to Tampa and waited for the attorneys of the Pardo brothers to set up a day and time to go to New York to close our deal. We sincerely believed that more than thirty million dollars could be made on recovering Titanic artifacts and putting them on a world tour. Producing a documentary film of the historic expedition and selling it on television, plus selling corporate sponsorships and Titanic merchandise would help make our $30,000,000 estimate a reality.

With the exchange rate of nearly six French Francs to the dollar, our proposed 11,000,000 FF expedition budget would only cost an investor about $2,000,000 U.S. If we let the Pardo brothers recoup their $2,000,000 investment first, a 50-50 split of the profits would still bring in plenty of money for all of us.

Our plan was set and our enthusiasm was high as Jerry, Carlos and I flew to New York City to meet with the Pardo brothers and negotiate the details of the funding of our Titanic Expedition 1987.

Almost immediately, things began to go south! One of the first things the attorneys showed me was a letter on IFREMER stationary dated March 19, 1987 that stated, "I hereby confirm that IFREMER entered into a final agreement with Mr. David PARDO and the Company he represents (WINHILL Limited) for the performance of the 1987 TITANIC expedition. For the avoidance of doubt, I confirm that there is no other ongoing negotiation with IFREMER on that subject." The letter was signed by Michel Stahlberger, Head of the IFREMER Legal Department.

I wasn't too happy to see that the two Pardo brothers were already negotiating with IFREMER and had some sort of an agreement with them, when I hadn't even seen the contract they said they had prepared for me to sign. David Pardo told me they got in touch with IFREMER just to make sure that what I was telling them was true. As good business men they wanted to confirm that I did have a 90-day exclusive contract from IFREMER to get the Titanic Expedition 1987 funded.

I knew that was a bunch of bull because they would have checked on my 90-day exclusive contract with IFREMER weeks earlier, or they never would have sent them $500,000!

We spent the day discussing how we would conduct the expedition and recover the Titanic artifacts. I also told them about John Joslyn and his promise to sell the television rights to the expedition for at least $1,000,000.

During this first long day of negotiations I did my best to keep Carlos sober, but during lunch and dinner Carlos managed to imbibe a few more drinks than his fair share.

I hoped no one would notice, but David Pardo did notice and casually asked me about Carlos' drinking. I tried to pass it off that he was just celebrating a little too much as he was delighted they had agreed to fund our expedition.

When the attorneys showed Carlos, Jerry and me the contract they had prepared, the three of us retired to a separate room where we could review it and discuss it privately. Everything was fine except for the part where they offered to give us only 5% of the project ownership. We had agreed in Switzerland with Pardo that it would be 50/50! Carlos and I were 50-50 partners. If we split the 5% equally, I would only end up with 2.5% of the ownership in a project that I had worked hard to get off the ground since the early 1970s.

I reasoned that I was the first to fund expeditions to search for the Titanic and I was also the first to produce documentary films of the Titanic searches. I was bringing IFREMER's technical expertise to the table. I was also bringing John Joslyn's television contacts to the table. Surely all of that was worth more than 5%.

When we raised our objections to David Pardo, he pulled me aside and told me that he and his brother didn't want Carlos to be a part of the expedition. They said it was obvious to them that he was a drinker, which, as they put it, would result in nothing but problems. David told me to drop Carlos from the team. He said I should have the total 5% ownership for myself. They told me emphatically that they wanted to work with me and would work with me, but they would not work with Carlos.

It took me less than one second to tell him I wasn't interested. I had known Carlos for a long time and considered him to be a good friend. I was not about to drop him from the project just to make a better deal for myself. I told David that 5% was way too small for us to accept. I told him that I would agree to let him take 100% of the profits until he got his money back but then I wanted to split the profits 50-50 after that.

He wouldn't even discuss such a scenario. David said 5% was all he and his brother were willing to offer, take it or leave it. I told him I certainly appreciated his interest, but I would not fire Carlos from my team—and I certainly wouldn't accept just 5% ownership after working so hard for so many years to make my dream a reality.

When we left the hotel where we met with the Pardo brothers I told Carlos to give George Tulloch a call. Carlos and I had met George several years previously when we delivered two MG sports cars to George's automobile dealership in Bridgeport. George was a charismatic person who knew quite a few wealthy individuals in and around the Connecticut area.

When Carlos got George on the phone with me, George immediately began telling me how much he knew about the Titanic and how interested he was in my early expeditions to find her. George said he had followed my previous expeditions with great interest.

He said that ever since he was a kid, he had been fascinated by the Titanic and the stories of her sinking. He knew how many people were on board, how many lives were lost in third class, compared with first class, how many famous people went down with the ship in 1912 and all sorts of other curious and interesting details.

George Tulloch

I was quite impressed with his knowledge about the Titanic, because personally, I had never been any great aficionado of what had happened to the Titanic or who was on board when she sank.

Growing up I had always heard stories about the unsinkable Titanic and how she struck a giant iceberg on her maiden voyage and sunk in the North Atlantic. But I never studied, nor was I ever particularly interested in, the details of how she was built or how many eggs were served during the voyage. I only became interested when *Deadly Fathoms* became a success and I began looking for another successful adventure to film.

Titanic was out there as one of the great marine catastrophes of all time, so it was only natural for me to want to lead another underwater expedition that hopefully would be even better than my diving adventure at Bikini Atoll.

I told George that Carlos, Jerry and I would come to Bridgeport and meet with him to go over all the material I had which showed how we planned to dive on the Titanic and recover her historic artifacts. I also told him that Carlos and I had recently formed ORE and that we were 50-50 partners.

George wanted to know what we were doing in New York. I told him about our meeting with the Pardo brothers and that they wanted to sign a contract with us to fund the expedition but would only give us 5% in the deal. I told George we turned down their 5% offer and that's why we were now calling him.

I didn't tell George about Carlos's drinking problem or about David Pardo wanting to kick Carlos out of the project because of his drinking. George said he didn't think 5% ownership was a fair offer given all that we were bringing to the table. He then went on to say that his BMW dealership had been very good to him for many years but that he had begun thinking about doing begun thinking about doing something

Carlos Piaget in Switzerland

different with his life. He reiterated about how much he'd always been fascinated by the Titanic and how he would love to get involved with what we were putting together.

To sell us on the idea and what he could actually contribute George told us that he knew quite a few very wealthy individuals that he had sold BMW automobiles to over the years and would start talking to them about getting financially involved in our expedition. When the phone conversation ended, both Carlos and I were enthused about George's long time personal interest in the Titanic and his seemingly real potential for raising money for the project.

Since George said it wasn't necessary for Carlos, Jerry and me to travel to Bridgeport to meet with him, the three of us got on a plane at JFK and flew back to Tampa. It was now early 1987 and the clock was still ticking on our exclusive contract with IFREMER. They had given us 90 days to come up with the funding—the same amount of time they had given Jack Grimm and John Joslyn.

At this point Carlos was basically out of money. He still had some good contacts both in the U.S. and Europe, but he had lost whatever money his family had given him when they backed his Watchaus of Switzerland venture in Michigan back in the 1960s. After that he tried to sell classic 1950 MG sports cars that were being built in Switzerland. Unfortunately, the car dealership deal didn't work out for Carlos. Whatever he got involved in he never seemed to do it straight. Nothing he ever tried worked out very well. So for a number of years, he had been living hand to mouth.

Evelyn and I, as two friends who had known Carlos for years (starting back when he was financially flying high) had been helping to keep Carlos afloat for several years. I had never done particularly well myself so also trying to help Carlos wasn't easy.

Carlos Piaget, Debbie (girlfriend), Evelyn and Mike Harris with Daughter Robin

Maybe because of his drinking, or maybe because of his unorthodox business dealings, Carlos' marriage to his longsuffering wife, Sylvanne—along with almost everything else in his life—had gone down the tubes.

When Jack Grimm told me he could no longer finance any more of my Titanic expeditions I asked my wife Evelyn if I should ask Carlos to help me find the money I needed for my Titanic project through his contacts in Europe. She cautioned me strongly that even though Carlos was a longtime friend, we also knew from past experience that his business dealings were, to put it mildly, questionable and he couldn't be trusted.

Evelyn also reminded me that I had put plenty of blood, sweat and tears into getting my Titanic project funded, and I shouldn't risk its success by getting involved with someone like Carlos—who we both knew deep down was only interested in Carlos.

But I was stupid and I was also desperate. I knew my wife was right, but I didn't listen to her. I could only see years of friendship with Carlos and didn't want to see or believe that he would ever do anything in a business relationship that would hurt me personally. But now, all of that was water over the dam. I did ask Carlos to help me get Titanic funded through his Piaget family connections.

Carlos was successful, in that through him we met M.F. Cardis, who introduced us to the Pardo brothers. It wasn't Carlos' fault that the Pardo deal turned out to be so unfair we couldn't accept it. On the other hand, his drinking problem didn't help the situation.

Now we were back in Florida with an IFREMER contract in our pocket, but still without money to fund our project. And the finances Mike Robinson had provided for our trip were now long gone. I told Carlos I was going to take Evelyn back to California to see if I could raise the money we needed out there. I asked him to stay in touch with George Tulloch in Bridgeport just in case he was able to get any of his rich friends to put money into our project.

Carlos didn't have long distance service on his apartment phone so he asked for my house key while Evelyn and I were gone so he could make long distance phone calls from my phone. I told him I couldn't afford for him to do that. I reminded him of several other occasions when he had charged calls to my phone without my knowing it and had run up hundreds of dollars in phone bills that I couldn't pay.

Carlos then asked if he could use my car while I was out in California looking for money. I again told him no. I was afraid he'd get drunk and have a wreck. He got angry that once again I wouldn't agree to help him.

I hated to tell Carlos that I wouldn't help him out. But I had my own family to take care of, plus I had to use the little money I still had left to try and get out to California so I could get the Titanic project off the ground for both of us.

I was afraid Carlos would go on a drinking binge because I was leaving town without letting him have the use of my phone or automobile. But I could never have anticipated what he would do next because of his anger and frustration.

I had not been out of town for more than a few days when Carlos called George Tulloch collect and told him that he owned 100% of Oceanic Research and Exploration Limited (ORE). I know this is true because when I confronted Carlos later, he sheepishly admitted what he had done. He also said he told George that he was president of ORE and the only Director.

"And George Tulloch went along with what you told him?" I questioned, beginning to get angry.

Carlos only shrugged, and added, "George did ask me, what happened to Mike Harris? I thought that you and Mike were partners!"

"Well, I guess it shows that George wasn't completely nuts," I blurted, becoming completely exasperated. "Is there anything more you want to tell me?" I asked sarcastically.

"I told George that I had in my possession two share certificates of ORE stock. One was for 50-shares and the other was also for 50-shares. I told him they were both Bearer shares which meant that as the bearer and person in possession of the stock, I was its 100% owner!"

As usual, Carlos was three-sheets-in-the-wind otherwise he probably wouldn't have so readily admitted his fraudulence. And to make matters worse, I found out he told George that I didn't own anything! I was speechless.

Carlos continued, reveling in his disreputable ways. "I told George that you were not the president. I was. And that I was ORE's sole Director. I also told him that under Swiss law, being Sole Director, gave me the right to do whatever I wanted with the corporation!"

I was flabbergasted! What Carlos told George Tulloch about the Bearer Stock was true. Because of my stupidity, Carlos was legally—but not ethically—owner of 100% of the corporation. Carlos knew that I never intended to give him my shares of stock to own. I was only letting him hold my shares for safekeeping. But because Carlos was angry and must have thought that I had abandoned him, he told George Tulloch that if he would back him on the expedition the two of them could become equal partners.

I figured George knew deep down that Carlos was lying about the ownership, but the opportunity to get 50% ownership in the Titanic project was just too great a temptation for him to resist. If Carlos was holding all the Bearer shares like he said, it might be too bad for Mike Harris, but it was certainly good news for George Tulloch.

When Carlos reminded George about John Joslyn and the $1,000,000 he said he could raise by selling the expedition television rights, they both quickly agreed it would be a good idea if they asked John to join forces with them.

George was sure he could raise part of the money through his BMW dealership contacts in Connecticut but he also knew it would be easier for him to raise the money if Joslyn and his $1,000,000 commitment were on the team.

George and Carlos called John in California and asked if he would like to join forces with them. John was also curious about what happened to Mike Harris, but not so curious as to turn down a deal, honest or not. John immediately said he would love to join forces with Carlos and George, as he didn't have any more allegiance to me than he had to Jack Grimm.

Joslyn then reiterated to Carlos and George that he was sure he could sell the expedition television rights to the Tribune Company for a million dollars. Consequently it didn't take Carlos and George long to decide that they would invite John to become an equal partner with them and they would split up the ownership in ORE, 33 1/3% for each of them. Obviously none of them had any compulsion about truth or integrity. All three knew I was the one who started the Titanic project. All three knew I was the one who led the first expeditions to search for the Titanic and produce documentaries of the deep ocean search. And all three knew that I had spent many years of my life researching the best way to locate and recover artifacts from the Titanic. Stealing my project from me through Carlos' bitterness and deception didn't seem to bother any of them one bit.

When Carlos told George Tulloch and John Joslyn that the Titanic project was his, they both knew that Carlos didn't know a thing about the Titanic. He didn't have any experience putting together an expedition. He didn't have a clue about how to recover Titanic artifacts or produce a film. And he certainly had no idea who IFREMER was until I introduced him. Neither George Tulloch, John Joslyn or Carlos Piaget had much in common except for greed and the desire to steal Mike Harris' project from him—whether it was legal or not.

20 ORE & Lawsuits

What happened next is not a matter of speculation. It's part of the public record. Multiple law suits over a number of years by the various parties involved have provided me with all the documentation needed to clearly see exactly what transpired.

The struggle for Titanic no longer involved just Harris, Ballard and Grimm. It now included Carlos Piaget, George Tulloch and a television producer named John Joslyn. Dividing up ORE equally Piaget, Tulloch and Joslyn set about raising money for the expedition with the French, which I had organized with Robert Chappaz and IFREMER, but from which I was now excluded.

While Joslyn was getting a television distribution company in California to put up the first million dollars in exchange for TV rights to the expedition, George Tulloch set about trying to convince his wealthy friends in Connecticut to invest in a company which he would later call Titanic Ventures.

One man who agreed to back George in his new venture was William Gasparrini of Greenwich, Connecticut. Bill had made quite a bit of money in the scrap metal business. George and Bill also got investment capital from a some of their friends in the area, including Lawrence D'addario, Ray Rocco, Peter Rocco, John Fasone, Kurt and Cheryl Hothorn and several others.

In June 1987 Carlos Piaget transferred 100 shares of ORE (Gibraltar) to George Tulloch and 100 shares to John Joslyn so they each had an equal share in the company that Carlos and I originally formed.

In July 1987 Titanic Ventures Limited Partnership was formed in Connecticut with ORE as the General Partner and George Tulloch as TVLP's sole Limited partner.

In August 1987 John Joslyn's company, Westgate, along with Robert Chappaz and Yves Cornet's company Taurus International were officially brought into the mix. A Titanic Ventures, Limited Partnership Agreement was executed which now included Bill Gasparrini, Lawrence D'addario and the other investors, as well as

Taurus International in Paris, and Westgate. Westgate was named as co-general partner with 12% ownership. ORE's ownership in TVLP was listed as 28%.

When money was put into the IFREMER account from the Connecticut investors and the Tribune Company that Joslyn got to invest for television rights, a specific expedition date was set for August and team members began to be hired.

One of the first people to be hired was Ralph White, who was on the expedition with Bob Ballard when he discovered the Titanic in 1985. I knew Ralph as someone who had an excellent reputation as a filmmaker and suggested to Joslyn that he hire him when Carlos and I were putting together the salvage expedition.

It's funny how things work out in life. Now it was Ralph going on the expedition and I was staying home. Adding insult to injury George, Carlos and Joslyn decided to hire Robert Chappaz of Taurus International as their expedition leader. I guess they figured that with Robert on board it would help smooth the way for them working with IFREMER.

The Titanic salvage expedition that I had tried so hard to put together was now going to be a reality. But without me. Unfortunately for them, however, things began falling apart before they ever got out to the Titanic site.

John Joslyn arranged for part of the television money to be put into the ORE account in Switzerland that he, Carlos and George had set up. But then Tulloch discovered that Joslyn and Piaget had taken money out of ORE's Swiss account without telling him about it—or offering to share any of the money with him. As president of their newly formed Connecticut Limited Partnership Titanic Ventures, Tulloch threatened to sue both of them if they didn't return the money fast.

But George couldn't make too much of a threat against John Joslyn since it was he who controlled the one million dollars that had been put up by the television distributor. I think they promised to give some of the money to George, but I never heard if they ever did.

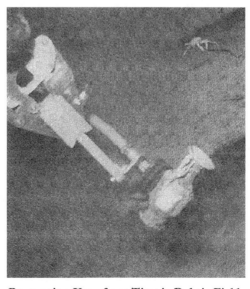

In any case, George Tulloch, now working closely with Robert Chappaz and IFREMER in Paris, managed to get the expedition together and during the latter part of the summer of 1987 began picking up Titanic artifacts from off the ocean bottom at 12,000 feet.

Recovering Vase from Titanic Debris Field

229

When the Titanic began to sink she broke in half, with the bow landing on the bottom about a half-mile from where the stern section came to rest. As she slowly sank, chairs, tables, light fixtures, bags, clothing, pieces of broken pipes, glass, pots, pans, boilers, anything and everything that was loose inside the Titanic—including bodies—began pouring out and settling to the bottom. All of it came to rest on the sandy bottom 12,850 feet deep in an area between the bow and stern sections that subsequently has been identified as the "debris field".

Carlos Piaget didn't go out on the expedition. I never knew why. He did tell me later there was a lot of mistrust and suspicion between Joslyn and Tulloch, who did go out on the expedition together, along with Bill Gasparrini—the single largest investor in the project and Tulloch's new best friend.

The expedition members spent 54 days at sea during 1987 and made 32 dives with IFREMER'S deep diving submersible Nautile, during which they recovered hundreds of

Megaphone Being Recovered

artifacts from the Titanic. Total cost for the successful expedition was $2,500,000.

TIME Magazine Photo, November 2, 1987.

The November 2, 1987 issue of TIME magazine carried a large article under the headline "Treasures Reclaimed from the Deep". A sub-heading exclaimed, "Exclusive photographs of a rich trove of artifacts from the Titanic". The extensive three-page article featured a large color photograph of the Nautile sitting on the surface of the ocean with divers in the water indicating that the submersible is prepared to dive.

Other color photographs showed the submersibles robotic arm picking up a porcelain vase from off the bottom, the captain's megaphone being recovered, as well as a large kettle from the Titanic's kitchen and a still-closed leather satchel.

Additional color photographs featured an ornate vase from the first-class deck, a metal and glass lamp from the stern bridge and a well-preserved crystal carafe.

Bridge Telegraph Recovered

One of the most beautiful and dramatic artifacts recovered was a magnificent cherub that had broken loose from the Titanic's grand staircase. Nautile's robotic arm also brought to the surface an array of sterling-silver cutlery, two ornately decorated coffee and tea pots, the bridge telegraph for signaling the engine room and a jar of skin cream that was still fresh in its glass container.

Doug Llewelyn, an executive producer for John Joslyn's Westgate Productions, described what it was like to view the sunken wreck of the ocean liner from inside the Nautile. "All around us," he stated, "there was this twisted mass of wreckage and tons of coal spread around. And then there was this lady's shoe. It was incredible, just haunting."

Grand Staircase Cherub

Yann Keranflech, a member of the French contingent, said, "You think about the victims. If you find a pair of shoes or a suitcase, you ask yourself if the person managed to survive."

Ralph White was hired to film all the artifacts as they came on board. Later Carlos whispered to me something that was truly shocking. He said that when the expedition returned Ralph White confided to him that a pair of, diamond cuff links were recovered from the Titanic's debris field. He said that Tulloch thanked Bill Gasparrini for helping him fund the expedition by giving him the diamond cuff links that had been recovered.

Titanic Silverware Recovered

I have no way of knowing if Ralph's claim or Carlos' story are true.

Crystal Carafe

I do know that taking any of the Titanic artifacts for personal gain was strictly against all the rules and aims of the expedition. When I negotiated the terms and conditions of the expedition with IFREMER, everyone agreed in writing that no Titanic artifacts would ever be kept as a souvenir nor would any of them ever be sold. They were to be recovered, catalogued and preserved. The artifacts could be filmed and shown to the public in museum-type settings, but no artifact could ever be kept as a personal souvenir or sold for personal gain.

A safe was also recovered from the Titanic's debris field. It was thought to have come from the Third Class Passenger section of the ship. Noted film and television actor Telly Savalas was hired by Joslyn and Westgate Productions to host the production of the first recovery expedition. To insure a large television audience, John Joslyn— who had also produced the live opening of Al Capone's vault in Chicago with Geraldo Rivera— promoted the fact that the Titanic's safe would be opened live during the broadcast from Paris.

The program was a great success and generated terrific television ratings. As expected, a large audience tuned in to see what had been recovered—and what was going to be in the safe when it was
opened live on international television.

Telly Savalas

As might have been expected, there was a little more hype surrounding the opening of the safe than the contents could live up to. It contained a number of soggy bank notes, some personal jewelry and a pristine collection of solid gold coins. An expected cache of diamonds, however, than many hoped would be in the safe never materialized.

The diamond cuff link "problem" would surface several months later when George Tulloch again sued John Joslyn claiming that over one million dollars was unaccounted for from television revenues. Joslyn counter-sued both Tulloch and Titanic Ventures claiming that Tulloch had stolen a bag full of diamonds that was never made part of the itemized list of artifacts brought to the surface.

Ralph White (from what I understood from Carlos) was the source of the rumor that claimed a bag full of diamonds was recovered during the salvage expedition but never made it onto the official manifest. The story floated around the project for years and I never discovered if it was true or not.

Newspaper columnist William F. Buckley was also on the 1987 recovery expedition. He wrote a column in support of Titanic Ventures efforts to tastefully recover artifacts from the infamous sunken liner. Despite Buckley's efforts to legitimize Titanic Ventures' expedition, there were still some who didn't wish to see the Titanic site disturbed. Bob Ballard, of course, continued to be the biggest detractor, making protestations to the media whenever he could about George Tulloch and his no-good cohorts "robbing Titanic's grave".

Dr. Robert Ballard is an outstanding oceanographic scientist, but when it comes to the Titanic, I believe he's also a hypocrite who's just sore

William F. Buckley

because he couldn't personally make money from recovering Titanic's artifacts himself. The only way Ballard was able to fund his own expedition was by using the U.S. Navy and public funds. Consequently, there was no way he could claim any personal ownership for himself. In my opinion, Ballard's crying about people robbing Titanic's grave was disingenuous to say the least.

Don't get the idea that I thought Piaget, Tulloch and Joslyn were a bunch of good guys. I had already learned the hard way that you can't make a good deal with bad people. And in my mind Piaget, Tulloch and Joslyn had all proved to me exactly what they were made of. Some might say Ballard falsely accused them of robbing Titanic's grave, but there was no question, whatsoever, they were certainly robbing me.

Before Joslyn's live Titanic show was broadcast internationally on television I tried to stop the program from going on the air. Deep down I didn't have the stomach for suing anyone. But several of my friends said that I should try to do something. They said it wasn't right for me to just sit back and do nothing and let the three of them steal the project from me that I had worked on for so long to put together.

Bobby Blanco and I had been friends for many years. He was in the zodiac boat with me when we were washed over the waterfall in Mexico. He also was with me on all three of my Titanic expeditions. Bobby said he had a cousin in Tampa who was an attorney, and that his law firm may be willing to represent me in a lawsuit against ORE and Titanic Ventures.

I quickly told Bobby that I didn't have any money to pay attorneys for anything. I figured that trying to sue someone in Connecticut from Tampa would be a very time consuming and costly proposition. Trying to come up with the money as far as I was concerned was totally out of the question.

But Bobby said that I might not need any money. He said that if I would just go and talk to his cousin and explain to him how Carlos had stolen the project from me, I might be able to work something out. That sounded good, but I still wasn't sure. But Bobby was persistent. He convinced Evelyn that I should try to do something. So mainly to please her, I told him that I would at least go talk with his cousin, but I was sure it would only be wasting his time and ours.

21 LEGAL RESPONSE

Bobby and I went to see his cousin, Elio Muller, who was part of the Tampa law firm Fernandez, Muller & Sanderson. Ralph Fernandez, Stuart Sanderson, Elio, Bobby and I met in their pleasantly furnished office on Moody Street close to downtown Tampa. I explained to them how Carlos Piaget and I formed ORE together in Geneve and how I stupidly handed my 50-shares of Bearer stock to him for safekeeping.

I told them that Carlos took my 50-shares and his 50-shares and told George Tulloch that he was the sole owner of ORE. I told them how I invited a television guy named John Joslyn to join forces with Carlos and me when we were putting together the expedition to go salvage Titanic artifacts.

I explained that Carlos, George Tulloch and John Joslyn split up the ownership in ORE equally among themselves, raised the money needed for the expedition and recovered over 800 Titanic artifacts that summer. I told them that Telly Savalas had been hired to host the television show, which was scheduled to be aired live from Paris in about a month.

Ralph Fernandez, Elio Muller and Stuart Sanderson said they wanted to talk among themselves for a few hours to consider what they should do—or could do—to take on such a huge, international project. I quickly reminded them that this was all Bobby's idea. I let them know I didn't have any money to pay for what I perceived could be a very expensive legal process.

When Bobby and I returned a couple of hours later, they surprised me by saying they would take on the legal work and do it on a contingency basis. They would take 25% of whatever they were able to collect in project ownership or money.

Here was an offer I couldn't refuse. I had no ownership and no hope of getting any. If these gentlemen could work their legal magic, maybe I'd be able to come out with something. And something was worth a whole lot more than nothing.

Fernandez, Muller and Sanderson decided they would sue ORE and Titanic Ventures in Federal Court for $300 million. They also filed an injunction to stop Joslyn's television broadcast which was scheduled to air live within just a few weeks.

The $300 million lawsuit stuck, but a Federal Judge refused to allow the injunction to stop the broadcast. Consequently, on October 28, 1997, "Return to the Titanic… Live", featuring Telly Savalas as host, aired as scheduled from Paris.

I should have sued them for using my documentary film title in their television production, but didn't. The film I had produced with James Drury as on-camera host and narrator in 1981 was also called *Return to the Titanic*. I guess they figured that since they had already stolen my Titanic project, they might as well steal the title to my second film as well.

I was disappointed that my law firm wasn't able to stop the popular television production, but the lawsuit certainly stirred up a hornet's nest of legal trouble for my three antagonists. Faced with my $300 million suit, claiming that Tulloch, Piaget and Joslyn had stolen my 50% share of ORE, the three of them fought back. They desperately tried to prove that Piaget had obtained 100% of ORE fair and square and that I had never owned any ownership in ORE whatsoever.

While a multitude of attorneys tried to defend their illegal and unscrupulous activities, the management of ORE and Titanic Ventures almost immediately began falling apart from within. When Tulloch and Piaget discovered that one million dollars was missing from television revenues, they quickly sued John Joslyn and Westgate Productions—who then counter-sued both of them.

Tulloch, Joslyn and Piaget each had attorneys defending themselves against my $300 million dollar claim, but they also had attorneys defending them against lawsuits from each other.

Not wanting to be left out, Jack Grimm got into the act by filing a lawsuit against Joslyn, claiming that he and his previous television partner had the rights to go on an expedition with the French before Carlos and I came along.

Jack Grimm

When Carlos and I renegotiated the contract with IFREMER and I invited Joslyn to jump over to our team, Jack Grimm, figuring that he should have also been included, sued John.

Everyone was suing everyone, except Bob Ballard. He was on the sidelines telling everyone who would listen how bad ORE and Titanic Ventures were for looting the Titanic of its artifacts. In fact, the January issue of DISCOVER magazine ran an article called "We All Loot In A Yellow Submarine"—a not-so-subtle reference that IFREMER's yellow painted submersible Nautile was helping to steal Titanic artifacts from the sunken ocean liner.

But time was not on Bob Ballard's side. It had been over three years since he discovered the Titanic and people were now fascinated with the artifacts that were being recovered and wanted to see more.

Consequently, in 1989 Titanic Ventures and ORE cobbled together another expedition with IFREMER and recovered even more artifacts from Titanic's debris field. Carlos didn't go out on the first expedition, nor did he go out on the second. He stayed home and nursed a deteriorating liver, which unfortunately for him, was continuing to get worse. I knew that if he didn't stop drinking soon it was going to kill him. Even though Carlos had stolen my project, I didn't like the idea of my friend killing himself with alcohol.

The Harris Group that was suing ORE and Titanic Ventures didn't just include me, it also included my son, Jerry, his friend Mike Robinson, my friend Bobby Blanco and George Grosz in Paris. Each was instrumental in one way or another in trying to help me get my Titanic project funded.

As expected, the lawsuits between my group, Piaget, Tulloch and Joslyn began to get ugly. In order to settle once and for all that what my law firm was telling the court was the absolute truth, Fernandez, Muller and Sanderson sent a Certified letter to Fidniam Fiduciaire S.A. in Geneve, the Swiss law firm that originally formed ORE for Carlos and me. My firm requested a statement from them certifying that 50 Bearer Shares of ORE were given to Carlos and 50-Bearer Shares of ORE were given to me the day the corporation was formed.

I don't know if attorneys representing Piaget, Tulloch and Joslyn got to the Swiss firm and threatened them in some way or not, but William Balzli from Fidinam Fiduciaire S.A., Geneve sent a letter back to my attorneys, which did nothing but complicate things further. Balzli stated that I had one share, Carlos had one share and Carlos and I jointly owned 98 shares. In effect, they were saying they really didn't know who owned the 98 shares. So much for honest attorneys.

I guess that now with over 2,000 Titanic artifacts recovered (with a reported value of fifty million dollars) a growing number of people were not really interested in the truth; they were only interested in the money.

While many attorneys from a variety of law firms filed claims and counter claims for and against a variety of clients, Titanic's legal situation began to get more and more complicated. Titanic Ventures wanted me to go away, but as long as Fernandez, Muller and Sanderson represented me on a contingency basis, I wouldn't.

Unfortunately for the Harris Group, Fernandez and Mueller were beginning to grow weary of carrying on the costly and time-consuming fight — especially with no

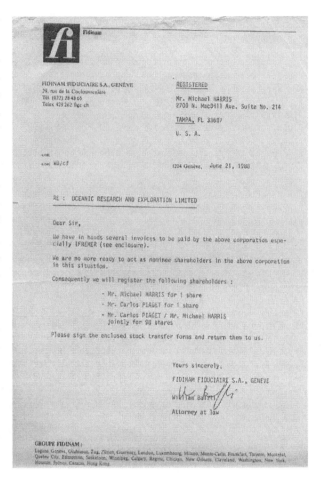

Letter from Fidniam Fiduciaire, S.A.

apparent favorable ending in sight. They invited Bobby, Jerry and me to a meeting one day and suggested that the only way we could break through ORE's continued stone-walling, was to hire legal counsel in Connecticut and sue them on their home turf.

I certainly didn't have the money to start the whole legal process over from the beginning in Connecticut. But our Tampa counsel made it clear that when Fidinam Fiduciaire S.A., Geneve didn't provide the legal backing we thought they would, Fernandez, Muller & Sanderson decided they'd better throw in the towel. They said the legal process had become a much too expensive and time-consuming undertaking. Consequently, they no longer wanted to continue what they perceived to be a losing battle.

It was now1990 and with seemingly no other choice available, I asked my legal team if they would stick with me long enough to make an effort to settle. They said they would, and sent a letter to Tulloch, Piaget and Joslyn, indicating that the Harris

Group would like to put an end to all the legal maneuvering and negotiate a fair settlement.

After several weeks my three adversaries made a benevolent offer to us of 2%. I couldn't believe it, but then of course I could. They were not interested in offering any ownership that was fair, even though deep down they knew they had obtained their ownership under fraudulent circumstances.

The Pardo Brothers that I turned down originally offered Carlos and me 5%. I don't know why Tulloch and Joslyn thought I would now accept a measly 2%. I asked my legal team to reject the offer, telling them that I rightfully owned 50% of the Titanic project and was going to hire a law firm in Connecticut with instructions to pursue my ownership rights to the fullest extent of the law.

It was, of course, a lot of bluff and bravado, because I didn't have the money to hire a law firm in Connecticut to pursue anything. But the threat must have worked, because within about three weeks Tulloch, Joslyn and Piaget had their law firm submit a less-than-favorable ownership offer of 2.5%, which was only slightly better than their first.

This went on back and forth for about six months, wrangling over this offer and that, until an ownership position of 5.04% was agreed upon. It obviously wasn't what I wanted or what I thought was anywhere close to being fair but Fernandez, Muller and Sanderson said they could not keep representing me and the Harris Group any longer. They didn't think it was a fair offer, but didn't think I could get anything better unless I hired a law firm in Connecticut, like they had suggested six months earlier.

Feeling I had no other choice, I allowed for papers to be drawn up in 1991 between the Harris Group, Tulloch, Joslyn and Piaget and filed with the Connecticut court. Carlos Piaget, now in very poor health and up to his eyeballs in debt to attorneys and creditors, sold out his interest in ORE and Titanic Ventures for $204,000. His buy-out agreement with ORE and Titanic Ventures was also made a part of the court's final settlement with me.

While I was trying to finalize the legal mess with Titanic Ventures, others saw the tremendous interest RMS Titanic continued to generate with the public and wanted a piece of the famous liner for themselves. She was resting on the bottom in 12,850 feet of water in international waters, so anyone who wanted to could legally go out and film her or try to recover artifacts.

Stephen Low was a Canadian film producer who wanted to get a job with me on my first Titanic expedition in 1980. I wanted to hire him, but because of the limited number of people who could actually go on the expedition, I had to turn down his request.

In subsequent years Stephen became a successful documentary film producer on his own and was instrumental in creating film specials for the large format IMAX-screen. In June of 1991 he put together his own expedition and went out to the Titanic site in a joint filming effort with the Russians.

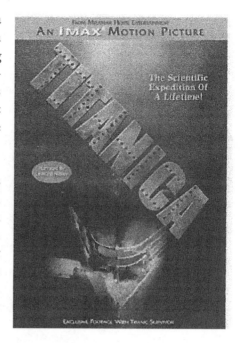

Filming from two deep-diving Russians submersibles, Mir 1 and Mir 2, Steven produced Titanica, a marvelous 70-mm film. Present with him on the expedition was Ralph White, the underwater cameraman I had asked John Joslyn to hire back in 1987 before Joslyn joined with Tulloch and Piaget in their illegal takeover of ORE. Repeated filming from the Russian deep diving submersibles enabled Ralph to gain extraordinary knowledge of the bow and stern sections of the Titanic

Stephen Low Film

and the incredible number of artifacts that were still resting on the bottom in her debris field. This very special knowledge would soon play a role in Ralph becoming a major player in the next round of Titanic greed.

Ralph White

22 TEAM PLAYER

The court had yet to decree my ownership in ORE and/or Titanic ventures, but George Tulloch and I, along with Carlos Piaget, had signed our agreement and I was anxious to help get the fledgling company properly financed and on its way to making money. Up to now it had recovered a lot of valuable Titanic artifacts that were purported to be worth fifty million dollars if they could be sold to interested collectors, which they could not.

There's no question the company had a potentially major asset, but only if the company could raise the money needed to preserve the artifacts and put them on an international world tour. Titanic Ventures had the potential to make money in the future, but the current debts were about to sink her just like Titanic.

Even though Titanic Ventures recovered a lot of valuable artifacts, they also generated substantial debt to attorneys for the numerous lawsuits they had to litigate, not only with the Harris Group, but among its own members and vendors as well.

Titanic Ventures also owed money to IFREMER and Taurus International for the cost of the recovery expeditions in 1987 and 1989. They also were accumulating bills from EDF, the French company involved with preserving the salvaged artifacts.

Now that George Tulloch and I had come to terms, I suggested to him that to protect Titanic Ventures investment it should go to court and legally "arrest" the Titanic, which would keep others from trying to recover any of its artifacts in the future.

In order to "arrest" a sunken ship a salvager needs to know the location of the ship and also needs to recover an artifact from the ship which would prove that the ship being "arrested" is, in fact, the specific ship in question. Titanic Ventures had already recovered 2000 artifacts so it could easily meet the legal requirements.

George surprised me by saying he was against the idea. He said that in his mind the legal process would be much too difficult and it would cost too much money. "We've already spent a lot of money on legal cases," he groused. "I don't want to spend anymore". Instead he asked me if I would use my own contacts to help him raise money for the struggling project—which he pointed out was also "my project" now.

George was not stupid. He knew that Carlos Piaget had lied about my ownership, but purposely manipulated Carlos to get the ownership in Titanic that he personally wanted. Now he was manipulating me, knowing full well that what he was telling me was what I wanted to hear. He also knew that I probably did have financial contacts that could help him keep Titanic Ventures afloat and he certainly wasn't beneath schmoozing with me or anyone else to get what he wanted.

Wanting to be a part of what I considered to be the company I originally started, I told George that I would help and immediately began spending my own money trying to contact everyone I could think of that I thought might help.

One of the first people I introduced George to was Gordon Cooper. Gordon lived in Van Nuys, California and was one of NASA's original Mercury 7 astronauts. From a previous experience I had with Gordon I knew he was a friend of Roy Disney.

Gordon Cooper

I had met Gordon through Clay Lacey, a friend who was a professional airline pilot. Clay also flew a P-51 Mustang at the National Air Races in Reno. I filmed the races in the early 1970s. During filming, Clay and I became friends and he introduced me to Gordon Cooper.

I knew that Bob Ballard had tried to get the Disney Company involved in funding a Titanic expedition in the 1970s when he, Bill Tatum, Ralph White and Emory Kristof solicited Roy Disney's support.

Bob Ballard had no luck in getting Disney to invest, and I had no better luck in 1989. As a favor to me, though, Gordon Cooper did contact Roy Disney and tell him about Titanic Ventures. He told him that Titanic Ventures had successfully salvaged 2000 historic artifacts from the Titanic and how millions of dollars could be made in exhibiting them worldwide. Though Roy had followed the Titanic project closely he wasn't interested in biting on the deal.

Gordon told me that because of the potential controversy that might ensue from those who claimed salvaging Titanic artifacts was tantamount to grave-robbing, Roy didn't think he should get the Disney name involved. I told Gordon the grave-robbing charge was just a smokescreen from Bob Ballard, but thanked him anyway for everything he had done in trying to help me raise funds for Titanic Ventures.

I next introduced George Tulloch to my friend Clive Cussler, successful author and a fellow member of the Explorer's Club of New York. Clive's book *Raise the Titanic!* caused quite a stir back in the 1970s and did much to reinforce the public's interest in the Titanic which has never waned.

Clive Cussler

I met Clive in 1984. I had moved to Evergreen, Colorado, which is near Denver just off Highway 70. Clive lived outside of Denver on Lookout Mountain, also just off Highway 70. since I had led three expeditions to locate the Titanic I made it a point meet with Clive at his home and talk to him about his fictional *Raise the Titanic!* story. Clive and I had several interesting lunches together talking about his fictional story and how it compared to the real expeditions I was leading to find the Titanic. We also talked about Clive's love of locating Civil War vessels that were lost or sunk during the War Between the States.

By the late 1980s I had moved back to Tampa so I called Clive at his home to let him know what I was up to. I told him about the recent turn of events with Titanic Ventures and how I expected to finally get a little ownership in the organization I started.

About this same time George Tulloch had made a contact with Sea World in Orlando. The popular Florida tourist attraction was looking for something special that would help their lagging sales. Disney World (just down the road) was really killing their attendance.

George talked with Bill Miller who in 1989 was president of Sea World in Orlando and suggested to him that he exhibit a collection of Titanic artifacts at the theme park. Miller immediately loved the idea and told George that he was sure exhibiting

Titanic artifacts at his theme park would give him a leg up on Disney for the annual tourist dollars.

Unfortunately there was one slight problem: August Busch the Chairman of Anheuser Busch in St. Louis actually owned the Sea World attraction in Orlando. Bill Miller would have to get Mr. Busch's permission for the Titanic artifacts to be exhibited.

Bill Miller told "Auggie" about his opportunity to exhibit Titanic artifacts at Sea World and said it was just what they needed to successfully compete with Disney. "Auggie" got back to Bill in just a couple of days, but turned down his request. He said that he was reluctant to associate the Anheuser Busch name with what he considered to be a terrible maritime disaster. He said in his opinion Titanic was still too fresh in people's minds.

But Bill Miller wasn't ready to cave in on what he perceived was a very good opportunity for Sea World without at least putting up some semblance of a fight. Since I lived in Florida, George asked me to talk with Bill Miller myself and see if I couldn't help him come up with an idea that might persuade the Busch chairman to change his mind.

I told Bill about my friendship with Clive Cussler and also about George Tulloch's friendship with newspaper columnist William F. Buckley. I suggested that maybe we could get them to write personal letters to "Auggie" Busch endorsing the idea of exhibiting Titanic artifacts at Sea World. Bill thought that would be a great idea.

Clive Cussler and William Buckley did write letters for us in support of Titanic Ventures recovering and preserving artifacts from the historic ship. I also got Titanic historian Walter Lord who wrote *A Night to Remember* to write a personal letter to "Auggie" Busch. But none of the letters did any good. Mr. Busch refused to change his position.

Bernie Little

I had one more idea. My friend Bernie Little lived in Lakeland, Florida which was located between Tampa and Orlando. Bernie owned the Busch beer distributorship in Lakeland, but more importantly he also owned and operated the famous race boat 'Miss Budweiser' that had generated tons of publicity for the Busch family for years.

I knew that Bernie and "Auggie" Busch were close personal friends. I asked Bernie if he would talk to Mr. Busch about my Titanic project as a favor to me. Bernie did talk to him, but "Auggie" Busch's mind was made up and nobody could persuade him to change it.

Figuring there was no use beating a dead horse I changed tactics and got in touch with David Hill, another friend of mine who lived in Atlanta. I had known David for quite a few years and knew that he was acquainted with quite a few influential people. One of those friends was a promoter by the name of Arnie Geller. Arnie's main claim to fame was that he had successfully handled the careers of a number of famous music stars—including singer Paula Abdul.

David Hill already knew about my many years of trying to find the Titanic then having George Tulloch, John Joslyn and Carlos Piaget steal the project from me because of my own stupidity. The first thing he wanted to know was why I was still trying to fool around with the Titanic?

I explained how my Florida attorneys finally got Titanic Ventures to offer me 5.04% ownership in the company if I would drop my lawsuits. I told him I had finally agreed to do that because some ownership in Titanic Ventures was better than no ownership at all.

Arnie Geller

I also told David that Titanic Ventures Limited Partnership (TVLP) in two expeditions had successfully recovered 2,000 artifacts from Titanic's debris field and if they were exhibited correctly around the world the company could end up being worth a lot of money.

David quickly became interested in what I was selling. I told him that what Titanic Ventures needed now was money, first to pay off debts to several French creditors, and second to put the Titanic artifacts on exhibit so they too could start making money. I reminded him of his promoter friend Arnie Geller whom David had bragged to me several years previously about promoting the career of Paula Abdul.

It didn't take David long to get Arnie on the phone and pitch him on the possibility of his getting involved in promoting and exhibiting Titanic artifacts around the world. Arnie requested that I send him some information on the project, including information on the number of artifacts that had been recovered. He also wanted to know if any additional Titanic artifacts could be recovered in the future?

I prepared an elaborate Titanic presentation and sent it to David Hill who in turn sent it on to Arnie Geller. In about a week Arnie got back to me and said my Titanic presentation looked interesting and that he might like to get involved. What he wanted me to do was set up a meeting for him with George Tulloch. I told Arnie I was sure I could do that and I'd be back in touch.

The reason I stalled a little was because I wanted to get a commission agreement in writing from George Tulloch before I put George and Arnie together. Just in case the rock and roll promoter decided to get in bed with Titanic Ventures and raise money for the project I wanted to be protected.

I contacted George at his Titanic Ventures office in New York City and told him about my conversation with Arnie Geller. I told George that I thought Arnie might just be the person we're looking for to help us raise the money that's needed to get Titanic Ventures rolling.

George wanted to know if I could set him up a meeting with Mr. Geller. I said I was sure I could just as soon as he put something in writing to me. I told George I wanted Titanic Ventures to give me a commission on any money that Arnie Geller raised for the project. I hated to be so blunt about wanting George to put

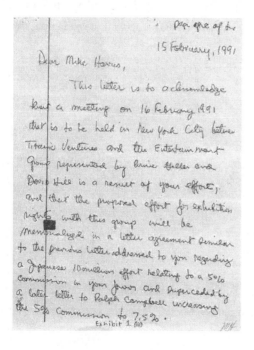
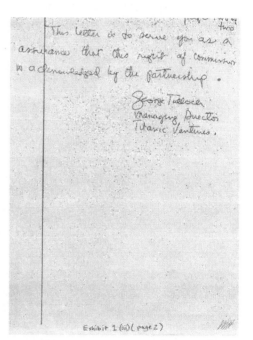

Two Page Commission Agreement George Tulloch Signed with Mike Harris

something in writing, but I had been cheated before and didn't want it to happen again. George said he didn't have a problem with giving me a commission contract and would be happy to put it in writing. We haggled briefly and agreed upon a commission amount of 7.5%.

I told George that once he and I had a signed contract I would set up a meeting between he and Arnie so they could meet together face-to-face.

George faxed me a letter on February 15, 1991, agreeing to pay me a 7.5% commission if the "Entertainment Group represented by Arnie Geller and David Hill" raised money for the project. It was signed with George's signature as Managing Director of Titanic Ventures. On February 16, 1991 Arnie and George met for the first time in Manhattan.

The lawsuit between George and I was finally handled by a Connecticut court and in a Stipulated Judgement the Harris Group was given 5.04% ownership in Titanic Ventures. Most of the shares came from Carlos Piaget who was still drinking heavily and now reduced to begging his friend George Tulloch for money.

When I asked George to disperse the shares to the Harris Group he told me he couldn't because what we now owned was .insider. stock which had to be held for two years before it could be distributed or sold. Not knowing any better I went along with not getting our Harris Group stock in hand as the court had finally decreed and continued to try to help George raise money for what I considered was now our Titanic project.

Unfortunately, as soon as George Tulloch and Arnie Geller began working together they no longer had any interest in communicating with me. Whenever I would call the Titanic office trying to find out information about what Arnie was doing for Titanic, neither Arnie nor George would speak with me. It didn't matter when I called, day or night, both were always too busy and stonewalled me completely.

Only by constant badgering was I able to obtain a more formal commission contract. On October 3, 1991, I finally received a contract that was signed by George Tulloch, Arnie Geller and my friend David Hill. The contract promised to do two things. They would pay me a 7.5% commission on any money they raised and would also allow me to co-produce a Titanic exhibition in Florida should Geller and his "Entertainment Group" be successful in raising money for Titanic Ventures.

The contract seemed to be pretty straightforward and I was anxious to do whatever I could to work closely with them in helping to get "our" Titanic project funded.

Unfortunately, once again, it was not to be. 1991 slipped into 1992 and Arnie Geller was now spending almost all of his time working closely with his new best friend

George Tulloch (both in Connecticut and New York) trying to raise money for Titanic Ventures. Neither of them had any interest in communicating with me all the way down in Tampa. I was completely left out of the fundraising loop.

Realistically speaking, it didn't make any difference whatsoever where I lived. I had been dropped by both of them like a bad habit. Trying to find out what was going on between Geller and Tulloch was virtually impossible. Even though I was the guy who put them together, it was as if I was some kind of a pariah that now neither wanted to have anything to do with.

From what I could surmise, Geller didn't actually bring in an outside investor who put money into Titanic Ventures, but he did cause money to be put into Titanic Ventures which kept it going. I don't know if he took money out of his own pocket or helped George raise money from some of the stockholders who were already a part of Titanic Ventures.

In any case even though Geller caused money to flow into Titanic Ventures I never received one dime of commission. I know that some money must have come in that I should have been compensated for because Arnie and George started exhibiting a portion of the Titanic artifacts in Europe.

Titanic Exhibit in Europe

I found out from Yves Cornet in Paris that the French preservation company EDF was still owed money for their previous preservation work on Titanic artifacts. They placed a lien on the artifacts and wouldn't allow them to leave the European continent. They would allow, however, for the artifacts to be exhibited at selected museum sites within Europe, such as Sweden and Norway. In that way most of the money generated could go to them to help pay for the artifact preservation costs they were owed.

Both exhibitions in Sweden and Norway were a tremendous hit, breaking attendance records at the marine museums where the artifacts were exhibited. I bugged Arnie and George for some compensation, since Arnie was now taking over exhibition of the artifacts. But they still wouldn't take any of my phone calls.

I had been shut out once again and was becoming more and more disgusted, not only with George Tulloch, but now with Arnie Geller as well. George would not give me the stock as he had been instructed by the court to do, nor would he or Arnie let me have anything to do with helping Titanic Ventures.

I offered to help them plan a new expedition to recover more artifacts, or help exhibit some of the artifacts that had already been recovered, but both ignored my requests like I never existed.

Arnie Geller (left) and George Tulloch at Titanic Exhibit in Europe

Discouraged again, I did not turn down Jack Grimm when he called in the spring of 1992 and asked if I wanted to go on another Titanic expedition. He said that Herbo Humphreys a friend of his in Memphis wanted to go out to the Titanic site and pick up artifacts. Considering how I was being treated by George Tulloch and Arnie Geller, my response to Jack was, "When do we go?"

23 MAREX EXPEDITION

It was 1992. I hadn't heard from Jack Grimm in years and here he was inviting me on an expedition. I asked him all sorts of questions. Was he funding the expedition? What submersible was he going to use to recover the artifacts? He just laughed and said his longtime friend Herbo Humphreys from Memphis called him and said he thought he could get the money together for an expedition if Jack was interested.

The two of them met in Memphis to put the proposed expedition together. Ralph White also flew in from California for the meeting. It turned out that Ralph was also a friend of Herbo's and had let him know that he had in his possession a bottle that came off the Titanic. When the three of them met, Ralph told Jack and Herbo that he had secretly acquired a small bottle from the sunken liner when he was out with George Tulloch on Titanic Ventures first expedition in 1987.

Ralph convinced Herbo and Jack that what they needed to do was arrest the Titanic, then they'd be able to claim all the salvage rights for themselves. Ralph explained that even though Titanic Ventures had been out to the Titanic site on two previous expeditions and recovered at least

Capt. Herbo Humphreys

2,000 artifacts they had never gone through the legal process to arrest her and legally claim the exclusive salvage rights for themselves.

Jack being an old poker player knew what Ralph was up to—and also knew a winning hand when he saw one. He told Herbo and Ralph to count him in. He didn't hold any loyalty to George Tulloch, and he certainly didn't hold any loyalty to John Joslyn who he was still suing for not including him in his deal, first with me then with Piaget and Tulloch.

Being a take-charge guy, Jack immediately began to take charge. He told Ralph and Herbo that he would get the best legal advice money could buy and they would go into court and start staking their salvage claim to the historic ship. Jack was thrilled by the thought that Titanic Ventures had been too stupid to arrest the Titanic for themselves. But their stupidity was not his problem. All it meant to Cadillac Jack was that the Titanic was still fair game to anyone who could afford to mount a salvage expedition and go after the artifacts. Come hell or high water that's exactly what Cadillac Jack was going to do.

Jack wanted me to come along with him on the expedition to produce and direct another documentary film of the salvage expedition. He had been pleased with both *Search for the Titanic* and *Return to the Titanic*. Realistically, he probably also figured I would produce a film for him cheaper than anyone else he could hire.

I had mixed emotions about helping Jack and Herbo recover Titanic artifacts. I had been named part owner of Titanic Ventures, but it wasn't looking like I would ever get my hands on the ownership shares the court had decreed. George always had excuses as to why he couldn't give the Harris Group the shares we were owed.

I was also very disappointed I had introduced Arnie Geller to George Tulloch and Titanic Ventures only to be shut out once both of them had gotten what they wanted from me. I didn't really want to go out on Jack and Herbo's expedition, but then again, I also didn't want to miss out on a Titanic adventure.

I told Jack and Herbo that I would go on the expedition with them and produce a documentary film of the artifacts they recovered. During a meeting with them in Memphis I found out their plan was to lease a research vessel that could carry a large remotely operated vehicle (ROV) equipped with lights, a television camera and two large manipulator arms. Their plan was to use the ROV to pick up artifacts that were scattered on the bottom in the debris field.

The reason they were using an ROV was because it was a lot cheaper to pay for two people to sit in a control room on board a research ship watching TV screens while directing the ROV's two manipulator arms to pick up artifacts on the bottom. Having to lease a research vessel large enough to carry a manned deep-diving submersible got into spending a lot of money fast.

Jack and Herbo wanted to recover as many Titanic artifacts as they could as cheaply as they could and sell them to the highest bidder. I had to agree that if you wanted to pick up Titanic artifacts from off the bottom, using an ROV was the cheapest way to do that!

I reminded Jack that I initially worked up the salvage contract with IFREMER and that we had agreed we wouldn't sell any of the artifacts once they were recovered. I also reminded him that ORE and Titanic Ventures kept basically the same contract intact that I negotiated with IFREMER when they went out on their expeditions with the French.

Jack scoffed at the agreement and said he didn't give a damn about any allegiances to the French, to Titanic Ventures, or to anyone else. If he and MAREX wanted to recover artifacts and sell them to the highest bidder then that's exactly what they were going to do. MAREX was short for Marine Exploration, Herbo's company. Up to that time they had been specializing in salvaging Spanish galleons in the Bahamas.

I told Jack I firmly believed that none of the Titanic artifacts should ever be sold. I thought at the time, though, that it would be a terrible waste not to be able to preserve and enjoy relics from 1912 (and still do today). I believe firmly that as many Titanic artifacts as possible should be recovered and put on display in museums around the world for the masses to appreciate the opulence and grandeur of the historic ship's bygone era.

Unfortunately I didn't have any authority over what Jack Grimm, Herbo Humphreys and Ralph White intended to do. If I wanted the job (and if I wanted to get paid for it) the only option I had was to keep my mouth shut and swim along.

I told Jack I would do my best to keep the film production costs to a minimum. I would need to rent lighting, sound and camera equipment and would also hire my cinematography friend Nik Petrik to go along and help me film the expedition. Jack agreed because he knew Nik and I were capable of producing a satisfactory film presentation, inexpensively, of the proposed recovery adventure.

We all flew from the United States to Lisbon, Portugal, and met the Bermuda flag oceanographic vessel Sea Mussel and its British Crew. Although not particularly large, she was a sturdy ship and perfectly suited for travel and work in the deep ocean.

On Sea Mussel's fantail sat the large ROV that the expedition team was counting on to recover artifacts from the bottom. Also on the stern portion of the ship was a large collection of scientific equipment, including 20,000 feet of wire and a motorized crane. The crane was needed to lift the ROV in and out of the water and allow it to work close to the bottom in more than 12,000 feet of water.

Before we left on the expedition, lawyers for Jack Grimm and Herbo Humphreys filed legal papers with the United States District Court for the Eastern District of Virginia, Norfolk Division, on behalf of MAREX TITANIC, INC. They officially requested to arrest RMS TITANIC and claim exclusive salvage rights for themselves. Their legal stand was based on Ralph White's statement that he had in his possession a small green bottle that he had recovered from the RMS TITANIC which was located at 41 degrees 43' 32. North Latitude and 49 degrees 56' 49. West Longitude.

In order to successfully file a claim to arrest a ship in the ocean it's necessary to provide the exact location of the ship that has been lost and also to provide an object from the ship that's been recovered. Both are needed to provide proof that the ship being arrested has in fact been found.

Consequently Ralph White's ability to provide, not only the location of where the Titanic ship was resting on the bottom, but also an item that had been salvaged was of utmost legal importance.

When the MAREX TITANIC, INC. claim to officially arrest the Titanic hit the newspapers all hell broke loose. George Tulloch and Arnie Geller probably had a corporate heart attack because as quickly as they could they filed a claim of their own in the same Norfolk District Court to arrest the RMS Titanic in the name of Titanic Ventures.

I had begged George to arrest the Titanic more than a year earlier so no one could go out and try to recover artifacts for themselves. Now here I was out in the middle of the Atlantic Ocean agreeing to film a Titanic salvage expedition that, if George had listened to me, would never have been.

It took seven days for us to travel on the Sea Mussel from Lisbon to the location of the Titanic site some 380 miles off of Cape Race, Newfoundland. While we were at sea another huge struggle for the Titanic began shaping up. Titanic Ventures literally sat on the steps of the courthouse in Norfolk, doing whatever they could to stop Jack Grimm and Herbo Humphreys from picking up Titanic artifacts in the North Atlantic.

Emotionally I was caught in the middle. I didn't really want to be a part of the Jack Grimm and Herbo Humphreys group that was dedicated to recovering and selling Titanic's artifacts to the highest bidder, but the company I had started—and now held at least some stock in—was refusing to give me my stock or let me participate in any way.

I had arranged for John Joslyn to hire Ralph White in 1987 and even though Ralph and I had known of each other for many years this was the first time we had ever been at sea together. I got to know Ralph pretty well during the MAREX voyage and I also got to know his long-time assistant Jennifer Carter. Many an hour was spent in the Sea Mussel's galley listening to them talk about their previous expeditions together.

Ralph was a great talker. He loved to pontificate for hours about his knowledge of the sea, the sinking of the Titanic, and how he had made more dives on the historic ship than anyone else in the world. Ralph was knowledgeable about the Titanic and he was an excellent marine cinematographer, there was certainly no doubt about that. But endless hours of listening to someone talk about himself can get to be a little tiresome—especially when you're a captive audience.

Ralph White at Sea

However, the many hours of listening to Ralph talk and tell stories about himself and his previous expedition shipmates revealed some very interesting information. Ralph liked to talk about Bob Ballard. He especially liked to talk about the time when he and Emory Kristof from National Geographic were with Ballard when he discovered the Titanic in 1985.

Ralph loved to say how Bob was only interested in glory for himself and how he tried to get Ralph, along with his friend Emory to break into the safe on board the Woods Hole research vessel Knoor to take the map that had the Titanic's location marked on it. He said Bob was determined that no one but Bob would ever get to know the Titanic's exact location.

Ralph made a big thing about how he told Bob to go to hell, as taking that map would be stealing from the U.S. Navy. "If we were ever caught," Ralph lamented strongly, "we'd go to jail for sure!"

I asked Ralph how he found out the Titanic's location if Ballard didn't give it to him. He allowed smugly that when he was in the control room one day with Bob he happened to see the navigation map laying on a table close by that had Titanic's coordinates written on it. Even though the map and coordinates were upside down from where he was standing he quickly made a mental note of the ship's latitude and longitude location.

Ralph also related that when Titanic photographs and videotapes were sent to Halifax, Nova Scotia they were supposed to be distributed among the various members of the world media who were anxiously waiting for the historic materials to arrive. Ralph said that Ballard paid money to a man in Halifax so that when he received the materials he wouldn't share it with the rest of the world media until NBC had broadcast everything first and promoted Bob as the sole discoverer of the Titanic.

I don't know if that's what really happened or not, but I do know that Bob Ballard had a deal with IFREMER in which they had agreed to announce that the discovery of the Titanic had been made jointly by Robert Ballard of Woods Hole and IFREMER in Paris. When NBC shouted from the rooftops that Robert Ballard had found the Titanic, with hardly any mention of any contribution made by IFREMER, the joint venture arrangement between Ballard and IFREMER unraveled.

I know this is true because back in 1986 when I negotiated with Yves Sillard to be the first to dive on the Titanic using IFREMER's submersible Nautile, Yves himself let me know in very strong terms that he wasn't happy with the way things had worked out with Ballard the previous summer.

Learning that Ballard was a huge opportunist wasn't news to me. Emory, Ralph and Ballard were part of the scientific team I had proposed to Jack Grimm in 1979 when the purpose of the mission was to recover artifacts from the Titanic and put them on a world tour. I understood from Emory that's what Ballard planned to do from the very beginning. Ralph White also confirmed that was the case.

I guess that changed when Ballard could only fund his expedition with help from the French and U.S. governments. Using public funds he couldn't recover the artifacts, put them on a world tour and make money personally. He had no choice but to change horses and declare that his goal was and always had been to protect the Titanic's lost souls from grave-robbing salvagers.

It sounded good, and people around the world bought into his holier-than-thou rhetoric. But as far as I'm concerned, what he really wanted to do was keep others off the wreck so he'd have all of it to himself.

In Ballard's book The Discovery of the Titanic he wrote, "at one point, Seaonics was approached by a Texas oil millionaire named Jack Grimm who wanted to back a Titanic expedition. Emory Kristof negotiated with him briefly, but neither of us liked Grimm's style and the negotiations never got far." That wasn't exactly true. I was the one who met with Emory several times, and neither he nor Bob (as far as I was led to believe by Emory) had any objections to my plan of locating the Titanic, recovering her artifacts and putting them on a world tour.

One of the most interesting things I overheard Jennifer Carter and Ralph White talking about one day in the galley during our MAREX voyage was how Ralph obtained his green bottle from off the Titanic.

Jack Grimm and Herbo Humphreys had based their case for arresting the Titanic on Ralph White's claim that he had in his possession several bottles from the Titanic. Ralph told Jack and Herbo that he had secretly collected the bottles for himself, which he wasn't supposed to do, when he was on George Tulloch's 1987 salvage expedition funded by Titanic Ventures. I had no reason to question Ralph's claim when he was telling the story.

But later Jennifer cornered me and told me Ralph was lying about where he got the green bottles. She said she was positive the bottles

Ralph White and Jennifer Carter

came from a Canadian wreck they worked on together the previous summer, as she had one of the green bottles herself.

When we finally arrived at the site where the Titanic was located, MAREX attorneys called us over the ship-to-shore phone and said that we couldn't put the ROV into the water. When we asked why, they told us that George Tulloch and Arnie Geller had filed their own claim to arrest the Titanic. They said the judge in Norfolk had placed an injunction on MAREX forbidding it to salvage any artifacts from the Titanic until the attorneys could argue their case in court.

We were told to wait at the Titanic site for a few days so the high-priced attorneys could sort out the situation. In the meantime, Jack Grimm told the MAREX attorneys about my background with the Titanic project and that I may not be too happy with George Tulloch and Arnie Geller. Jack told them I could probably be persuaded to put, what I knew about Tulloch and Geller in writing, so the attorneys could present whatever I said to the court.

I was asked to write my feeling about Tulloch and Geller before I learned the truth about Ralph White's green "Titanic" bottles. Consequently, at the time, I didn't mind helping out Jack Grimm and doing what I could to help save the MAREX expedition.

IN THE UNITED STATES DISTRICT COURT
FOR THE EASTERN DISTRICT OF VIRGINIA
Norfolk Division

MAREX TITANIC, INC.
a Tennessee Corporation,

     Plaintiff,

v.   CIVIL ACTION NO. 2:92cv618

The wrecked and Abandoned Vessel,
its engines, tackle, apparel,
appurtenances, cargo, etc.,
Located within one (1) nautical
mile of a point located at 41 degrees
43' 32" North Latitude and 49
degrees 56' 49" West Longitude,
believed to be the RMS TITANIC,
in rem,

AFFIDAVIT OF MIKE HARRIS

    The Deponent, Mike Harris being first duly sworn deposes and says:
    My name is Mike Harris. I am an emancipated adult, and I live at 3903 Jamesville Drive, Tampa, Florida 33617.
    I am presently embarked aboard M.V. SEA MUSSEL, a Bermuda flag oceanographic vessel en route to the site of the wrecked and abandoned vessel, its engines, tackle, apparel, appurtenances, cargo, etc., located within one (1) nautical mile of a point at 41 degrees 43' 32" North Latitude and 49 degrees 56' 49' West Longitude, believed to be the RMS TITANIC, on an expedition to salvage artifacts from the wreck.

The 1987 expedition which recovered artifacts from the R.M.S. TITANIC was initiated by me in January/February of that year. I negotiated the initial charter agreement with Robert Chappaz (Taurus), for use of IFREMER's surface vessels, submersible "Nautile" and ROV "Robin". I named the corporation O.R.E. (Oceanic Research and Exploration, Ltd.) and along with Carlos Piaget, a Swiss national, was the original incorporators of

Page One of Mike Harris Affidavit to Court

I sent a two-page statement to the court in Norfolk, whereby I told them the absolute truth about how I started ORE with my Swiss friend Carlos Piaget. I told them how George Tulloch, John Joslyn and Carlos Piaget stole my ownership in

ORE and how I introduced Arnie Geller to George Tulloch but never received a commission I was promised under contract. I also said in my statement that I was eventually awarded stock in Titanic Ventures by the court, but so far had never received it. I knew that what I was telling the court could be damaging to Titanic Ventures, but feeling cheated by both Tulloch and Geller, I figured I had no choice but to just tell the truth and let the chips fall where they may.

 For the next three days the court heard arguments by attorneys for both sides while we continued cruising back and forth in the North Atlantic over the site of the Titanic's sinking.

When the MAREX legal team phoned the Sea Mussel, Nik Petrik and I had our cameras rolling. We wanted to record on film, firsthand, whatever the attorney's reported that the Norfolk judge had ruled. Unfortunately the attorneys reported nothing but bad news. They said the judge had upheld Titanic Venture's injunction. They said MAREX was forbidden from recovering any Titanic artifacts, at least until the matter could be finally resolved in court.

Everybody on the Sea Mussel was stunned. All that time and money and expertise was going down the drain because of Titanic Ventures success at being able to influence the court. I don't know what they said, or how they said it, but it was obvious that George and Arnie's big-shot attorneys were better than the big-shot attorneys working for Grimm and Humphreys.

Everyone on the Sea Mussel was disappointed at not being able to carry out the salvage mission. We were at the site ready to go, but we were ordered by the court to stand down and do nothing.

But I wasn't disappointed in the least. Actually I was secretly relieved. By that time I had found out, thanks to Jennifer Carter, that Ralph White's claim of having green bottles in his possession from the Titanic was phony.

There was a lot of happy talk among MAREX expedition members that as soon as the lawyers did their legal thing we would be allowed to go back out to the Titanic site later in the summer and continue the salvage expedition that had been cut short by the legal maneuvering.

But knowing that Ralph White's claim wasn't true, I didn't share their enthusiasm. I didn't think that Grimm and Herbo should have been allowed to arrest or steal salvage rights to the Titanic for themselves especially when it was based on fraudulent information.

When I got back home I called George (who actually took my call) and told him what I knew about Ralph and his fake Titanic bottles. He never said anything about the affidavit I filed from the Sea Mussel. He immediately became my best friend again and asked if I would write and sign an affidavit for Titanic Ventures telling the court everything I knew about Ralph White's bogus claim. This I was willing to do because, once again, it was the absolute truth.

I don't know if my affidavit was the deciding factor, but I do know that within a few months the judge ruled in favor of Titanic Ventures and against MAREX, who now had no choice but to give up on their fraudulent venture. Meanwhile George Tulloch and Arnie Geller continued with their own legal claim to arrest the Titanic and secure exclusive salvage rights for Titanic Ventures.

24 RMS TITANIC, INC.

On May 4, 1993, George Tulloch and Arnie Geller purchased a shell corporation in Florida called First Response Medical, Inc. They changed its name to RMS Titanic, Inc. and began selling over-the-counter (OTC) Titanic stock shares at eleven dollars each. None of the Titanic Ventures shares had been issued to the Harris Group as George continued to argue that the two-year holdback was still in effect. Consequently we didn't receive any of the new RMS Titanic, Inc. shares that were being sold over-the-counter to the public.

Geller managed to work out an agreement with Titanic Ventures whereby he would receive in excess of 2,000,000 shares for helping form RMS Titanic, Inc. which was now a public company. George threw in extra shares for himself, in addition to the 7,066,000 shares Titanic Ventures stockholders were supposed to receive for contributing the more than 2,000 recovered Titanic artifacts.

I did the math and figured out what 5.04% of Titanic Ventures stock should be worth. When the two-year hold back was no longer in effect (sometime in May 1995) the Harris Group was to receive a little over 350,000 shares. If the stock stayed at $11.00 per share, our ownership would be worth $3,850,000. Not nearly the millions that Arnie and George had penciled in for themselves.

In order to impress the Norfolk court that Titanic Ventures (now doing business as RMS Titanic, Inc.) deserved to be declared Titanic's exclusive salvor in possession, George led another expedition out to the Titanic site and began recovering even more artifacts.

When George went back on the high seas to recover more artifacts, once again, I was not invited to go along. I knew he now considered Titanic to be his project. I'm also sure that he thought if I went along he would probably have to share some of the spotlight with me, which he definitely didn't want to do.

Deep down though, I had long ago given up any hope of having anything to do with the Titanic. So while George was out doing his thing on another Titanic expedition, I was out doing my thing: leading a group of aviation enthusiasts from Texas on another expedition to Bikini Atoll.

Aircraft Carrier Saratoga Sinking at Bikini Atoll

When I led my first expedition to Bikini in the early 1970s and produced my first documentary feature film, *Deadly Fathoms*, we dove on and filmed the famous WWII aircraft carrier Saratoga.

The Texas group saw my film and wanted me to lead them back to Bikini so they could salvage some of the fighter planes that had been knocked off Saratoga's deck into the water during the atom bomb tests.

Although we found several of the planes during dives into Bikini Lagoon, their condition had deteriorated so badly over the years that it wasn't financially prudent to salvage them, much less try to have them restored back to their former glory.

I had a wonderful trip back to Majuro and Bikini and got to get reacquainted with many of my old friends in the Marshall Islands, but the goal of recovering planes and restoring them for aviation collectors around the world could not be met.

Although George's third expedition to recover Titanic artifacts was another big success, there was very little money flowing back into RMS Titanic from the several small artifact exhibitions being held in Oslo and Stockholm. Plus, newspapers continued to run a number of negative articles about various lawsuits that questioned who actually owned the recovered artifacts. Consequently the newly released RMS Titanic, Inc. stock that opened at a respectable $11.00 per share quickly began dropping like a rock.

BayLife Section **F**

The New York Times.

TITANIC SINKS FOUR HOURS AFTER HITTING ICEBERG; 866 RESCUED BY CARPATHIA, PROBABLY 1250 PERISH; ISMAY SAFE, MRS ASTOR MAYBE, NOTED NAMES MISSING

The New York Times of April 16, 1912, reported the sinking dramatically.

German artist Willy Stoewer visualized the sinking, above.

Tribune file photographs

Titanic's grave awaits disturbance

By ROB STEIN
of United Press International

WOODS HOLE, Mass. (UPI) — Seventy-five years after the "unsinkable" Titanic went down in the icy North Atlan-

al.
Among outspoken critics of the French plan is Dr. Robert Ballard, who explored the vessel with robot cameras last year.

"The ship is finally at rest. It's over."

live television next summer and retrieve artifacts.

"This is a scientific project," says Grimm. "Some of the artifacts will be put on display in museums. If we can return

would still stay afloat. The iceberg, however, opened five compartments to the sea.

The Titanic was double-hulled as high as E deck. With five compartments flooded, the weight of sea water pulled E deck

Typical Negative Newspaper Article on Recovering Titanic Artifacts

If a person bought stock OTC the individual who received the stock could buy or sell it on a daily basis. But George Tulloch refused to give any of the Titanic Ventures or Harris Group investors their shares in the public company. None of us were happy. Everyone was shouting for George to give them their stock so they could sell it on the market before it dropped any lower.

But George wouldn't budge. He still claimed he didn't have the authority to issue shares until the two-year, hold back, period was completed. I didn't like the fact that George wouldn't give the Harris Group shares that it was owed, but he obviously wasn't just picking on us. He refused to give RMS Titanic shares to the original Titanic Ventures investors as well.

RMS Titanic publicized the fact that it now owned over 2000 artifacts that had been recovered from the Titanic. Newspaper and magazine articles suggested that the potential value of the recovered artifacts could be as high as fifty million dollars.

The hope was that such publicized claims would keep RMS stock from dropping any farther.

But it didn't seem to help. The RMS Titanic court case to obtain exclusive salvage rights had yet to be settled. And to make matters worse, a British Insurance company that originally said it had insured the Titanic in 1912 filed a claim in court against RMS Titanic demanding a share of the artifacts that had been recovered.

Suddenly it was feared that people would start coming out of the woodwork, all wanting Titanic artifacts that had previously been recovered. With continuing bad publicity and recurring stories speculating about who would eventually end up owning the Titanic artifacts, RMS's OTC stock continued to drop.

Then a miracle happened. RMS Titanic was awarded the exclusive rights to salvage the Titanic by the Norfolk District Court. The Court stated officially that RMS TITANIC was now the official "salvor in possession".

I suppose I played at least some positive roll in the court's decision, since it was my personal testimony that exposed Ralph White's fraudulent claim to the Titanic.

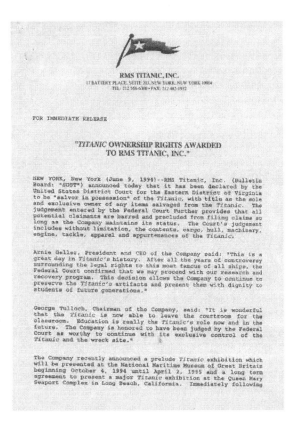

Press Release on Exclusive Salvage Rights

MAREX, Jack Grimm and Ralph White had officially lost, but it still didn't help me get what I believed was legally mine. As far as receiving additional stock, or at least a commission from what Arnie Geller had brought to the table, I received absolutely nothing. Once Arnie and George got what they wanted from me it was back to the same old stonewalling and business as usual.

But I wasn't the only one upset. Bill Gaspirrini, Titanic Ventures' largest stockholder, didn't like the fact that Arnie Geller had taken over the company that he and his friends had helped start with millions of their own money. Geller was running things and the original investors weren't even allowed to hold any of the shares they supposedly owned.

To make matters worse Arnie Geller and George Tulloch assigned millions of additional RMS shares for themselves so that now they owned, on paper at least, more of the company than Gaspirrini and the original Titanic Ventures stockholders.

Gaspirrini was also mad that money was finally being made from exhibiting a portion of the Titanic artifacts in Europe but none of it seemed to be getting back to the States. Geller and Tulloch were having a grand time traveling back and forth to Europe on RMS money while Bill Gaspirrini and the rest of the Titanic shareholders could only cool their heels and wait for their stock.

The problem was there was no confidence that Tulloch and Geller would get around to issuing them any of their shares before the price slid below $5.00.

With RMS Titanic now in full possession of the salvage rights to the Titanic, George used the good news to set up a large exhibition at the Maritime Museum in Greenwich, England.

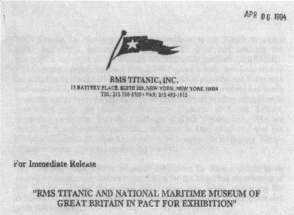

National Maritime Museum Press Release

Record breaking crowds toured the historic exhibit, but again, no money ever trickled back to the States and into the coffers of RMS Titanic.

There was a pretty good reason why no money ever made it into RMS coffers. Almost half of the exhibition money earned had to be paid to the Greenwich museum for exhibiting the artifacts. The other half had to go to attorneys in Connecticut who were still owed more than a million dollars for defending law suits against John Joslyn, the Harris Group and MAREX for salvage rights and the British Insurance company's claim to the artifacts.

As months passed, Bill Gaspirrini wasn't getting any happier and neither was I. The Titanic artifacts were being used to make money but none of the shareholders, including the Harris Group, were seeing any of it. George Tulloch and Arnie Geller continued to fly around the world living off the Titanic and promoting RMS to the media but not a dime was being made for the shareholders back home.

I knew Tulloch didn't want to issue any shares to me or my Harris Group, but I was surprised that he still refused to issue his good friend Bill Garpirrini or any of the other Titanic Ventures shareholders their shares as well. Eventually there was a fight, this time between Bill Gaspirrini and George Tulloch. George's friend and main financial backer finally had enough and was going after him personally.

As Chairman of the Board, Bill figured he could influence enough votes to get Arnie Geller fired and cut him down to "only" 2,000,000 shares. He was also sure he could cut Tulloch down to the shares he was supposed to receive for his original stolen ownership in ORE.

Maritime Museum Greenwich, England

I'm not exactly sure how many extra shares George had penciled in for himself, as I was too far on the outside to know everything that was going on within. In the end, Bill did allow George to remain president, but he put him on a very short leash.

In the summer of 1994 George went on a third expedition—partly to recover more artifacts (although he hadn't put the money up that was necessary to preserve the artifacts recovered the previous year) and partly to help strengthen RMS' standing as official "salvor in possession."

As "salvor in possession" George knew that RMS couldn't just sit on the legal right given them by the court and expect to keep others off the wreck indefinitely. Legally, to protect their exclusive salvage rights, they had to go out at least every other year. George knew the court needed to be convinced that RMS was doing what it needed to do in order to legally maintain its exclusive salvage rights to the Titanic.

George also went out that summer to generate good publicity for himself and the company. He liked the personal adulation he received when asked to conduct newspaper and television interviews, but he didn't relish the personal and corporate criticism that also came his way from the negative press.

Bob Ballard was still out there making waves, along with a few of the original Titanic survivors who considered RMS Titanic to be nothing but grave-robbers. Thank goodness most Titanic survivors didn't feel that way. Most were very supportive of my expeditions in the 1980s, as well as what ORE, Titanic Ventures and RMS Titanic were trying to do.

The stock did bump up a little with the news that RMS Titanic had been given the exclusive salvage rights to the ship. But it didn't take long for the stock to start slipping once again when it became clear that all the money was being spent on the expeditions and law suits and nothing was being made for stockholders.

I still couldn't get my hands on any of the stock the Harris Group had been promised by the court, so I started working almost full time on developing other projects. One was a project I actually started back in the 1980s when I traveled to China four times to meet with Ming historians, trying to learn all I could about their great maritime explorer Admiral Zheng He. In the mid-'80s, at the end of my fourth trip, I presented the Chinese government (through the China Film Co-Production Corporation) with a 100-page report on my research.

Admiral Zheng He, I learned, commanded an incredible fleet of Ming Treasure Ships sixty years before Christopher Columbus discovered America. During February 1995 I traveled to Beijing with my French partner George Grosz who was by then a close friend and also a member of the Harris Group. Within thirty minutes of our arrival at

Zheng He's 430-Foot Long, 9-Masted Treasure Ship

the Beijing Hotel several Russian-made limousines picked us up and took us to the Great Hall of the People on Tiananmen Square where we were met by Wang Guangying, Vice-Chairman of the Standing Committee of the Chinese National People's Congress. Mr.Wang was the third most powerful man in all of China and very interested in helping me develop my project, which I call Silk Dragon.

Zhang Mingzhi, George Grosz, Wang Guangying, Evelyn Harris, Mike Harris, Du Wei

Silk Dragon will be the largest cultural exchange project ever undertaken between China and the West. It involves building two Baochuan Treasure Ships to historical accuracy, filling them with original Ming treasures from China's leading museums and sending them out as floating cultural exhibits, over an eight-year period, to the major coastal cities of the world. The project also involves publishing a book I've written called *Silk Dragon* and producing a feature film that's based on the book.

In 1995 Vice-Chairman Wang said I should travel to Nanjing, the capital of China during the early Ming period, and visit a museum there dedicated to the voyages of Admiral Zheng He. When I got to the museum, the director presented me with a book written totally in Chinese that described the voyages of their famous Ming admiral. It looked interesting but I couldn't read a word of it.

In the back of the book, though, written in Chinese and English was a list of the names of people and the research materials they created the Chinese author used as reference material. Surprisingly, I found my name listed, along with the name of the 100-page report I presented to the Chinese government ten years earlier entitled "Cheng Ho - Eunuch of the Three Jewels". It described the work as "An Original Storyline Idea, Feature Motion Picture Script Outline," that I had presented to China Film Co-Production Corporation in the early 1980s. It also gave my name and listed my address as being from Tampa, Florida.

The museum director seemed quite impressed. It was nice to find my name in the back of that Chinese book on Admiral Zheng He. My 1980's report used the name Cheng Ho, which was the Anglicized version of Zheng He, but it's the same person.

Zhang Mingzhi and Mike Harris at Zheng He Museum

In early 1995 I was keeping busy trying to get Silk Dragon off the ground with my friend George Grosz in Paris. I was also traveling back and forth to Beijing, meeting with Vice-Chairman Wang and officials from China International Culture and Art Center (CICAC). I had hired them to help organize the project and help me set up meetings with the various Chinese officials needed to provide support.

With my attention firmly focused on developing Silk Dragon, I had little time to worry about what George Tulloch and Arnie Geller were doing with the Titanic. In fact, when the two-year hold up was finally lifted on my Titanic stock in May, I didn't call him about the disbursement until I had returned from Paris several weeks later.

Mike Describing Project to Fujian Design in Fuzhou

When I called Tulloch about issuing shares to the Harris Group as he had promised to do in May, it didn't come as a complete shock when he came up with yet another excuse as to why he couldn't release any of the Titanic stock. Even though the District Judge in Norfolk two years earlier had ordered George Tulloch and Titanic Ventures to issue the Harris Group its shares, George continued to find a way to defy the judge's order.

It soon became clear what he was up to. As long as he held the stock in his own name no one could vote him out of his position as president of RMS. He really didn't have to worry about the Harris Group, though, because in our stipulated we allowed George to have our vote.

But with Bill Gaspirrini and the other stockholders it was a different story. George knew they would kick him out of office in a New York minute for the way he had been running the company. They believed he only used the Titanic project for his own personal aggrandizement with little or no thought of making any money for the early Titanic Ventures shareholders who had put up the first money to make it all happen.

But George didn't want to take any chances. I'm sure he figured that if he gave any shares to the Harris Group he would also have to issue shares to Bill Gaspirrini, Arnie Geller, John Joslyn and the other early Titanic Ventures stockholders.

John Joslyn was getting especially itchy, knowing that his lawsuit with Tulloch and Titanic Ventures was still unsettled. Even if George relented in the future and decided to give others their shares, John figured that without his own case officially being settled there was little chance George would settle with him. If he didn't figure out how to break the status quo he might get stuck on the sidelines and never get any of the Titanic shares he thought legitimately should be his.

To make matters worse, with George Tulloch at the helm and nobody able to get any of the shares of RMS stock they were owed, the price drifted down further to less than $3.00 a share. I remember how excited everyone was years earlier when RMS Titanic became a public company and the shares came out with an opening price of $11.00. We believed at the time that RMS Titanic was going to be a terrific investment.

Everyone hated that the stock had dropped all the way from $11.00 down to $3.00 (and looked like it was going to drop even lower), but with George Tulloch controlling everyone's stock, there appeared to be nothing we could do.

Complaining and praying didn't seem to be working. If something wasn't done to change the current situation fast, Joslyn and the other stockholders reasoned among themselves that the RMS Titanic stock wouldn't be worth salvaging.

25 TAKING STOCK

John Joslyn knew that bugging George for his shares of RMS Titanic stock wasn't going to get him anywhere. He figured that being one of the three original members of ORE with Carlos Piaget and George Tulloch, plus his having arranged for the first million dollars in funding from his television contact, he was entitled to more than a million shares. But if George wouldn't give John his shares and he wasn't giving anyone else their shares, he figured he'd better come up with an alternate plan or he might end up with nothing.

About this time in early 1995 Jack Grimm arrived back on the scene. It seems he had sued Joslyn for some of John's shares if and when he would ever get them. Jack claimed that when I called Joslyn back to Paris after Carlos and I were given the funding rights to the Nautile by IFREMER he should have been included. I had called John Joslyn because he seemed to be the only person who had any chance of raising money quickly through his television contacts.

During the summer of 1995, Carlos Piaget was found dead in a rundown motel on the outskirts of Tampa. I hadn't even known he was in town—neither had his ex-wife Sylvanne. Carlos hadn't called anyone. He had long ago worn out his welcome, not only with his few friends in the U.S. but even with his family in Switzerland.

When I found out about Carlos' death I agreed to go to the small funeral service Sylvanne planned. I asked my son Jerry, his friend Mike Robinson in Orlando, plus my close friend Bobby Blanco—all of whom had known Carlos when he lived in Tampa—if they wanted to go and pay their last respects. They all declined saying spitefully that his death couldn't have happened to a more deserving guy. In their minds Carlos was nothing but a crook. He was a liar and they all knew he had cheated me bad. None of them thought that I should go to his funeral either.

But I did go to Carlos' funeral and I was glad that I did. Carlos had once been my friend. We had spent many happy times together in Switzerland and other places around the world. When Evelyn and I were married he arranged for us to have our honeymoon together in his parent's private chalet in Grimentz. That chalet high in the mountains of the Swiss Alps provided a wonderful start to our marriage, which has lasted for forty years.

Usually a person's life is long and a lot of things happen, some of which are good and some bad. Carlos' last years were definitely not good. Maybe because of his drinking he became desperate and felt he had to cheat me just to get by. I went to his funeral because I wanted to remember the good things he had done in his life and the fun times we had had together for many years.

Piaget Maid in Grimintz Chalet

It turned out that I was one of only eight people other than family members and friends of Sylvanne who bothered to show up. Carlos' mother came over from Switzerland along with his son Carlitos. A day after the small gathering they carried Carlos' ashes back to Neuchâtel where he was born and his family still lived.

The death of Carlos Piaget didn't affect the plans of George Tulloch and Arnie Geller one bit. They had already made a cash-settlement with him two years before when they worked out a settlement with me. Unfortunately for him the attorneys got most of the money. What money was left Carlos probably spent on alcohol, which eventually killed him before he reached the age of fifty.

The Titanic exhibit at the Maritime Museum in Greenwich, England was so successful George and the museum management decided to extend the exhibition for another six months.

Mike in Front Yard of the Piaget Chalet

This enabled George to begin paying a few RMS Titanic bills, but there was still no money left that could be distributed to any of the shareholders. Since almost all of the money continued to flow to the attorneys in Connecticut there was little left to pay IFREMER for recovering the Titanic artifacts or for CP3, the new French company that had been hired to preserve the recovered artifacts.

With IFREMER and CP3 getting stiffed for their bills, they got in line to sue Tulloch and RMS Titanic as well. I learned from Yves Cornet at Taurus International in Paris that CP3 had not been paid for previous artifact preservation work they had completed in the past. Consequently when they received the new artifacts from Tulloch's 1994 expedition they just stuck them in buckets of seawater. This created a real danger the artifacts wouldn't be preserved correctly, but would in fact continue to deteriorate.

I also learned from Yves that his long-time partner Robert Chappaz also died recently from some type of blood disease. Robert and I had become friends when I first approached IFREMER back in 1986. When Jack Grimm and John Joslyn lost their contract with IFREMER in 1987 I introduced Robert to Carlos Piaget, which resulted in Robert dropping me and concentrating all his interest on Carlos. Then when Carlos stole my ownership and joined forces with Tulloch and Joslyn, Robert Chappaz got to be Expedition Leader for their first Titanic recovery expedition in 1987. I didn't wish Robert any bad luck—

Evelyn at Piaget Chalet in Winter

and certainly didn't want him to get sick and die—but it is curious that some of those who stabbed me in the back through the years didn't live long enough to enjoy their ill-gotten gains.

Thanks to Yves Cornet I knew of the continuing problems with the preservation of Titanic artifacts and the continuous dropping of RMS Titanic stock, but I was in no position to do anything about any of it. Consequently I made a second trip to Beijing and met with my Chinese friends on Silk Dragon, which was now my primary project.

About this same time, I also led an archaeological expedition to Qumran, Israel, where we tried to discover additional Dead Sea Scrolls. The expedition to Qumran was very interesting. Qumran is an ancient archaeological site that I had visited several times previously with Dr. Jim Strange, recognized as one of the top three Biblical archaeologists in the world. Jim arranged for us to dig on the Qumran plateau where we hoped to find a hidden underground repository for additional clay tablets similar to those found previously in caves close to the Qumran ruins.

Unfortunately no hidden underground cave was found. But when the digging site was being cleaned up Dr. Strange did discover an important clay tablet known as an Ostracon that dated back to the time of Christ. It had nothing to do with the Dead Sea Scrolls, but biblical scholar Hanan Eshel believed Dr. Strange's tablet was probably a letter or deed of some kind.

Dr. Jim Strange

The inscription began, "In the 2nd year, in Jericho, Elazar, son of Nehumia," Unfortunately it was only a fragment so no more of the document could be deciphered. I wished that we could have found a repository for more Dead Sea Scrolls but making at least a small archaeological discovery was better than nothing.

It was now early 1996. I was spending most of my time on my Silk Dragon project in China. I was also spending more and more time in Paris with my French partner George Grosz who traveled with me on a number of trips back and forth to China.

While in Paris one evening I received a phone call from John Joslyn who asked me if I would join forces with him in a lawsuit against George Tulloch. John had figured out that with the percentage of ownership the court had promised to the Harris Group and the percentage of ownership he was supposed to have, when combined, added up to more share ownership than George Tulloch's ownership.

I asked Joslyn about the percentage of ownership that Carlos had owned before he died. He explained that Tulloch had been paying Carlos money on and off for years. He did it to buy Carlos' loyalty but it mostly just supported his bad drinking habit. When our lawsuit was settled in 1993, Carlos received over two hundred thousand dollars, most of which went to his attorneys. John said that from what he understood Carlos ended up with basically nothing and his shares of stock were dissolved by Titanic Ventures. Consequently they no longer exhisted.

I didn't really want to be carrying on a conversation with John Joslyn. He obviously was not one of my favorite people. When he asked me again if I would join forces with him I basically told him to go to hell and reminded him forcefully that he was still the same son of a bitch who cheated me back in 1987.

John didn't want me to hang up on him. He desperately needed my help, so he immediately started to grovel. He acknowledged that what he had done was not right and begged for my forgiveness. He then began giving me a number of lame excuses in a weak attempt to absolve himself.

He was sure that he could make everything up to me if I would just agree to go along with his plan for the two of us to join forces. I remembered what Jim Broughton, my friend in Memphis, had told me years earlier: "Mike, you can't make a good deal with bad people!"

Again, I told John to quit wasting my time. I told him I wasn't interested and hung up the phone. No matter what John Joslyn was pitching, I wasn't buying!

Consequently I continued to concentrate my time on Silk Dragon. As far as I was concerned, with George Tulloch and Arnie Geller in charge of RMS Titanic and refusing to give anyone their stock, the project was doomed to sink just like the infamous ship.

Within a few days my son Jerry, who was a member of my Harris Group, called me in Paris and told me that he had been talking with John Joslyn and Jack Grimm. He said he thought their plan to oust George Tulloch did make a lot of sense. As far as he was concerned joining forces with Joslyn might be the only way the Harris Group would ever get its rightful shares.

I told Jerry that Joslyn didn't say anything to me about Jack Grimm getting into the act. Jerry allowed that since Grimm was suing John they

Jerry Harris with Dad

could maybe patch things up by joining forces with me. I related to Jerry about what I told Joslyn on the phone. He said, "Yeah, I heard you called him a son of a bitch." I told Jerry I should have called him worse than that.

Now it was my son who started begging me to reconsider. I told him not to hold his breath but to give me a little time and I'd think about it.

When I got back to Tampa a few weeks later I consented to go with Jerry to see Fernandez and Muller, our original attorneys who had handled our lawsuit with ORE and Titanic Ventures back in 1987. Their fee was to be 25% of whatever stock we received or $2,000,000 whichever was greater. Since we had never gotten any money or any stock, the attorneys had never received anything.

When Jerry and I presented them with this latest option, Ralph Fernandez told us that we were just wasting our time and we would never get anything from George Tulloch or RMS Titanic. He told us strongly that having anything to do with the Titanic was nothing but a lost cause. Ralph also made it clear he didn't want to spend one nickel or make one phone call to help us get our stock.

We were disappointed, but not particularly surprised. If they wanted to drop us as clients there wasn't anything Jerry or I could do about it.

I immediately got in touch with Bobby Blanco and told him what had happened with his cousin's law firm. He apologized for their not sticking with us, especially now that maybe we had a chance for the situation to turn around. I told him not to worry about it. It wasn't his fault. I tried to put a positive spin on the situation and told him that somehow we'd find another attorney.

Jerry found another attorney who looked at all of our legal paper work and confirmed that it just may be possible to kick George Tulloch out of Titanic Ventures if we joined forces with Joslyn and Grimm. The attorney didn't want to work on a contingency basis, so I said to let me think about it and I'd be back in touch.

I immediately called John Joslyn in California and told him I would consider joining forces with him, but I had a condition. I told him he would have to pay for my attorney fees.

It didn't take long for John to call back and agree to my demand. Within days he hired the Washington, D.C. law firm, Storch and Brenner, who specialized in corporate matters. John told me that Jack Grimm also agreed to step up to the plate and help pay attorney fees both for them and for the Harris Group. Finally, things began moving forward.

Since I was traveling out of the country quite a bit on my China project, and also because I basically didn't want to have anything to do with Joslyn, Tulloch, or Arnie Geller, I asked Jerry to handle all of the legal matters for the Harris Group.

I don't like confrontation. I don't like arguments and I definitely don't like to deal with people who I think are devious and dishonest. My experience with Piaget, Joslyn, Tulloch and Geller had not been favorable. All of them seemed to think nothing at all of shouting threats, cursing and saying whatever they wanted with no regard for the truth.

Jerry had been the business manager of several local and nationally recognized comedians. He seemed to relish the fast life and sometimes-crazy clientele he had become closely involved with for a number of years. I had been around him on several occasions when I heard him shouting at someone on the other end of the phone trying to make a point. It wasn't necessarily my style, but if it worked for him, God bless him. I'm sure he prided himself on being a hard-nosed wheeler-dealer who nobody would or could get the best of.

Since I had no experience or interest in dealing with people like that I told Jerry that if he wanted to get involved with the people running RMS Titanic, then please have at it. But I cautioned him strongly that Joslyn, Tulloch and Geller would probably end up eating him alive. He laughed and told me he was sure I was wrong and to just let him "handle it".

I'm sure one aspect of his bravado was the fact that he wanted to prove to me his dad that he was no longer a kid. He was grown up now and could handle himself in a business situation with the best of them. I'm also sure he figured that Titanic was a major project his dad had started but if he didn't step in and save the day it was also a project his dad might lose.

Consequently with an over abundance of enthusiasm (not to mention a heavy dose of piss-and-vinegar) Jerry jumped in with both feet and quickly got in touch with John Joslyn, Jack Grimm and their attorneys in D.C. While Jerry started banging heads to get our Harris Group stock, I flew back to Paris and once again concentrated on my Silk Dragon project in China.

The first thing Jerry, John Joslyn and Jack Grimm did was have their D.C. law firm, Storch and Brenner, legally shut down Titanic Ventures and RMS Titanic so neither company could operate in any way. I can only imagine what George Tulloch and Arnie Geller must have said when they received the legal documents. Whatever was said it got their attention fast. Within two weeks they had their attorneys in Connecticut talking with the attorneys in D.C. to negotiate some sort of settlement.

Neither George Tulloch nor Arnie Geller liked John Joslyn, and neither thought they could have a meaningful dialogue or negotiate any type of stock settlement with him. I found out later they asked Jerry to act as a mediator between the three of them.

I'm sure Jerry loved every bit of that. He relished the idea of getting right in the middle of all the negotiations between Joslyn, Grimm, RMS Titanic, and their attorneys. I suppose it was because he spoke their language and wasn't intimidated by their noisy shouts and numerous threats. Jerry was, in that regard, an ideal negotiator to help get their legal problem resolved.

George Tulloch was now being assaulted from all sides. His own stockholders wanted to kick him out as president and now outsiders like Jerry were threatening to take over not only his position as president but the entire company as well.

There wasn't much Arnie Geller could do. Bill Gaspirrini had never liked the fact that when Geller came in he and George started running everything together and basically pushed Bill to the side. When Gaspirrini got his back up and started exercising his clout as Chairman of the Board, he cut some of the shares Geller was supposed to receive and made certain most of the control he had was cut as well.

When Arnie was forced out by Bill Garpirrini, George hired a corporate attorney named Alan Carlin to come in and help him run the day-to-day operations. Alan did what he could to help keep RMS on an even keel but with all the law suits swirling around there was little he could do about anything. All the three of them could do at this point was keep their head down and hope the legal storm would somehow pass.

But it didn't pass—and it wasn't about to. Still, George wasn't overly worried. He had paid a lot of money over the years to his Connecticut attorneys. He figured that somehow they were smart enough to hold off the takeover threat from John Joslyn, Jack Grimm and the Harris Group.

As long as George continued to hold all the stock in his own hands he didn't think anyone could gather enough votes together to challenge his control. There were, of course, public shares being sold on the open market, but no one person owned very many. As long as George kept his immediate detractors at bay, I'm sure he figured he could hold his position as president and everything else would be fine.

But he knew his friend Bill Gaspirrini owned—at least on paper—more stock than anyone else. He also knew he'd better start doing something quick to show Bill and the other local stockholders he was capable of getting RMS Titanic on a sound financial footing so the stock would start going up.

What George decided to do was go back out on another expedition. Not just "another expedition," but a larger-than-life, blockbuster expedition. If he could do that he reasoned that people would stop trying to kick him out of the job he loved and cherished more than anything else in the world. Maybe Gaspirrini would even cut him a little slack. Maybe with money in the bank he could actually start feeling secure enough to release stock to those that had been hounding him for so many years.

But first he had to resolve his immediate problem. Joslyn, Grimm and the Harris Group had him tied up in court and he could do absolutely nothing. So he called Jerry with a suggestion. He told Jerry that it was counterproductive for RMS to be shut down so they could do nothing, and that to keep their exclusive salvage rights to the Titanic they needed to go back out to the site that summer and recover more artifacts. George asked Jerry if he would negotiate a compromise on their legal shutdown so that RMS Titanic could conduct a forth expedition to the North Atlantic.

Jerry knew that what George was saying was true. RMS Titanic did need to carry out salvage work at the Titanic site in order to safeguard its exclusive salvage rights. Jerry also knew that it would be counterproductive for Joslyn and Grimm to stop Tulloch from carrying out a salvage activity that could possibly affect RMS' bottom line. Everyone wanted to get their RMS stock in hand and when they did, they wanted the stock to be worth something.

Jerry helped work out a compromise so that RMS Titanic could go out on another expedition that summer. Jerry and George quickly became new "best" friends. But George didn't waste too much time on trying to be friendly. He quickly began concentrating on organizing his new blockbuster expedition that would not only start making money for RMS, but would also begin to ingratiate himself with RMS' chairman Bill Gaspirrini. He chafed at his short leash and figured that a successful blockbuster expedition would be a cure to all of his personal and corporate ills.

George's blockbuster expedition wasn't going to go out to the Titanic site with just one ship and pick up a few artifacts. He had done that several times in the past and it was getting to be old news. The "excitement" had worn off just picking up artifacts. Their recovery didn't generate the same amount of publicity for the company and shareholders as they once did.

What George wanted to do this time was hire two passenger ships to go along on the expedition, fill them with paying customers who wanted to be present on the site in the middle of the North Atlantic as Titanic artifacts were being recovered. George heavily promoted the fact that on this historic expedition a large section of Titanic's hull would be salvaged from the wreck, brought back to the surface and returned triumphantly to New York, the historic ship's destination in 1912. Certainly with two passenger ships close by watching the recovery operation on closed circuit television the expedition would generate a lot of new publicity not only in the U.S. but around the world as well.

George was certain that such a heavily promoted stunt would again generate a lot of interest in the Titanic which in turn would help buoy the stock of RMS Titanic which by now had sunk to a price below $3.00 per share.

George's blockbuster expedition and Titanic hull recovery plan did get a lot of publicity. He was even able to get the Discovery Channel involved. They sent out a production crew and filmed the entire adventure. The large piece of Titanic's hull they recovered made it all the way up to the surface, but because of its tremendous weight—and the fact that not enough lifting bags were attached—it dropped back to the bottom of the ocean more than 12,000 feet below.

Luckily for George, the IFREMER team had enough experience and foresight to attach a communication beacon to the large metal section so that if it did drop back to the bottom they could easily locate it again on a subsequent expedition.

Even though the Discovery Channel's television program made pretty good ratings and generated publicity for George Tulloch as expedition leader, the price per share for RMS Titanic stock refused to budge over $3.00.

Several months after the expedition Jerry got back in touch with me and said that, although George and he had developed a pretty good working relationship, George was beginning to complain that Jerry didn't have the legal right or authority to negotiate on behalf of the Harris Group because he was not a major shareholder of the group.

Jerry said it would help his credibility if I would get the other members of the Harris Group—Bobby Blanco, George Grosz and Mike Robinson—to sign a special agreement with him whereby 41.67% ownership in the Harris Group would be assigned to him, 41.67% to me and 5.56% ownership to each of the other three members. In addition Jerry said that he also needed to be named as the official Trustee of our Group. He assured me that he would give us a letter stating that he would give each member of the Harris Group our correct ownership amount once he was able to get the RMS Titanic stock in hand.

On my assurance to George, Bobby and Mike that Jerry would indeed honor the original ownership commitment we signed together in the Harris Group, we all signed the new document Jerry presented to us on March 1, 1996, and returned it to him for his use in negotiating with Tulloch.

I made another trip to China during the summer of 1996 and quietly hoped Jerry would be able to "do his thing" and somehow come up with a miracle. But unbeknownst to me at the time there was another problem, already at full boil, between John Joslyn and George Tulloch.

When Tulloch went out on his fourth expedition during the summer, John Joslyn had made a deal with NBC to also go out on an expedition to the Titanic site and produce a show for their television network. John, of course, hadn't said anything to George about what he was planning to do.

When Tulloch found out, he was furious. He went back to court and filed an injunction to stop John from going out on the site. George had plenty of experience in filing injunctions to keep people off the Titanic site because that's what he did when he stopped Jack Grimm and Herbo Humphreys from using an ROV back in 1992.

This made Joslyn even more furious at Tulloch because he had already received $600,000 from NBC as an advance payment on the program he was supposed to produce for them. Now with Tulloch's injunction keeping him from diving on the Titanic there was no way he could make the promised television show for NBC.

Tulloch could care less that he had caused problems for Joslyn, as he was part of the group that was trying to shut him down and take the company away from him. If George could do something to make Joslyn's life miserable, then so much the better.

Another incident that fueled Joslyn's anger was the fact that he knew Tulloch had allowed a Hollywood producer named James Cameron to go out to the Titanic site earlier that same summer so he could shoot some underwater footage. Tulloch knew that Cameron was a famous Hollywood producer and also knew he had a studio commitment for $100,000,000 to produce a major film he was going to call *Titanic*. The excitement Cameron's film was sure to create, George reasoned, could only help the sale of RMS Titanic stock and the Titanic artifacts it was now exhibiting.

George was under no illusion that Joslyn's NBC television show would create any such popular interest. Probably for that reason—plus his overall personal disdain for his former partner—he had no qualms about shutting down Joslyn's proposed television production with NBC. NBC now threatened to sue Joslyn for non-performance and there wasn't one thing he could do about it!

During this same period Jerry began spending more and more time out in California at Joslyn's company Blackhawk Television in Burbank. Since they were both spending time together, trying to negotiate a stock settlement with Tulloch, they decided they might as well try to make a little extra money together as well working on another project that involved Titanic.

Jerry got in touch with Anatoly Sagalavitch, Director of the P.P. Shirshov Institute of Oceanology at the Russian Academy of Sciences in Moscow. He sold Anatoly on the idea of taking a select group of V.I.P. passengers down to the Titanic in the Institutes deep diving submersibles, Mir 1 and Mir 2. Jerry and Joslyn could make money and the P.P. Shirshov Institute could also make money by renting out the use of their two submersibles.

The plan was simple. Jerry and Joslyn would try to attract wealthy individuals who wanted to dive on the Titanic and be an eyewitness to a part of history. The promotional sheet they created is as follows:

"VIP PRESS RELEASE - DIVE THE TITANIC

Los Angeles-based Blackhawk Television has secured an exclusive agreement with Moscow's prestigious P.P. Shirshov Institute of Oceanology to charter the Russian vessel Akademic Keldysh. The Keldysh, a 402-foot research vessel, is uniquely equipped for deep submersible exploration. Our destination is 2.5 miles below the unforgiving waters of the North Atlantic Ocean. In teams of three, we will dive to the final resting place of the legendary RMS Titanic.

A limited number of V.I.P.s will participate in this adventure of a lifetime and join our dive teams in three-man deep submersibles. Our V.I.P.s will in no way be disclosed in any related filming of the project, as identities will be held in the strictest confidence.

Be advised that the Keldysh is a working research vessel, not the Love Boat. The dive will be a once in a lifetime experience, but not a guided tour. Every dive remains a working dive with all vehicle exterior lights and cameras functioning while exploring new areas of the Titanic wreck yet unseen by anyone."

They did snag Hollywood producer/director Oliver Stone, who paid $50,000 for the privilege of diving on the historic wreck with his son. But they had to give him his money back when Tulloch put a stop, not only to his television show with NBC, but also to taking V.I.P's down to the Titanic in the two Russian submersibles Mir 1 and Mir 2.

Since things didn't work out with their V.I.P. dive promotion, Jerry began to concentrate once again on getting Joslyn and Tulloch to settle their lawsuits and end their long-running acrimonious relationship. Joslyn, unfortunately, was still so mad at Tulloch for giving him unwanted grief with NBC he refused to talk with him directly. As before Jerry was used as a middleman between the two combatants to see if something couldn't be worked out between them.

Jerry told Tulloch that he would bring Joslyn to the table but he wanted as consideration extra shares for the Harris Group. Jerry confided to me later there was a lot of yelling and cursing and threatening going on back and forth but in the end, George did agreed to settle with Joslyn and also to give Jerry and the Harris Group an additional 80,000 shares for mediating the deal. So instead of the 350,000 shares our group was to receive, we would get 80,000 more shares for a total of 430,000.

When Jerry proudly explained to me what he had pulled off, I could hardly believe it. I thanked him profusely for doing such a good job and let him know that I thought what he did was nothing short of a miracle. I also told him he should keep the extra 80,000 shares for himself because he had brokered the deal on behalf of the Harris Group and had earned them.

He said cheerily that he didn't want the 80,000 shares for himself and would let me know when the closing was supposed to take place, probably at the office of Tulloch's attorneys in Bridgeport, Connecticut.

In the middle of December 1996, Jerry called me in China to tell me the good news. He said that the deal was done and that I'd better get home as soon as possible to sign the papers.

I jumped on the first flight I could find and managed to arrive in Connecticut just in time to sign final papers at Tulloch's law firm. While Jerry

VIP PRE-PRESS RELEASE
DIVE THE *TITANIC*

Los Angeles-based Blackhawk Television has secured an exclusive agreement with Moscow's prestigious P.P. Shirshov Institute of Oceanology to charter the Russian vessel *Akademic Keldysh*. The *Keldysh*, a 402 foot research vessel, is uniquely equipped for deep submersible exploration. Our destination: 2.5 miles below the unforgiving waters of the North Atlantic Ocean. In teams of three, we will dive to the final resting place of the legendary RMS *Titanic*.

A limited number of V.I.P.'s will participate in this adventure of a lifetime and join our dive teams in three-man deep sea submersibles. Our V.I.P.'s will in no way be disclosed in any related filming of the project, as identities will be held in the strictest confidence.

Be advised that the *Keldysh* is a working research vessel, not the Love Boat. The dive will be a once in a lifetime experience, but not a guided tour. Every dive remains a working dive with all vehicle exterior lights and cameras functioning while exploring new areas of the Titanic wreck yet unseen by anyone.

For further information, please contact G. Michael Harris at (818)238-0015.

BLACKHAWK TELEVISION
4444 Riverside Drive Suite 202 Burbank, CA 91505
(818) 238-0015 FAX (818) 238-0016

Blackhawk Television VIP Pre-Press Release

and I were flying back to Tampa together with RMS corporate stock finally in our hands Jerry pointed out to me a very interesting fact. He remembered that it was the middle of December 1986 almost ten years to the day, when Carlos Piaget and I got together on the Titanic project and planned our first trip to Paris to get it funded.

Who would have thought it would take ten long years of problems and heartache to get ORE formed and funded, only to have it taken away from me by Piaget, Tulloch, Joslyn, and eventually Geller. But now, ten years later, I was finally getting something for all my effort.

Exhausted from returning on a long flight from Beijing and the quick meeting in Bridgeport with Tulloch and his attorneys, I fell asleep on the two hour flight back to Tampa. In my hand were two RMS Titanic certificates worth 215,000 shares. My son Jerry sitting next to me also had two RMS Titanic certificates in his hand worth another 215,000 shares. When we got home the shares would be divided up with the other members of the Harris Group as we had previously agreed and my Titanic struggle for the Titanic would finally come to an end.

With my Titanic struggle behind me, another wonderful adventure was about to open up, not for me this time, but for my son Jerry and his son, Sebastian. I had been a member of The Explorer's Club of New York for many years. Now my son and grandson were going to be members as well.

26 A NEW GENERATION

With the seemingly breath of fresh air now blowing through RMS Titanic several positive things started happening all at once. George put together a new Board of Directors consisting of Allan Carlin, Curt Hawthorne (one of the early TVLP partners), Arnie Geller, my son Jerry (now going by his preferred name, G. Michael) and himself. G. Michael was delighted at his new status as an official Director of RMS Titanic.

He told me that being a Director in RMS TITANIC and a serious stockholder would allow him to accomplish what he and John Joslyn were now working on together. Through Joslyn's contact with SFX Entertainment, a huge entertainment company in New York City, G. Michael said that he and Joslyn wanted to develop a Titanic exhibit of their own in Orlando, which they would call "Titanic: Ship of Dreams".

When I asked him if they were going to be able to exhibit any of the artifacts that had been recovered, he wasn't sure. He said they would still need to get permission from George Tulloch and the other RMS Directors but now that he was one of the Directors he thought he could find a way to swing it.

It turned out that my industrious son and Joslyn had another card up their sleeve. They planned to introduce George Tulloch to SFX Entertainment. SFX had the experience necessary to manage and exhibit the recovered Titanic artifacts anywhere in the world. Under Tulloch and Geller's management the artifacts had only been exhibited at a few venues in Europe. This was largely due to the fact that they still owed money to IFREMER and the preservation companies, who wouldn't allow the artifacts to be removed from France before they were paid in full.

But now with the fresh wind blowing through RMS, the opportunity to finally make some real money with the Titanic artifacts just might become a reality.

G. Michael told me that he wanted my early expeditions to be featured in the "Ship of Dreams" exhibition. I was a little skeptical, as I didn't understand the vision he had in mind. But G. Michael knew he had my interest so he quickly began regaling me with visual pictures of how their "Ship of Dreams" exhibition would be different from the bland Titanic exhibitions that Tulloch and Geller had promoted in the past.

He said their exhibit would feature the Titanic's grand staircase, which would be constructed entirely out of wood to its original specifications. Tulloch and Geller, he pointed out, only exhibited a large photograph of the staircase in their European exhibition venues.

He then went on to explain how his "Ship of Dreams" exhibit would employ actors in period costumes who would walk around the exhibit and interact with customers. One actor would play the part of Edward John Smith, Captain of the Titanic, while he strolled through the exhibit informing customers about his magnificent ship. Other actors would recreate what it was like working on the Titanic as a laborer at Harlan and Wolf Shipyard in 1912. Still others would interact with customers as they played the part of a First Class, Second Class or Third Class passenger enjoying their voyage to New York in 1912.

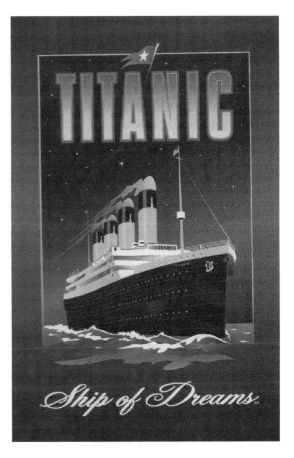

"But that isn't all that would be different!" G.Michael exclaimed proudly as he grew more and more excited explaining what he and Joslyn were planning. Their "Ship of Dreams" exhibit would feature a real iceberg so customers touring the exhibit could reach out and actually touch a large chunk of ice similar to one that sunk the famous ship.

Another clever innovation he explained was letting people stand at the rail of the Titanic and look out into the starry night sky just as passengers experienced that fateful night when she hit the iceberg in 1912. G. Michael said they planned to refrigerate one gallery so that the temperature would remain in the low 30's as customers shuffled through. Customers could lean on an exact recreation of the Titanic's rail and gaze out into the cold night sky as computer generated

Titanic: Ship of Dreams Exhibit Poster

Illumination would recreate the night sky exactly as it was on April 14, 1912.

I had to admit that their proposed exhibit sounded like nothing I had ever heard of or imagined before. It they could pull it off, it would be a grand exhibit indeed. But to get me really excited he went back to explaining that Tulloch and Geller had never given me the recognition I deserved for leading the first Titanic expeditions in the early 1980s. They also never gave me any recognition for being the person who founded ORE, which eventually became their public entity RMS Titanic.

I told G. Michael that was true then asked him how he intended to change what had happened in the past. He explained that he wanted to sell my two films *Search for the Titanic* and *Return to the Titanic* in the exhibit gift shop in Orlando. He also wanted to display my 1980 Expedition Jacket along with photographs of me during my early exhibitions.

I then asked him about the note I owned that came from one of the persons who was actually on the Titanic when she sank. "Don't you want to exhibit that?" Taking my cue he said that he definitely wanted to exhibit my Titanic note and allowed that my note was just as valuable as any of the other Titanic artifacts that had been recovered to date.

While G. Michael and Joslyn were trying to develop their Titanic exhibit in Orlando George Tulloch began trying to promote the sale of coal that had been salvaged at the Titanic site as a historic souvenir. He couldn't sell any of the Titanic artifacts to make money. Selling artifacts was still prohibited from the agreement I originally negotiated with IFREMER back in 1986. But with the publicity the coal sale generated, coupled with magazine and newspaper exposure from the production of Jim Cameron's blockbuster Titanic film, interest in anything Titanic increased and RMS' stock began to be more valuable.

Meanwhile, I flew to London to meet with the management of Inchcape Shipping Service, the largest ship services company in the world. I needed to sell them on providing ship services for the two Baochuan Treasure Ships I planned to build and put on world tour as part of my now developing Silk Dragon project.

George Grosz met me at Waterloo Station when I arrived on Eurostar, the super fast train service that travels daily under the English Channel from Paris to London. While George and I worked together on my China Project in Paris, the bloom was coming off the rose back in Connecticut.

George continued to run RMS Titanic as his own personal company. Even Arnie Geller who had backed George and made it possible for him to start exhibiting Titanic artifacts, not to mention his help in making Titanic Ventures a public company, became more and more disgusted when he realized that he didn't have the authority that RMS' attorney Allan Carlin now enjoyed. It was George and Allan who were calling the shots, not George and Arnie.

With unrest becoming pervasive throughout RMS, G. Michael and Joslyn began trying to see if they could orchestrate the current corporate situation to their mutual benefit. It was no secret that people like Arnie Geller and Bill Gaspirrini were no longer enamored with George Tulloch. Consequently my son and Joslyn began exploring how they might gather enough votes to kick George out of RMS and not be bothered by him once and for all.

The only way they could do that, of course, was to find a way to control more RMS Titanic votes than George Tulloch. If they found the votes, they decided, they would ask Bill Gaspirrini to call a special stockholders meeting and try to vote him out as president. It wouldn't be easy. George controlled a lot of shares. But it also wasn't an impossible amount of shares that couldn't be overcome.

G. Michael and Joslyn began getting in touch with disgruntled stockholders who were upset over the way George was running the company. Hopefully they'd be able to talk them into joining forces so they could remove George as president of RMS.

They knew Arnie Geller controlled some 2,000,000 shares and Bill Gaspirrini another 2,000,000. Between Joslyn and the Harris Group, another 1,000,000 shares could be cobbled together. But Tulloch controlled over 7,000,000 shares which was the original amount given to Titanic Ventures Limited Partnership when it was taken over by RMS. G. Michael and John knew they had to come up with more than 7,000,000 shares if they were going to be able to legally vote George Tulloch out as president and take over the operation of RMS Titanic for themselves.

While all the behind-the-scenes negotiations were going on to search for RMS Titanic votes, a play about the sinking of the Titanic opened on Broadway in New York City. It opened on April 10, 1997, almost 85 years to the day from when Titanic sank in 1912. It was an immediate success and started generating publicity again for anything and everything Titanic.

About the same time, James Cameron's *Titanic* was also taking shape and generating publicity around the world. There was talk in magazines and newspapers about how Cameron was having a tough time cutting his Titanic film down to a viewable length and how much he had gone over budget. In any case, the buzz that surrounded Cameron's film only helped fuel growing expectations about its scheduled release later in the year.

To take advantage of this upsurge in Titanic publicity, George Tulloch decided that what he should do is go back out to the Titanic site on another expedition and try to recover the large piece of Titanic's hull that was unceremoniously dropped to the bottom the previous summer.

James Cameron's Titanic Film in Production

He got back in touch with Anatoly Sagalevich of the Shershov Institute in Russia and arranged to once again lease the two deep submersibles Mir 1 and Mir 2 for the summer's proposed expedition.

When George went out to recover the large piece of Titanic's hull the expedition was covered extensively by The Discovery Channel. On October 13, 1997, they broadcast "TITANIC: The Investigation Begins" which again was able to generate a large audience and excellent reviews. George, of course, was delighted as the salvage program once again promoted him as Expedition Leader and president of RMS Titanic.

While George was busy in the North Atlantic I made a trip to Guangzhou, not far from Hong Kong on the southern coast of China. I visited the large shipyard there to talk with them about building the two Baochuan Treasure Ships I wanted to build for my Silk Dragon project. I had previously visited a shipyard in Shanghai and now wanted to see what Guangzhou had to offer. The cost to build two Ming Treasure Ships to historical accuracy would not be easy and it wouldn't be cheap. Ming experts estimated the total cost for building my two tall treasure ships would be a little over $30,000,000.

G. Michael was now working full time in Orlando trying to get his "Ship of Dreams" exhibition opened before the end of the year. John Joslyn visited Orlando from time to time from his office in Burbank, but it was my son who was mostly in charge of getting their exhibit designed, built and up and running.

Titanic: Ship of Dreams Grand Staircase Gallery

Sometime in July 1998 John Gao Productions, a film production company in London, decided they wanted to produce a television show on the Titanic. They came to my home in Tampa with a small film team and interviewed me while I told them about my expeditions in the early 1980s. They paid me a little money for my appearance in their film and also paid to use some of the film footage from my 1980 and 1981 expeditions.

G. Michael and Joslyn signed a contract with SFX Entertainment earlier in the year and were now working closely with them to get "Titanic: Ship of Dreams" opened in Orlando by Thanksgiving. I, too, began working closely with them, at least on my portion of the exhibit. My photos, motion picture poster, 1980 expedition jacket and personal note from Jack Steward all had to be framed and professionally prepared for inclusion in the Orlando exhibit.

There was one glaring problem though that G. Michael and Joslyn had to face. Their "Ship of Dreams" exhibit featured many wonderful things like Titanic's rebuilt grand staircase, Verandah Café, recreated first, second and third class cabins and actors who moved among the paying customers recounting what it was like to be on the unsinkable Titanic during her maiden voyage.

Titanic: Ship of Dreams Verandah Café Gallery

But the exhibit didn't feature any artifacts that had been salvaged from the Titanic. A few collectors provided a Titanic deck chair, life preserver, clothing, and other objects, but they weren't able to show any actual artifacts that had been recovered.

The problem of course was George Tulloch and RMS Titanic. They refused to allow G. Michael or Joslyn to exhibit any of the recovered treasures. The two entrepreneurs rationalized their exhibit would be successful without them but there was no getting around the fact that a Titanic exhibit definitely needed to exhibit Titanic artifacts.

Titanic: Ship of Dreams Harland and Wolff Gallery

Titanic: Ship of Dreams Boarding Gallery

When the big day arrived for their Grand Opening, executives from SFX Entertainment came to Orlando, as did Gloria Stuart who played Rose DeWitt-Bukater in James Cameron's hugely successful film *Titanic*. It was a wonderful celebration with plenty of rousing Irish music, champagne and food.

Titanic: Ship of Dreams Expedition Gallery

Through their association with SFX Entertainment, G. Michael and Joslyn had the good fortune to meet a gentleman named Joe Marsh. Joe was president and owner of a company called Magicworks in Cleveland and represented, among others, the celebrated magician David Copperfield. SFX had recently bought out Joe Marsh and his Magicworks Company for quite a bit of money. Consequently Joe was looking around for something else to get into that might be not only interesting, but profitable as well.

When my son and Joslyn told Joe Marsh about the recovered artifacts that RMS Titanic owned and the potential money that could be made from exhibiting them around the world, the entrepreneur began thinking that maybe getting involved in RMS wouldn't be such a bad idea. Then G. Michael and Joslyn explained to Joe that their exhibit would be a lot better if they were able to exhibit some of the recovered artifacts. Unfortunately they couldn't, they told Joe, because George Tulloch wouldn't let them have any artifacts.

Joe, at first, wasn't sure what any of that had to do with him. But then they began explaining to him about their plan to take over the company. They suggested that if he would purchase shares of SOST (the stock symbol for RMS Titanic, which combined the Morse Code distress signal SOS and the name Titanic) on the open market, then maybe, with the other shares they controlled they would be able to gather enough shares together to legally vote out George Tulloch as president and take over RMS Titanic.

Titanic: Ship of Dreams Deck Chair

Once they had control of RMS they could run the company better than George Tulloch, plus they could also release some of the artifacts for their exhibit in Orlando. It would be a win-win situation for everyone.

G. Michael and John did everything they could to convince Joe that George Tulloch was nothing but a used car salesman from Connecticut and didn't know how to properly promote the artifacts that had already been recovered.

With Joe Marsh's help they emphasized and his experience as a successful marketer, millions could be made from the exhibitions, not to mention the potential run up of the RMS stock.

Joe must have bought what G. Michael and Joslyn were selling because he and several of his friends began purchasing small blocks of SOST stock on the open market. They didn't purchase large amount of shares all at once as they didn't want to alert George Tulloch or Allan Carlin that someone was accumulating large ownership blocks of shares in the corporation.

In January of 1999 while all this surreptitious buying of stock in RMS was going on, I went back to London and signed an agreement with Inchcape Ship Services. Inchcape agreed to supervise the construction of my two Baochuan Treasure Ships and handle all ship services for the two Ming vessels while they were docked at the major coastal cities of the world. Having Inchcape locked into my Silk Dragon project was, for me, a very big deal. I had already secured full cooperation from high-ranking officials of the Chinese government. Now all I needed to do was sign a contract with my good friend Jim Broughton in St. Petersburg to handle the exhibition part of the project and I'd be set!

Jim Broughton

Jim is recognized as one of the leading exhibitors of museum artifacts in the world. He has received critical acclaim for his "Rameses" and "Napoleon" exhibitions in Memphis, his "Treasures of the Tzars" and "Splendors of Ancient Egypt" exhibitions in St. Petersburg, and his "Nicholas and Alexandra," "Treasures of Imperial Japan" and "Faberge" exhibitions in Wilmingon, Deleware. I had no doubt that a contract with Broughton Productions would go a long way toward helping me get my Chinese project up and running.

In February G. Michael and Joslyn's "Ship of Dreams" exhibition in Orlando was open for business and pulling in crowds but not the huge numbers they envisioned. It was a struggle to pull tourists away from Sea World and Disney especially when word got out that even though their exhibit was professionally done and quite unique it still did not feature any artifacts that had been recovered from the Titanic.

Titanic: Ship of Dreams First Class Gallery

On February 12, G. Michael, Joslyn and Joe Marsh formed the Titanic Acquisition Group or TAG for short and began trying to line up shares they would need to complete their hostile takeover of RMS.

In August of 1999 I signed a contract with Broughton Productions to be the official Director of Exhibitions for my Silk Dragon project. About the same time my son attended a meeting of RMS stockholders at the corporate headquarters in New York. Directors nominated were George Tulloch, Allan H. Carlin, Arnie Geller, Gerald Michael Harris, Kurt Hothorn and Paul-Henri Norgelet. George Tulloch was again elected president of RMS and Allan Carlin secretary. There was no hint of the widespread discontent boiling beneath the surface or the secret continuous search for additional votes.

Even though there was an underground swell to get rid of Tulloch, things seemed to be going better for the embattled company president. By now thanks largely to Jerry and Joslyn's previous introduction, George was able to negotiate a contract with SFX Entertainment whereby SFX would have the exclusive right to exhibit Titanic artifacts for twelve months in exchange for a multi-million dollar annual fee.

An arrangement was also worked out whereby SFX and RMS would allow a few Titanic artifacts to be exhibited at my son and Joslyn's "Ship of Dreams" exhibition in Orlando. They would have to give up 20% of the net profits to RMS but it did give their exhibit a lot more credibility being able to exhibit artifacts that actually came off the Titanic and recovered by RMS.

At the end of November, on Thanksgiving evening, Jerry, Joslyn and Arnie Geller figured they had enough shares of stock that they could make a hostile takeover of RMS Titanic. In the dead of night they went to RMS Titanic headquarters at Battery Place in New York City and broke into the corporate offices. They quickly changed the locks on the front door so Tulloch or Allan Carlin couldn't get back in Monday morning even if they wanted to.

Titanic: Ship of Dreams Bridge

When police arrived to see what was going on they told them they were engaged in a hostile takeover, then showed them legal paperwork their attorneys had prepared which proved what they were saying was true.

Since it was a long holiday weekend, G. Michael, Joslyn and Geller had plenty of time to confiscate all the company computers and go through all the corporate files. They were anxious to figure out how Tulloch and Carlin had been able to run RMS Titanic for so many years without making a profit.

When Tulloch and Carlin arrived back at the offices after the Thanksgiving holiday, they were surprised to find out they couldn't get in their own front door. When they called the building superintendent and asked him why their office keys wouldn't work, they both almost went into cardiac arrest when they learned what had happened.

When they did let them in, G. MIchael, Joslyn and Geller told them they were no longer in charge. Their personal items had already been placed into individual cardboard boxes that they unceremoniously handed to them as they said "goodbye".

Tulloch and Carlin didn't just walk to their attorney's office, they ran. But my son, Joslyn and Geller had done their legal homework. There wasn't anything the previous management could do except try to negotiate a buyout of some kind which they did. I'm not exactly sure what Tulloch and Carlin received but I do know that between them they received several millions of dollars, which I thought was more than generous.

It certainly was a whole lot more generous than what I received. It seemed that everyone I brought into the Titanic project was now making more off the project than me, but I had no complaints. My son G. Michael, who was instrumental in spearheading the hostile takeover, was named RMS' new Chairman of the Board. As his father, I couldn't have been prouder.

A lot of "takeover news" was generated in most of the major newspapers around the country that was not bad for RMS' stock. The stories featured statements from my son, the new Chairman and Arnie, the new President, about how it was a new day at RMS Titanic.

One of the first things G. Michael and Arnie did was publicize the exhibition contract RMS had with SFX Entertainment and started promoting heavily that a major exhibition was going to open in early 2000 at the Museum of Science and Industry on Lake Michigan in downtown Chicago. Newspaper and magazine articles let everyone know that RMS, in association with SFX, was going to present a major Titanic exhibition of never-before-seen recovered artifacts. As an added feature, they exclaimed, the huge piece of Titanic's hull that was brought to the surface and recovered in 1999 would become a major focal point of the Chicago exhibition.

At this point in my son's life he was flying high. Not only was he co-owner of a Titanic exhibition in Orlando, Florida that was doing well, he was now Chairman of the Board of RMS Titanic, Inc., a successful New York company that owned more than $50,000,000 in recovered Titanic artifacts. RMS had a multi-year contract with SFX Entertainment in New York so that annual income to RMS Titanic was almost assured.

Things for my son were going good, no doubt about that, but soon they were going to get even better.

Titanic: Ship of Dreams Engine Room Gallery

Titanic: Ship of Dreams Cargo Galley

27 CONCLUSION

As I mentioned previously, my son wanted to go by the name G. Michael and drop the name his mother and I had given to him at his birth. Now that he was on his own it didn't really matter to me that he preferred going by the name G. Michael. I was just happy that things were turning out so well for him. He was now busy getting ready for the major Titanic exhibition in Chicago. Plus he wanted me to work with him on organizing another Titanic artifact recovery expedition that was scheduled for the summer.

I had let some of my old contacts know what had transpired with RMS Titanic. I also let them know that my son was now the new RMS Board Chairman. Many of them had seen the publicity about the takeover and seemed genuinely happy about the way everything had turned out.

G. Michael suggested I get in touch with Anatoly Sagalevich at the Shirshov Institute to invite him to the Grand Opening of the Chicago exhibition. The idea was to finalize negotiations with Anatoly for the use of his two submersibles Mir 1 and Mir 2 in the summer's proposed new salvage expedition.

When Anatoly arrived for the exhibit I met him at the hotel and proudly showed him around the very impressive looking Titanic exhibit. The professional designers and exhibitors who worked for SFX really knew how to put together a dramatic looking exhibition.

Anatoly said he was well aware of my early contribution to the Titanic project and said it would be an honor for him to personally be in charge of the Mir submersible that carried me down to the Titanic during the 2000 expedition. I thanked him profusely and let him know how much of an honor it would be for me to have him be the pilot of Mir on my very first dive to the Titanic.

Before I ever led my first Titanic expedition I used to dream about diving on the Titanic. I saw myself more than once lying on my stomach inside a submersible looking out a view port at the bow of the Titanic that was just in front of me. These dreams occurred prior to 1980 when I was trying to fund my first expeditions to find the Titanic. Now it looked like they were going to be a reality.

When it came time for the 2000 expedition, G. Michael wanted me to go along with him, but I began having second thoughts. I would have loved to go, but was afraid I would take a little luster off his official title as the Expedition Leader. That's the same title I had when I led the first Titanic expeditions in 1980, 1981 and 1983. It was now his time, I told him. It was now his show. I hated that I wasn't going to be able to dive in one of the Mir Submersibles with Anatoly

G. Michael Planning his 2000 Titanic Expedition

Sagalevich. I was really looking forward to that. But it was now G. Michael's show and I didn't want to interfere with his expedition.

G. Michael Prior to Leaving on 2000 Titanic Expedition

I think deep down he would have liked for me to be there, if for no other reason than to prove to me what he had accomplished. But I also believe that deep down he was glad I chose not to go. This was his chance to shine and he didn't need his father around to detract from his own opportunity in the sun.

Picture of Titanic's Bow Taken by G. Michael on a 2000 Dive

When G. Michael dove to the Titanic in one of the Mir submersibles he accomplished something I had only dreamed of doing for years. But one afternoon on a return trip back to the Russian mother ship, there was bad weather topside and the Russian divers were unable to secure the Mir to the lifting harness. G. Michael and the two-man Russian crew were stuck in dangerous seas for over an hour and couldn't be lifted out of the water.

Inside Mir oxygen was running low. To make matters worse the propeller section of the Mir accidentally smashed against the stern of the recovery ship, which caused smoke and noxious gas to enter the crew compartment.

On this particular dive, it was no longer fun and games. The thrill of adventure had suddenly become a serious confrontation with life and death.

My son was never particularly interested in God and religion when he was growing up, but in that Mir submersible in the middle of the stormy Atlantic Ocean, he found that he'd better reach out to God and reach out fast. G. Michael began praying for all he was worth and promised God that if He would just save his life he would start going to church and do his best to do right by everyone.

God must have heard his frantic prayer because just as the last of their air was running out the brave Russian divers managed to secure a tether to the lurching submersible and G. Michael and his small crew were literally pulled from the jaws of death.

G. Michael did give God the glory for their deliverance and did start going to church. But it seems God was not through with his conversion. John Joslyn and Arnie Geller were not out on the expedition. Neither liked the fact that a wet-behind-the-ears youngster like G. Michael was now Chairman of the of the Board of RMS Titanic

Mir Submersible Returning from Dive

and was garnering all the worldwide publicity as the company's new Expedition Leader.

I guess in their minds they figured that being in partnership with him was no better than being in partnership with George Tulloch. So while G. Michael was fighting for his life on the high seas John and Arnie conspired together to do him in before he got home.

John accused my son of stealing money from their "Ship of Dreams" exhibition in Orlando. The charge was not true but it was enough to catch the attention of SFX who was a major partner with G. Michael and Joslyn in their exhibit.

With SFX going along Joslyn and Geller initiated a quick phone conference with the other major RMS stockholders. They told them that G. Michael was a loose cannon and he was a crook. They said that he couldn't be trusted to be Chairman of the Board of RMS Titanic. To rub salt into the wound, they also said he shouldn't be getting all the publicity representing RMS as leader of their current expedition.

When Geller and Joslyn called G. Michael at the expedition site they told him he was being accused of stealing money and that when SFX heard of the charges they threatened to pull out of their contract with RMS. "Under the circumstances," Arnie Geller intoned seriously, "we have no choice but to remove you as Chairman of the Board of RMS and also as Expedition Leader."

This ugly and false accusation came from John Joslyn and Arnie Geller over the ship-to-shore telephone right after G. Michael had barely survived his life and death experience. He couldn't believe what his supposed two friends were telling him. "You can't be serious!" he shouted back into the phone. "I didn't steal anything from anyone!" But with SFX believing Geller and Joslyn's lies, there wasn't anything G. Michael could do.

Well, there was one thing. He got on his knees and asked God what he should do. He didn't know why his life had suddenly and unexpectedly turned upside down but he wasn't going to turn away from God, not this time, not after God had just saved his life.

When G. Michael returned home he immediately hired a lawyer and fought the bogus charges that John Joslyn had leveled against him. When he won his lawsuit, G. Michael ended up with total ownership of their "Ship of Dreams" exhibit in Orlando. Maybe in the long run what happened to my son wasn't such a bad deal after all.

My admonition to G. Michael that you "can't make a good deal with bad people" certainly turned out to be true. He no longer had to worry about all the backbiting and surreptitious scheming that was going on in RMS Titanic. He now had total ownership of his own Titanic Exhibit in Orlando and was free to do whatever he wanted with Titanic in the future. And G. Michael also found religion. God is now a major part of his life for which I am very grateful.

One of the first things G. Michael did after he was free from Joslyn, Geller and all the other problems associated with RMS Titanic, was get back in touch with his old friend Anatoly Sagalevich at the P.P. Shirshov Institute of Oceanology in Russia. He told him he wanted to lease the Mir 1 and Mir 2 submersibles in 2005 and take them on a dive to the Titanic.

Anatoly asked how he was going to pay. G. Michael told him his 'Ship of Dreams" exhibit in Orlando was going to pay for all of it. He also told him he was going to take his oldest son Sebastian with him in 2005 when he'd be fourteen years old. Anatoly rubbed his nose and questioned if maybe fourteen might be a little young for diving 12,000 feet down to the Titanic. G. Michael laughed and said, "I'll have him ready, Anatoly! You just make sure your Mir submersibles are ready!"

Sebastian and G. Michael in the Mir Submersible in 2005

In 2005 G. Michael and his son Sebastian went out on an expedition and dove together in the Mir 1 submersible to the deck of the RMS Titanic. After taking pictures the sub's robotic arms left a plaque on Titanic's deck to commemorate the historic occasion. After G. Michael and his son returned home Sebastian discovered that he had set a world record that was recorded in the 2007 Guinness Book of World Records. On page 184, Sebastian's picture was shown inside Mir 1 during the dive. The caption underneath read:

YOUNGEST PERSON TO VISIT THE WRECK OF TITANIC. On August 4, 2005, while he was an 8th grade honor student in Florida, U.S.A., Sebastian Harris (U.S.A., b. September 19, 1991) dived to the wreck of RMS Titanic aboard the submarine Mir 1 at the age of 13 years 10 months and 15 days. For his record-breaking feat – commemorated by an engraved plaque placed at the site of the wreck (inset) – Sebastian has been made a full member of the Explorers Club.

Placing Plaque on Deck of Titanic

Sebastian Receiving Recognition of World Record from Guinness

What can be better than that? Mike Harris, G. Michael Harris and Sebastian Harris—three generations—are all proud members of The Explorers Club. I've been an Expedition Leader, my son has been an Expedition Leader and one day I'm willing to bet my grandson will be an Expedition Leader as well!

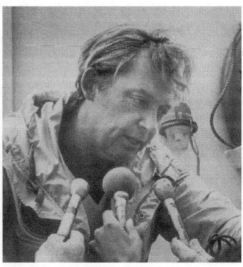

Anatoly, Sebastian & G. Michael   **Mike Harris**

Looking for adventure must be in the blood. I first started diving on ships sunk by atom bombs at Bikini Atoll in the Central Pacific. Then I was attracted to search for Noah's Ark on Mt. Ararat in Turkey and Pancho Villa's treasure in the mountains of Old Mexico. Next, trying to locate the Titanic in the North Atlantic almost took over my entire life. But, thankfully, I was saved by my interest in finding Amelia Earhart, hunting for the Ark of the Covenant and tracing the voyages of China's great Ming explorer Admiral Zheng He.

My search for adventure is just about over. But the life of my son and grandson is just getting started. What great adventures await them on this small planet or beyond? I can only imagine and dream.

As Professor Anatoly Sagalevich stated so beautifully in the Forward, "after opening of the hatch and view to blue skies…life is started again!"

Mike Harris

Mike Harris is an accomplished writer, explorer and film producer. He has led several major expeditions throughout the world, including the first expeditions to search for the RMS Titanic in the North Atlantic. His first expedition in 1971 was to Bikini Atoll in the Marshall Islands where atom bomb tests were conducted after WWII. His film *Deadly Fathoms* featured Rod Serling and won a Silver Medal at the Atlanta International Film Festival. In his second expedition Mike led a group of climbers and Biblical scholars to Mt. Ararat in Turkey to search for Noah's Ark. His film *Expedition to Noah's Ark* featured Joseph Cotton as his on camera host and narrator. Mike's third expedition took him to the mountains of Old Mexico in search for hidden treasure. Mike's film *Pancho Villa's Treasure* featured acclaimed actor Cesar Romero. In 1980 Mike led the first expedition to search for the Titanic. His film *Search for the Titanic* featured legendary actor Orson Welles as his on camera host and narrator. His second Titanic film *Return to the Titanic* featured James 'The Virginian' Drury. Mike's projects have taken him from Guyana to the Arctic Circle, Greenland to Israel and have included multiple studies of the Ming Dynasty in China. Harris is a member of The Explorers Club of New York, Fellow of the Royal Geographical Society in London and has been listed in Who's Who in America since 2000.

Made in the USA
Charleston, SC
10 January 2012